DIVE!

WORLD WAR II STORIES
OF SAILORS & SUBMARINES IN THE PACIFIC

BY DEBORAH HOPKINSON

SCHOLASTIC INC.

Copyright © 2016 by Deborah Hopkinson

This book was originally published in hardcover by Scholastic Press in 2016.

All rights reserved. Published by Scholastic Inc., *Publishers since 1920*. SCHOLASTIC and associated logos are trademarks and/or registered trademarks of Scholastic Inc.

ISBN 978-0-545-42559-9

10 9 8 7 6 5 4 3 2   17 18 19 20 21

Printed in the U.S.A. 40
First printing 2017

Book design by Phil Falco

*In memory of all those on eternal patrol,
and of my father, WWII veteran Russell W. Hopkinson,
whose favorite boat was a trout fishing canoe*

ALL SHIPS HAVE SOULS, AND ALL SAILORS KNOW IT.

—EDWARD L. BEACH JR.

TABLE OF CONTENTS

PART ONE: DARK DAYS
1941 – THE SPOTLIGHT IS ON: SEAWOLF

PART TWO: BRAVE MEN AND TERRIBLE TORPEDOES
1942 – THE SPOTLIGHT IS ON: SEAWOLF, CANOPUS, SPEARFISH, AND TRIGGER (PLUS WE MEET THE WAHOO)

AFTER SECTION

WELCOME ABOARD!

While I was researching this book, my husband, Andy, and I toured the USS *Blueback* (SS-581) at the Oregon Museum of Science and Industry in Portland. Before we boarded the submarine, which is moored in the Willamette River, our guide briefed us on what we were about to see. In the same way, here's a preview of what you'll find in this book.

The book is divided into four parts and an epilogue. It begins in December 1941 with America's entry into World War II and closes with the Japanese surrender in 1945. Three kinds of breakouts (sidebars, notes, or short pieces that add information to our main story) are interspersed throughout the book. *Briefings* provide analysis and background information about aspects of the war; *dispatches* are stories of interest or first-person accounts; and *submarine school* breakouts focus on submarines or life as a submariner. Occasionally, I've included a "skipper's recommendation" of a book or website I think readers will enjoy.

In the After Section, you'll find back matter that, like the propeller of a boat, is an important component of a work of nonfiction: facts and figures, a roster of names of key people (and dogs), a glossary, source notes (which indicate where quotations come from), a bibliography, and an index. The accounts of the men and boats featured here represent only a small portion of this fascinating story, and I hope you'll want to read more.

In Dive Deeper, the resources section, I've included a link to an online list of submarine museums throughout the United States. Some museums provide diagrams, layouts, and photographs of submarines online. If you've never been inside a submarine, you might want to take a virtual tour as you begin reading. There's nothing like climbing down the hatch yourself!

Writing this book was a wonderful learning experience and a challenging one. While every attempt has been made to be accurate, any errors are my own.

In telling these stories, I've been inspired by the fierce dedication, infectious humor, and undaunted bravery of the men who volunteered in the "silent service" during World War II. I hope the audacious spirit of these gallant submariners touches you too.

—Deborah Hopkinson

SKIPPER'S RECOMMENDATION: *Before you begin to read, take the San Francisco Maritime National Park Association's online tour of the USS* Pampanito *(SS-383) at www.maritime.org/tour/index.php. The website includes photographs of the submarine as well as diagrams, manuals, and technical information related to WWII submarines.*

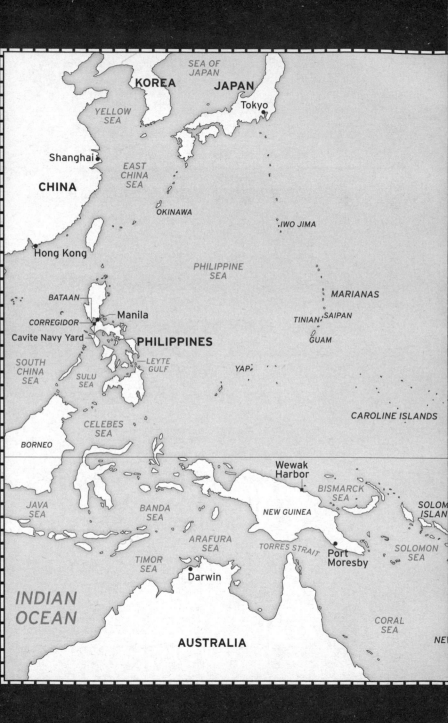

A MAP OF THE PACIFIC

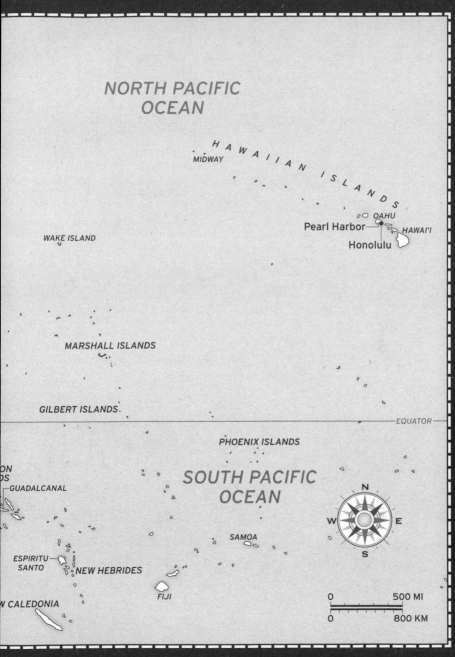

A LIQUID CHESSBOARD

The U.S. Navy fought the Pacific Ocean phase of World War II on a liquid chessboard with an area of more than 70 million square miles—the largest water mass on earth . . .

Usually operating alone, without recourse to their fellow warships and with only their relatively fragile submarine hulls to protect them from aerial bombs, surface ship guns, and depth charges, America's submariners wrote an unsurpassed chapter in the annals of the U.S. Navy's history for courage, dedication, and loyalty to their country.

—ADMIRAL BERNARD A. CLAREY

PART ONE
DARK DAYS

• 1941 •

To the Congress of the United States:
Yesterday, December 7, 1941—a date which will live in infamy—
the United States of America was suddenly and deliberately attacked
by naval and air forces of the Empire of Japan . . .

—President Franklin D. Roosevelt, Joint Address to
Congress Leading to a Declaration of War against Japan
December 8, 1941

Washington, Dec. 11—The United States declared war today on
Germany and Italy, Japan's Axis partners. This nation acted swiftly
after Germany formally declared war on us and Italy followed the
German lead. Thus, President Roosevelt told Congress in his message,
the long-known and the long-expected has taken place.

"The forces endeavoring to enslave the entire world now are moving
toward this hemisphere," he said. "Never before has there been a greater
challenge to life, liberty and civilization."

—*The* New York Times

Execute unrestricted air and submarine warfare against Japan.

—*Chief of Naval Operations*
December 7, 1941

The USS *Arizona* ablaze after the Japanese attack on Pearl Harbor on December 7, 1941.

Aerial photograph taken by a Japanese pilot during the Pearl Harbor attack.

WAVE AFTER WAVE
SUNDAY, DECEMBER 7, 1941

Fifteen-year-old Martin Matthews woke before six that bright Sunday morning, even though it was one of the few times he could have slept in. Like many sailors based in Hawai'i in peacetime, he had weekend leave and didn't need to report back for duty until that night.

On this day, though, the teenager from Texas was much too excited to lie still. Of all the new experiences he'd had since joining the Navy two months before, he was enjoying this the most. He'd had the chance to spend the night on a real battleship, the USS *Arizona* (BB-39). After breakfast, he'd be treated to a tour of every nook and cranny.

Through nothing but an extraordinary coincidence, Martin Matthews was in the wrong place at the worst possible time.

• • •

Just after his fifteenth birthday in October, Martin had lied about his age to join the Navy. A sailor friend home on leave had encouraged him, although it hadn't taken much to convince Martin. "He was wearing a uniform, and it seemed like he got all the attention from all the girls," Martin said, "and I decided that was the route I wanted to go."

Martin convinced his dad to sign an affidavit claiming he was seventeen. Since then, he'd already seen more of the world than he'd ever dreamed possible. He'd completed a few weeks of basic training at the San Diego Naval Training Station in California, where he discovered he wasn't the only underage recruit—one boy he met was only fourteen. After a short stay in Washington State, Martin had boarded a troop ship from Bremerton to the US Naval Base in the territory of Hawai'i. Martin was delighted with the assignment. "Anybody fifteen years of age and who had been very little of anyplace in his life would look forward to it."

Martin was assigned to the Naval Air Station on Ford Island, in the middle of Pearl Harbor. In November he'd begun taking a metal smith course to learn how to repair aircraft. Everything was new—especially the strict discipline. "It was to bed early at night and up early in the morning with liberty basically reserved for weekends only."

There were definitely pluses, though. "The chow was good," Martin recalled. "When you grow up in the Depression days and eat what I had to eat, anything looks better. Of course, at twenty-one dollars a month, that's more money than I had ever seen in my life anyhow."

• • •

On Saturday, December 6, Martin and a friend from the USS *Arizona* had spent the day in Honolulu, sightseeing and shooting some pool before returning to Battleship Row. Seven glorious stars of the Pacific surface fleet were moored there, with another, the USS *Pennsylvania* (BB-38), in dry dock nearby. Once Martin showed his pass, the officer on duty on the *Arizona* had given permission for Martin to stay overnight.

After breakfast on Sunday, Martin got his chance to explore the impressive six-hundred-foot-long ship. " 'I wish I could get duty aboard a battleship,' " he told his friend.

That's when it began.

• • •

When the young sailors first heard the planes, they didn't think much of it. Martin, now on the aft section of the *Arizona*'s deck, remembered that he simply glanced up. Nothing seemed amiss— it was just some planes in the sky. Even after it became clear that something was wrong, the reality was so unthinkable, so horrific, it was almost impossible to process what was happening.

"We heard noise over to our starboard side. . . . You could see a bunch of planes coming in; nobody's paying any attention to it. Then you could hear what seemed like thundering in the background, which actually were bombs starting to drop at that time," Martin said. "But none of us thought about bombs, because we didn't even know what a bomb was. I had yet even to see one in my life.

"But as these planes got closer, the thunder got closer, and then we started seeing clouds of smoke . . . Then we see fire and explosions," he went on. "Well, we knew that something was wrong, but we thought that maybe it was gunnery practice or something. We did not know, even at that time, that the Japanese were actually attacking us."

Martin wasn't alone in feeling confused. On the *Arizona*'s deck, Major Alan Shapley vividly recalled a sailor standing at the rail and remarking that this was the best drill the US Air Force had ever put on. Another sailor who spied the aerial torpedoes had a similar thought—it just had to be a mistake. " 'Oh, oh, some fool pilot has gone wild.' "

On shore, Rear Admiral Husband E. Kimmel, commander of the Navy's Pacific Fleet, understood what was happening in an instant. From the front yard of his house, he had a view of the harbor; in the moments before his driver arrived to whisk him to headquarters, he had stared in horror as buzzing hordes of planes approached Battleship Row. "'I knew right away that something terrible was going on, that this was not a casual raid by just a few stray planes. The sky was full of the enemy.'"

In fact, Kimmel (who was replaced in the aftermath of the surprise attack) was seeing the first wave of 183 Japanese planes—fighters, bombers, dive bombers, and torpedo planes—launched from six aircraft carriers about two hundred miles away. The pilots had instructions to target the pride of the US Navy's fleet: her battleships. The attack's mastermind was Admiral Isoroku Yamamoto, commander in chief of Japan's Combined Fleet, who hoped to decide the outcome of the war by landing a mortal blow on the first day. For the USS *Arizona* and her sister battleship, the *Oklahoma* (BB-37), the attack would indeed be fatal.

Frozen in fear on the *Arizona*'s aft deck, Martin heard the alarm for general quarters (GQ) sound. Martin's friend rushed to his battle station, leaving the young teen on his own. "Pandemonium broke loose; sailors were running everywhere," said Martin. "I had no place to go; I was basically just trying to get myself under cover, but, still, at my age and not prepared for any of this, needless to say, I was scared to death."

It was clear even to Martin's untrained eyes that the *Arizona* wasn't ready for battle. He watched as sailors rushed to uncover guns; another frantically tried to break a locked container to get at ammunition to load antiaircraft guns. No counterattack could save the *Arizona*. The ship had already been hit by one torpedo when a bomb fell on the starboard side. Martin could feel the deck beneath his feet shudder.

Then he was no longer on deck at all, but flailing in the churning waters of the harbor. It might have been from the force of the impact; maybe he had jumped—for the rest of his life, Martin was never quite clear. "I can't remember to this day whether it was the explosions or from sheer panic within myself, but I wound up over the side of the *Arizona* in the water."

The sea was salty and warm on Martin's lips. He'd lost his cap. He managed to keep his head above the surface, while his soaked clothes and shoes dragged him down. Gigantic plumes of dark smoke were now erupting along Battleship Row, spiraling upward into huge, roiling columns, like an army of angry tornadoes. Acrid smells of burning fuel oil singed Martin's nostrils and eyes. Black oil slicks spewed into the water from the *Arizona*. It's hard to know whether Martin could even hear the buzzing of the Japanese attack planes still overhead—or the screams and shouts of men.

• • •

Instinctively, Martin made for cover, swimming twenty or thirty yards to a large mooring buoy that was about eight feet across and slimy with green algae. He reached the far side and held on, trying to put as much distance between himself and the *Arizona* as he could. "I was just more or less hanging on a thread for dear life."

Overhead, Japanese planes were still on the attack. "All I can remember, it seemed like they came in constantly, wave after wave, and it seemed like they were completely uncontested, unmolested."

Martin got a horrific, close-up view of the attack. "When the *Arizona* finally started blowing up, it was ammunition, gun lockers, shells, steel fragments, and pyrotechnics coming, it seemed to

The USS *Arizona* burned furiously as she sank on December 7, 1941.

me, from all parts of the ship," he said. "It was a series of explosions; it wasn't just one deafening one. It came to one final one where she seemed like the middle part just raised up in the water and kind of half-buckled and then settled back down. Of course, she never completely sank, because the water at that time wasn't deep enough. But her bridge and masthead were above water."

The *Arizona* had been struck by a bomb that had detonated in the forward magazine with an "indescribably fearful explosion and concussion that seemed to suck the very life out of the air." That blast alone killed nearly a thousand men. One ensign who survived said " 'the ship was sinking like an earthquake had struck it, and the bridge was in flames.' "

For Martin, each moment brought ever more terrifying sights and sounds. "There was steel in the air; there was fire; there was oil . . . pieces of timber; pieces of the boat deck; canvas; and even pieces of bodies . . . I saw a thigh and leg; I saw fingers; I saw hands; I saw elbows and arms. It's far too much for a young boy of fifteen years old to have seen."

Flames were leaping from the ship, yet somehow they didn't reach him. He might easily have been struck by debris and shrapnel, but Martin's luck held out. "I never got hit by any of it. I did have quite a bit of oil and sludge and diesel oil all over me. In fact, my white uniform didn't look white anymore; it was black."

• • •

Martin wasn't quite sure how much time passed; he guessed he'd been in the water an hour or more when the attack seemed to end. He'd seen smoke and flames on Ford Island, and could only imagine the damage done to the planes on the ground. Martin figured his best chance to survive would be to swim to his base

Admiral Isoroku Yamamoto, mastermind of the attack on Pearl Harbor, sought to destroy the pride of the US Navy fleet on Battleship Row.

there, less than a mile away. Somehow he made it, despite the chaos, the smoke, and the oil-slicked water.

Martin clambered over the rocks and crawled onto the beach. That's when he faced a new danger: He was so covered in black sludge he was totally unrecognizable. As he scrambled to his feet, the young sailor found himself staring straight into the barrel of a gun. The sentry was nervous and not much older than Martin himself. In the chaos, the guard thought Martin might be an invading Japanese soldier.

Martin screamed, " 'I'm Navy! I'm with the United States Navy! Don't shoot!' "

The sentry lowered his gun.

As he stood catching his breath, Martin got his first chance to take in the entire scene of destruction. "Ships were still blowing up in the harbor; hangars were still blowing up; gasoline was still blowing up; planes on the ground on fire were blowing up and rupturing their fuel tanks."

Exhausted and shaken, Martin made his way to his barracks. He peeled off his wet, oil-clogged uniform—the whites he'd planned to wear as he strolled through the Honolulu streets. Then he reported for duty. The destruction hadn't been confined to the ships on Battleship Row. The Navy planes on Ford Island had been parked wingtip to wingtip—like "sitting ducks" for the enemy's attack, Martin thought.

Now Martin and other sailors went to those planes "to rescue people who might still be alive, to remove damaged aircraft from the runways, and to do just about any and everything that was needed there—whatever could be done to put Ford Island Naval Air Station back in operation."

They worked throughout that night and into the next day without even stopping to sleep. No one knew what might happen next—was the surprise attack just the beginning? Rumors flew fast and furious. "We were told numerous times that the Japanese had landed," Martin recalled. "Then that rumor would be quelled, and then they'd say the Japanese had landed in another island. Then we'd be informed of the rumor that the Japanese were going to attack again in the morning."

Martin was kept busy: helping to put out small fires, assessing damage to hangars, and hauling away damaged planes. Crews searched the wreckage for survivors. "Every now and then, we would come across somebody who was pinned in the wreckage. In fact, one time—it was three days later—there was a plane on the end of the runway; we found out there was a pilot in it who had been injured and trapped in it for three days."

• • •

That was the beginning of fifteen-year-old Martin Matthews's war. He probably could have petitioned to get out of the Navy because of his age. Instead he stuck with it. In an interview nearly forty years later, Martin reflected that being at Pearl Harbor that day had only solidified his determination to serve.

"I knew then that even if I had to wait the two years that I still would join up," he said, "because it was my country."

Crew abandoning the damaged USS *California* around ten o'clock on Sunday morning.

On the USS *California* (BB-44), twenty-year-old Musician First Class Warren G. Harding had reason to be grateful to sailors like Martin Matthews who kept up rescue efforts long after Japanese planes disappeared from the sky.

Like Martin, Warren was off duty on Sunday, December 7, with plans for a picnic in Honolulu. That morning, though, Warren missed the first "liberty launch," the boat that took sailors ashore. The delay saved his life. Later he learned everyone on it had been killed.

"'So I leaned against the rail and waited . . . I looked over to the right because I heard this drone, a ROAR-R-R-R. It was a plane diving. I thought: "My goodness, this is Sunday! Who practices dive-bombing on Sunday?" I'm looking up in the air, and immediately I spotted that red ball. I said, "That's a Zero!"

"'I saw it and recognized the red ball, and just like that I saw the bomb being released. It burst on the runway on Ford Island. . . . So I headed, automatically, to my battle station. That's all I thought—get to my battle station.'"

Warren raced four decks below to his station, called repair fore port (on the port, or left, side of the forward part of the ship), and grabbed his headphones. His job would be to relay orders coming from repair central. "'All at once I heard POW, the first explosion. It was an extraordinary feeling. When you fire a broadside on a battleship, it feels like the battleship is picked up in the water, then it kind of shakes and then settles back down.'"

The ship began to list. Water and oil seeped under the nearest watertight door. Warren's radio crackled to life. While the other repair stations were ordered to abandon ship, Warren and six others were told to maintain watertight integrity and stay put. Someone would be back to get them. And so they waited. The smoke got so thick one man passed out. Minutes ticked by.

"'Nobody panicked because I don't think we realized the full impact of what had happened. We couldn't believe our ship was sinking,' said Warren. 'We could still breathe good, fresh air, and we could see the lights were on. There were no bullets flying around, no shrapnel. But the ship kept sinking down. . . .

"'Time went on. Some guys went to sleep. There was a guitar and an electrician who knew how to play. He started strumming, and we started singing. We sang and we sang. Hours passed. Finally we ran out of songs and just sat there.'"

Warren could no longer reach repair central on his headphones. When the water rose over their legs, the sailors concluded that they'd been forgotten. They chose the smallest man to crawl into an air duct to inch his way through it up to the boat deck to try to get help. And then they waited some more.

Finally, about three in the afternoon, they heard a knock. Rescuers opened the watertight door from the outside, and the men escaped. On deck, Warren was so shocked by what he saw that his legs gave way. "'Smoke and fire were still on the water around the *California*. There were dead bodies in the water and bodies hanging over the gun turrets. . . . After a while I got up my strength and went over the starboard side. I crawled down and swam to shore. There was oil all over me, but I was alive. I crawled under a small building up on piers and just laid there until it started to get dusk. . . .

" 'There was no sleep at all that night. The next day we went back and started digging bodies out of the *California.* . . . I helped . . . and then I slipped off to check my trombone to see if it was all right. A clothes locker had fallen over on the trombone and had protected it.' "

Later, when the *California* was in dry dock for repairs, Warren got his first real look at the damage and realized how lucky he'd been. " 'I couldn't believe my eyes. I almost fainted. You could have driven a Mack truck through either one of the torpedo holes, and I was in the place right between them.' "

In an interview on the thirty-ninth anniversary of the attack, Warren said, " 'There was a dent in it, but I still have the trombone today. I haven't played it in almost thirty years, but it's in my bedroom, on a stand. I keep it shined. I shine it every December 7 and when I go back tonight, it'll get its shine.' "

SKIPPER'S RECOMMENDATION: *Visit the National Park Service's World War II Valor in the Pacific National Monument at http://home.nps.gov/valr/learn/index.htm.*

2 EXECUTE UNRESTRICTED SUBMARINE WARFARE

"Probably no man in Japan more earnestly wanted to avoid war with the United States than the one who planned the Pearl Harbor attack," wrote historian Gordon Prange, who spent nearly forty years researching the assault.

That man was Admiral Isoroku Yamamoto, commander in chief of Japan's Combined Fleet. Yamamoto was no stranger to the United States: Educated at Harvard, he spoke English and had lived in Washington, DC. Yamamoto had a keen appreciation of America's military and production capabilities. Ultimately he believed that Japan was outmatched and could not win a war against the United States.

However, in the years leading up to the war, the tide was against Yamamoto and other moderate voices. Conflict became increasingly likely after Japan joined in a military alliance with the Axis powers Germany and Italy in the September 1940 Tripartite Pact. World War II pitted the Axis powers against the Allies: Great Britain, France, and the United States, among others.

Once war seemed inevitable, Yamamoto believed Japan's best chance for victory would be to deal a crushing blow at the very outset. If the Japanese could destroy the US Navy's main fleet at Pearl Harbor, they could then launch assaults on strategic British and American military bases in Singapore and the Philippines.

Pearl Harbor, with Ford Island in the center, shown in October 1941, just months before the attack.

With the Philippines secured, Japan would be positioned to expand southward to Malaya and the Netherlands East Indies and other islands, eventually achieving dominance throughout the entire Pacific region. Destroying the US fleet at Pearl Harbor had another advantage: It would help keep the sea lanes open so that Japanese oil tankers and freighters could move freely, delivering fuel and supplies to Japanese airfields and military outposts on the islands it conquered.

In January 1941, nearly a year before the December 7 surprise attack, Yamamoto wrote that the Imperial Japanese Navy must "'fiercely attack and destroy the U.S. main fleet at the outset of the war, so that the morale of the U.S. Navy and her people'" would sink so low it could not recover. In other words, Japan wanted to win the war on the very first day.

That didn't happen.

• • •

The Japanese attack at Pearl Harbor killed more than 2,400 and wounded more than 1,000 people. Eighteen vessels, including battleships, cruisers, and destroyers, were sunk or heavily damaged; Navy planes on Ford Island suffered heavy losses.

The surprise assault did give the Imperial Japanese Navy a distinct advantage. Even before the attack, Japan boasted thirty-five heavy and light cruisers, compared to twenty-four in the combined US Pacific and Asiatic Fleets; Japan had 111 destroyers, while the United States had 80; it had ten aircraft carriers, while the US had only three; and it had ten battleships, while all eight of America's battleships at Pearl Harbor had suffered damage. Japan also boasted sixty submarines, more than the fifty-one subs the US had operating in the Pacific.

Despite these advantages, the attack at Pearl Harbor did not result in a quick, decisive victory for the Japanese. Yamamoto and other Japanese officials underestimated the crucial role that the submarines of the US Navy would be asked to play in the conflict ahead: to decimate Japanese ships and cut off the lines of supply.

Nor did the attack at Pearl Harbor shatter America's morale. Just the opposite.

The next day, Monday, December 8, 1941, the US Congress declared war on Japan. Three days later, America formally declared war on Germany and Italy.

• • •

Japanese military planners had underestimated the American people's resolve. The surprise attack galvanized the country into war. Japan had made another miscalculation as well: overlooking the potential impact that submarines might have in the war. The four submarines at Pearl Harbor that day had escaped damage; no bombs fell on the submarine base itself, nor were supplies of torpedoes and fuel damaged in any way.

One reason Japan may have discounted the importance of submarines was that in 1939, when World War II broke out in Europe, there were only fifty-five boats in the small American submarine fleet. Yet those numbers had been increasing as American military planners anticipated being drawn into war. The US Congress had authorized funds for the construction of more ships, including submarines. By December 1941, the US Navy could boast 111 submarines, with more scheduled for construction. Of these, 60 boats were part of the Atlantic Fleet operating in the Atlantic Ocean and other European waters. (The fleet also included eight battleships and four aircraft carriers, as well as cruisers and destroyers.)

During World War II, the Atlantic submarines (which are beyond the scope of this book) were charged with defending the US East Coast and the Panama Canal and, in collaboration with the British, raiding enemy shipping. They were also tapped to defend supply ships bringing food and munitions to Great Britain against German submarines, called U-boats.

At the start of the war, fifty-one US submarines were based in the Pacific. Twenty-nine were attached to the Navy's Asiatic Fleet (which included both surface ships and submarines), which was based in the Philippines. The other twenty-two were part of the Pacific Fleet housed at Pearl Harbor Naval Submarine Base. Only four happened to be at Pearl Harbor the day of the attack, and all escaped damage.

What role were the Pacific submarines expected to play? To understand that, it's helpful to take a look at the big picture and review the major combatants in World War II. The Allies were led by the United States, Great Britain, and the Soviet Union. This faction also included France, Poland, Canada, Australia, New Zealand, and South Africa, with other countries joining the effort after 1941.

The Allied nations were pitted against the Axis powers: Germany, Italy, and Japan, which had formed close ties in the 1930s. While all three pursued aggressive actions toward other countries and were opposed to the Allies, they did not mount a combined war effort.

America's overall strategy, according to naval historian Theodore Roscoe, called for "a concentration of effort to defeat

Nazi Germany while the Japanese offensive was contained by a holding action in the Pacific. This strategic plan recognized Germany as the most formidable Axis power and the Atlantic threat as the one more immediately menacing to the security of the United States.

"Defeat of Japan was considered inevitable once the Nazis were beaten, whereas a victory over Japan did not assure defeat of Germany, were the Nazis able to crush Britain and Russia in the meantime," wrote Roscoe. "This meant winning the Battle of the Atlantic while American naval forces in the Pacific went on the defensive."

This would be a two-ocean war for the United States Navy. And on December 7, 1941, it was clear that the battle for control of the vast Pacific region had already begun.

The call to action came that same day, only six hours after the Pearl Harbor attack. The Navy Department issued an order overturning an international agreement that restricted the actions submarines could take against nonmilitary ships, including merchant ships such as oil tankers or supply freighters.

The order read: *"Execute Unrestricted Air and Submarine Warfare against Japan."*

World War II in the Pacific was a complicated conflict involving many nations and territories. To help understand the overall goals of Japan, it's helpful to turn to esteemed naval historian Samuel Eliot Morison, who proposed to his friend President Franklin D. Roosevelt in the spring of 1942 that he write a maritime history of the war—a project that would involve Morison going to sea to be an eyewitness to battles and operations.

The result was a fifteen-volume masterwork, *History of United States Naval Operations in World War II*. Though Morison wrote in great detail, he also understood the value of being able to simplify and summarize complex historical events. Below is his summary of the Japanese war plan.

> *First, prior to a declaration of war, destruction of the United States Pacific Fleet and the British and American air forces on the Malay Peninsula and Luzon [the Philippines].*
>
> *Second, while the British and American Navies were decimated and disorganized, a quick conquest of the Philippines, Guam, Wake, Hong Kong, Borneo, British Malaya (including Singapore) and Sumatra.*
>
> *Third, when these were secure, the converging of Japanese amphibious forces on the richest prize, Java, and a mop-up of the rest of the Dutch Islands.*

Fourth, an intensive development of Malayan and Indonesian resources in oil, rubber, etc.; and, to secure these, establishment of a defensive perimeter . . . With these bases the Japanese Navy and air forces could cut all lines of communication between Australia, New Zealand, and the Anglo-American powers, which would then be forced to sue for peace.

Fifth and finally, Japan would proceed completely to subjugate China.

Had this ambitious plan succeeded, Morison noted, over half the world's population would have been under Japanese control.

"This scheme of conquest was the most enticing, ambitious and far-reaching in modern history, not excepting Hitler's," he concluded. "It almost worked, and might well have succeeded but for the United States Navy."

SKIPPER'S RECOMMENDATION: *Samuel Morison didn't want to be an armchair historian. Read how he went to sea to experience history as it happened, in this* Smithsonian Magazine *article: http://www.smithsonianmag.com/history /revisiting-samuel-eliot-morisons-landmark-history-63715 /?no-ist.*

THE PHILIPPINES
MONDAY, DECEMBER 8, 1941

Like young Martin Matthews, submariner Joseph Melvin Eckberg was on liberty that first Sunday in December. However, Mel Eckberg, known as Mel to his wife, Marjorie, and as Eck to fellow submariners, wasn't anywhere near Pearl Harbor but thousands of miles away in the Philippine Islands, which had been owned by the United States since 1898 and was in transition to becoming an independent nation.

Cavite Navy Yard, Philippines, in October 1941, before war broke out.

Mel Eckberg was one of thousands of Americans in the Philippines at the time. The US had pledged to protect the Philippines in the event of conflict with Japan, and had built a substantial military presence in the islands. The Navy's Asiatic Fleet of surface ships and submarines was based in the Philippines. In addition, General Douglas MacArthur was in charge of US Army Ground Forces, the Philippine Army, and military fighter planes there.

On that Monday, Mel Eckberg and his crewmates were waiting for their submarine, the USS *Seawolf* (SS-197), to undergo routine maintenance at Cavite Naval Station (sometimes called the Cavite Navy Yard) on Manila Bay in the port town of Cavite, south of the capital city of Manila.

Due to the time difference, with Manila being about eighteen and a half hours—nearly a day—ahead of Honolulu, the news about Pearl Harbor didn't reach the Philippines until the early hours of December 8. Nothing had interfered with Eck's free weekend; in fact, he'd gone out on the town to celebrate a reunion with an old shipmate named Jim Riley.

It wasn't until Monday morning, when Eck and Jim stopped by a local café for some much-needed coffee, that they noticed an unexpected tension in the atmosphere—something seemed to be wrong.

" 'What's the matter with everybody? They're jumping around like a bunch of jitterbugs,' " Jim remarked.

A young Filipino waiter broke the news: Pearl Harbor had been attacked. Eck glanced out the window. Already he could see people rushing along with grim and anxious faces.

Everybody—American and Filipino alike—feared that Japan would take aim at the Philippines next. They were right to be afraid.

In an instant, Eck and Jim had scrambled to their feet and dashed outside, where a cab screeched to a stop in front of them.

"'Going to the docks, sailor?'" the driver asked.

They climbed in and the cab sped away.

• • •

"The port was as busy as a beehive with submarines," remembered Eck. "Two of them, the *Sealion* and *Seadragon*, our sister ships, were undergoing a complete yard overhaul. That meant removing all engines, tearing down the electrical systems, and then rebuilding the ship—a six-to-eight-weeks job."

Seawolf's maintenance would have to wait. Eck hurried on board, passing workers busily loading the submarine with food and supplies. A little later, as he stood on deck for his turn at watch, Eck still found it hard to believe what he'd heard, especially on such a lovely tropical day. "The air was mild, the sun shone. War seemed impossible. Suddenly, in toward Manila, a light began blinking."

It was, Eck realized, a searchlight signal being broadcast from the old, faithful USS *Canopus* (AS-9), one of the submarine tenders serving the Asiatic Fleet. (As its name implies, a submarine tender is a ship that has been specially equipped to serve, or "tend to," submarines, an especially important role since subs have limited storage space to carry food, fuel, or torpedoes.)

"I read the flashes, and with each word my blood pressure shot up," the veteran submariner recalled. It was a dispatch from Admiral Thomas Hart to the men and officers of each ship:

From . . . Commander Asiatic Fleet . . . To Asiatic Fleet . . .
Urgent . . . Break . . . Japan . . . has . . . commenced . . .
hostilities . . .
Govern . . . yourselves accordingly.

America had been in the war for only hours when *Seawolf* and other pioneering Pacific submarines were ordered out on their first patrols. Mel Eckberg had been preparing for this a long time. He couldn't help reflect back on how he—and his beloved *Seawolf*—had gotten this far.

USS SEAWOLF (SS-197)

This story has 80 heroes and one heroine. The heroes are the officers and men of an American submarine. The heroine is the ship herself. More than 80 feet long, with eight torpedo tubes and a surface speed of better than 20 knots, she was commissioned December 1, 1939. Since that day, she has led an exciting and secret life.

—Office of Naval Records and History
Ships' Histories Section
Navy Department

MEET THE SEAWOLF

"'Kid, why don't you come into this outfit? We could use you.'"

Mel Eckberg had been eighteen when those words from his brother Paul spurred him to join the US Navy Submarine Service; in the thirteen years since, Eck hadn't regretted his choice.

"We know we're different from other services of the armed forces," he reflected. "Most of us went into the Navy as soon as we were old enough—seventeen, eighteen, nineteen.

"With all due modesty we know we're picked men, paid 50 per cent more in our jobs than men in any other branch of the service, and that few of us will be in it actively after we're forty—because it's so tough. . . . Submarines are our lives and our careers."

• • •

Eck first set eyes on the *Seawolf* in August 1939 as the boat was nearing completion at Portsmouth Naval Shipyard, a major submarine construction yard in Kittery, Maine, and near the city of Portsmouth, New Hampshire. He and his wife, Marjorie, had moved to Portsmouth so Eck could be part of the *Seawolf*'s shakedown crew—the group of highly qualified men tapped to put the new submarine through her paces and work out any kinks. They'd become her "plank owners," members of the crew when the ship was placed in commission, or active service.

"Yard workmen were laying the *Wolf*'s teakwood decking, riveters were assembling her periscope shears, painters were daubing a thick black coat of paint on her sides, which swelled outward so gracefully at the waterline," Eck recalled. "Her heavy bronze bell was being rigged. Under the scaffolding I could make out her clean, trim lines. She was pretty."

Not only would Eck be on a beautiful new boat, he'd be serving under Lieutenant Commander Frederick Warder, a respected skipper with an engineering background and unwavering moral compass. Warder would later become known by a nickname he didn't much like, but which stuck nonetheless: "Fearless Freddie."

Frederick "Fearless Freddie" Warder.

Eck, who handled radio and sound duties, explained his job this way: "I'd be her eyes and ears under water. A submarine is blind below periscope depth, and her only contact with the world is by sound. She feels and gropes her way along the bottom of the sea, between shoals, over reefs—all by sound. She recognizes the enemy's approach by sound and measures the success of her attacks by sound."

Once the *Seawolf* was finished, her crew assembled. The men spent long hours studying blueprints so they knew the boat inside and out. "A submarine such as the *Wolf* needs . . . three complete crews each on an eight-hour shift, and specialists all. Officers, electricians, machinists, radiomen, firemen, signalmen, torpedomen, fire-controlmen, cooks, mess boys," Eck explained.

Serving on a submarine required more than just understanding one's own duties, Eck explained. "Each of us had to know as much as possible about every other man's job. Every submarine man is a specialist, but he must be prepared to take over any other post at a moment's notice, whether it be frying eggs or firing torpedoes."

The *Seawolf*'s crew learned to take the boat apart, and put her back together again. Eck figured his job wasn't much different from being a surgeon who has to know each and every bone and muscle of the human body. In wartime conditions at sea, that depth of knowledge might just save a submariner's life.

The *Seawolf* was "glory itself," and easily the most impressive boat Eck had ever encountered. "I'd seen a lot of submarines, but the *Wolf* topped them all. More than 308 feet long, weighing 1,480 tons, built to make over 20 knots surface speed, air-conditioned and equipped with every modern device, she combined the best we knew in submarine construction.

"I ducked into her conning tower and let myself down the narrow perpendicular steel ladder leading to the control room directly under it. I turned around—and whistled. I'd never seen so many instruments—dials, valves, gauges, controls—in one control room. The room was white, glistening white, and the instruments shone and gleamed. Here was the glittering 'Christmas Tree,' a small panel of green and red lights which gave the legend on every hatch of the *Wolf*, and whether it was open or closed. . . . I almost swelled with pride as I stood there and drank it all in."

The most exciting part, of course, was Eck's own station, his "shack," a space of about six by eight feet. The panel rising from a glass-topped table reminded Eck of the control board of a radio station. Overhead were the familiar wires and cables of a submarine ceiling space.

"Seated at this table—my desk—I had before and behind me the last word in submarine radio and sound gear, an instrument of electrical echo-ranging and sonic devices so sensitive that when the *Wolf* was submerged I would be able to detect the beating of a ship's screws when she was still far away. On the surface I'd switch from sound to radio, and send and receive with an antenna strung topside."

• • •

Once crew members had become thoroughly familiar with their new boat, they began to move in. "The first thing I did was to paste a photograph of Marjorie on the panel of my sound gear, and fix another above my bunk," said Eck.

"My locker was built into the bulkhead next to my bunk, and I packed away my clothing: four suits of blue dungarees; four changes of underwear, one set of gray wool, one heavy all-wool with double back and chest; a dozen pair of socks, six wool, six cotton; two pairs of black shoes; dress and undress blues; sandals; six hats (blue and white, and one warm blue knitted watch cap for cold nights on deck)."

His crewmates put up photos of loved ones, and brought in books, magazines, dice, and decks of cards. (Cribbage was a favorite game on submarines, as well as poker and backgammon, sometimes called acey-deucey.) Eck recalled that one machinist's mate, "a wizard softball player, came in lugging a sackful [sic] of bats, balls, and mitts. We were making the *Wolf* our home."

• • •

By February of 1940, the *Seawolf* and her crew were ready for her first test dive. Despite the thorough preparations, tension hung in the air the day Marjorie Eckberg drove her husband to the dock. And for good reason.

Less than a year before, on May 23, 1939, another new submarine, the USS *Squalus* (SS-192), had met with a tragic accident during a dive off the coast of Portsmouth, New Hampshire. Twenty-six members of the crew of fifty-nine perished. (The submarine was recovered and later renamed the *Sailfish*.) Eck had known many of the victims.

Now as they rounded a turn, Eck caught a glimpse of the *Seawolf*: "Black, shining black, in the cold morning sun, long, sleek, and black. . . . The deck force was scampering about, chopping the ice clear from our lines, and even in the distance the orders echoed crisp and clear. . . . The flag was blowing at the stern. I got out of the car.

" 'Well, here goes, honey,' I said.

" 'Oh, Mel,' she said.

"I leaned down and kissed her. She turned the wheel sharply and drove off. I came aboard the *Wolf* as a voice boomed through a megaphone from the bridge: 'Preparations for getting under way!'

"There was a terrific roar from deep within the *Wolf*; then a series of sharp, ear-splitting reports . . . Her powerful Diesels were turning over."

As Eck hurried to his station in the radio shack, the "familiar odor of burned fuel oil came to me, and the old excitement swept over me. . . . I put on my earphones; the intercommunication system was switched on, and all through the *Wolf*'s compartments little grilled loudspeakers awoke and chatted.

"When the Captain went into the conning tower, not a whisper but his echoed through the ship. We were all one family, all wrapped together in that extraordinary intimacy of men who go down to the sea in the sealed steel chambers of a submarine."

The *Seawolf* sailed through her shakedown with flying colors.

• • •

Eck loved the *Seawolf*, but after shore leave in November of 1941, it was harder than usual to say good-bye to Marjorie. Their baby, David, nicknamed Spike, had been born just five weeks earlier in San Diego, where they'd been living since that spring.

"Marjorie and I did little that last night but sit around and ogle Spike," Eck recalled. "We couldn't get our fill of him. We put him on the carpet, and he lay on his back gurgling . . . Then we put him to bed and began to pack."

Following a brief stop at Pearl Harbor, the *Seawolf* traveled across the Pacific to her home base with the Asiatic Fleet in the Philippines. Hours after the news of the Pearl Harbor attack reached him, the new father was ready to put his long years of training and preparation to the test.

US Navy submarines are categorized by the class, or type of boat. Often the class is named after the first boat to be built in that category. World War II submarines fell into several classes.

At the outset of the war, a number of older submarines, known as S-boats, were still in service, some dating back to 1916. These boats had shorter cruising ranges and no air-conditioning, which made them ill-suited for long patrols in the Pacific.

Between 1935 and 1939, so-called fleet-type submarines were built, including P class (sometimes called *Porpoise* class), as well as *Salmon* and *Sargo* class boats. As Navy historian Theodore Roscoe explained, planners gave priority to improvements in "diving speed, cruising range and torpedo power." These submarines could cruise for longer periods, remaining on patrol for about seventy-five days, and could cover ten thousand miles at normal cruising speeds before being refueled. *Salmon* and *Sargo* class submarines built in 1938 and 1939 had eight torpedo tubes and were 308 feet long with a machine gun on deck. In 1940, the *Tambor* class submarines were built; these had ten torpedo tubes as well as a three-inch deck gun and two machine guns.

In 1941, *Gato* class boats became the standard for mass production during the war years. Like the *Salmon* and *Sargo* classes, the *Gato* boats were named after marine creatures and, Roscoe noted, "embodied the best features of the previously built long-range submarines—all-welded construction, all-electric drive, oceanic cruising range, ten torpedo tubes . . . length 307 feet . . . surface speed 20 knots. This was the submarine produced by American builders throughout World War II."

Submarines have hull numbers as well as names. (And to make things even more confusing, the "names" of submarines were also sometimes numbers.) Hull numbering for submarines is consecutive, dating back to the *Holland* (SS-1), launched in 1897. The *Seawolf* was SS-197 (ship-submarine 197); the USS *Diablo*, a *Gato* class boat, which set out on her first patrol days before hostilities ended in August 1945, was SS-479. (The abbreviation for battleship is BB; for a submarine tender, it is AS.)

While the practice is in decline today, traditionally, ships were considered feminine. This may date back to the Latin word for ship, *navis*, which is feminine; to female figureheads on boats; or to the fact that male shipowners named boats after women in their lives. In any case, most of the submariners in World War II (including the official Navy Ships' Histories) considered boats feminine and I have done so here as well.

SKIPPER'S RECOMMENDATION: *If you're fascinated by submarine construction, take a look at John D. Alden's* The Fleet Submarine in the U.S. Navy: A Design and Construction History *(Annapolis, MD: Naval Institute Press, 1979). Ask a librarian about using Interlibrary Loan to locate a copy.*

Even in the tiny galley of a submarine, a good cook could work miracles, and *Seawolf*'s Gus Wright was no exception. At seven p.m. on December 8, Wright served up a tasty dinner of steak, french fries, asparagus, and ice cream.

Mel Eckberg had just finished his meal when he began to sense restlessness in the men around him. Crew members murmured:

"'What are we waiting for?'

"'Time's a wastin', ducks on the pond, let's be away!'"

Thirty minutes later, Captain Frederick Warder called everyone together. Just as they'd guessed, the *Seawolf* would be heading out from Cavite Naval Station that night. Admiral Thomas Hart, and his second-in-command for submarines, John Wilkes, had divided responsibilities among the twenty-nine submarines of the Asiatic Fleet. Some would remain close to help defend the Philippines.

The *Seawolf*, along with the USS *Sculpin* (SS-191), would escort a convoy, or group, of three ships being sent south to safety, out of the range of Japanese aircraft based in Formosa (now Taiwan). One ship, the USS *Pecos* (AO-6), was a valuable oil tanker carrying much-needed fuel for the fleet. The two subs would act like herding dogs, protecting defenseless sheep from marauding wolves.

That wouldn't be *Seawolf*'s only job on her first patrol. Once her escort duties were done, she'd join other Asiatic Fleet submarines out on the high seas as a raider, searching for Japanese ships—especially oil tankers and cargo freighters crucial to supplying the Japanese military expansion.

After the attack on Pearl Harbor, restrictions on submarines attacking merchant ships such as oil tankers had been abandoned. The submarines would be deployed to target freighters and tankers and destroy Japanese shipping. Until the Navy's battleships could be repaired, submarines would be taking on this challenge pretty much on their own—becoming lone raiders in a vast ocean.

Submarines in the Pacific Fleet based in Pearl Harbor would focus on areas where high enemy ship traffic was anticipated and where shipping lanes converged. Boats like *Seawolf* in the Asiatic Fleet had a more complicated assignment in the early days of the war. As Japan moved aggressively to occupy islands throughout the Pacific, the submarines would patrol "a fluid front that constantly shifted with the advance of the Japanese offensive. Where opportunity presented they might penetrate this front to harry the sea lanes behind the lines or raid the harbors captured by the Japanese invasion forces."

The Pacific Ocean was immense. No matter how you looked at it, US submarines were spread very thin indeed.

• • •

Eck noticed his captain's left hand opening and closing again, something he'd seen the skipper do before when he was deeply moved. Frederick Warder told his men, " 'Needless to say, you all know we're not playing any more. We're out after them now. Let's get them.' "

Warder repeated the directive from command headquarters: "*'You will sink or destroy enemy shipping wherever encountered.'*"

That night, Warder made the first brief entry in what would eventually become hundreds of pages of *Seawolf*'s patrol reports: "Under way with convoy as directed."

● ● ●

"We had no chance to cable our families that we were all right," reflected Eck. By now, Marjorie would know they were at war and be wondering whether he was safe. He had no way to reassure her. "We'd have to wait for that later—somewhere, somehow. We knew we had our work cut out. Philippine waters are dangerous for submarines.

"Coral reefs, treacherous rocks, shoals, and in many places little depth to maneuver in, all add to trouble. And the waters themselves are so clear that planes can easily spot submarines."

Moving swiftly under the cover of darkness, the *Seawolf* made her way cautiously through Manila Bay. "We were constantly on the alert. The night lookouts kept their eyes glued to their binoculars . . . We strained every sense watching and listening."

Eck said, "As the sun rose on the ninth of December, we made our first day-long dive. We were on our first mission of the war; and from now on, unless we found ourselves in the safety of our own ports, the *Wolf* would never show more than her periscope in daylight."

Whenever the *Seawolf* ran submerged during the day, she needed to surface at night to recharge batteries. Like other submarines of the time, the *Seawolf* was diesel engine–driven when on the surface; underwater, the boat relied on battery-powered electric motors. This meant the submarine depended on fuel supplies for its diesel engines and stored energy from batteries to propel her underwater motors.

To conserve batteries, submarine captains preferred to run on the surface as much as possible. While submarines could make faster time this way, they were also vulnerable to attack from aircraft (sometimes even from friendly planes) and from other ships. So when submarine skippers needed to avoid detection or make a stealthy approach on an enemy target, they usually ran submerged.

Even submerged, the men on the *Seawolf* could track news through dispatches and radio broadcasts. What they heard made them realize just how close they'd come to being caught by the Japanese.

• • •

The enemy had wasted no time. Earlier on December 8, while the crew of the *Seawolf* had been rushing to leave port, Japanese planes had attacked Clark Field in the Philippines, wiping out seventeen B-17s—half of General Douglas MacArthur's force of Flying Fortress heavy bombers. In one swift move, the Japanese effectively established control of the air in the Philippines.

Not only did this clear the way for a land invasion, Japan could now send its own bombers over Manila Bay at any time, making any ships or submarines in the water "sitting ducks" as shells and bombs rained down from above. The Navy's submarine fleet was spared at Pearl Harbor. The same would not hold true in the Philippines.

• • •

On December 10, two days after the *Seawolf* left on patrol, her sister subs USS *Sealion* (SS-195) and USS *Seadragon* (SS-194) were still at the shipyard at Cavite undergoing overhaul. Workers were hurrying to finish. Nearly ready, the *Seadragon* was being painted. Empty and half-empty cans of black paint littered her wooden deck.

When the air-raid alarm sounded, sailors raced to man the machine guns, but the bombers were too high to be within range. *Seadragon* crew member A. J. Killin was standing on the bridge beside Ensign Samuel Howard Hunter, Jr., when the first bombs fell. Looking up, Killin realized, "We did not have a gun that could touch them. They didn't even break formation."

It's estimated that fifty-four Japanese planes, in two groups of twenty-seven, carried out the two-hour attack, which started fires that would last for days and create clouds of smoke seen thirty miles away in Manila.

On their second run, two bombs hit the *Sealion*, sending fragments through the air, which hit Ensign Hunter on the *Seadragon*. Hunter became the first submarine sailor killed in World War II. Four men in the *Sealion*'s engine room also died.

"Topside there was chaos," wrote historian Clay Blair. "The paint shop blew up, spreading fire all over the yard. Then the torpedo repair shop was hit. . . . A barge carrying forty-eight Mark XIV torpedoes for *Seadragon* and *Sealion* was hit. It capsized, and its valuable cargo rolled overboard. The paint cans on *Seadragon*'s deck blazed. The *Sealion* . . . listed to starboard, half sunk by the stern. Her crew, including three wounded, ran up the hatches and onto shore."

Seaman Ernie Plantz was on the USS *Perch* (SS-176), which was anchored nearby in Manila Bay to undergo some repairs. Plantz had transferred into submarines from a battleship for one

An illustration of the attack on the *Sealion*,
first submarine lost in WWII, December 10, 1941.

simple reason: better food. He'd never gotten enough to eat on his
previous ship, where the junior seamen were served last. After
being invited to dine on a sub, where there was plenty of delicious
food for all, he'd made up his mind. " 'Man, this is the place
for me.' "

Now Plantz and other crew members of the *Perch* looked on
helplessly as smoke rose into the air from Cavite. " 'The Skipper
was watching through the periscope in the Control Room, and he

let some of us look through the scope at what was happening. . . . Things were really blowing. They knew exactly where things were at, they knew exactly what they wanted to hit, and they proceeded to do it.'"

Luckily, the *Perch* wasn't struck, and was able to finish repairs and leave the Philippines two days later unharmed. The *Sealion* would never sail again. If there had been repair facilities available, she might have been saved, but those were destroyed in the attack. With the closest overhaul five thousand miles away at Pearl Harbor, the *Sealion* became the first submarine casualty of the war.

• • •

As the attack on Cavite raged, A. J. Killin, still on the deck of *Seadragon*, scrambled for cover. He almost didn't make it. "While I was rushing down the ladder into the conning tower, another concussion knocked me fourteen feet below to the control room deck.

"Four knobs about two inches long were all that remained of the ladder railing into control. I fell onto one of the knobs sticking up, landing full force on the tip of my spine. I lay there senseless on the control room deck for quite awhile."

Killin heard skipper Pete Ferrall give the order for the crew to abandon ship. Killin and the other sailors rushed ashore to find refuge from the assault; moments later, though, the captain ordered his crew back on board. He hoped that if they acted quickly, there might still be a chance to save the *Seadragon* by moving her away from the fires raging at the dock.

Men from the USS *Pigeon* (ASR-6), a rescue vessel designed to help submarines in distress, threw *Seadragon* a towline. As the sailors worked desperately to maneuver the two boats into deeper water, an oil tank exploded nearby, and a wave of fire threatened to engulf *Seadragon* and *Pigeon*. *Pigeon* managed to get *Seadragon* away from the blazing inferno just in time.

Badly wounded, *Seadragon* limped to the deep waters of Manila Bay, where crews worked frantically to patch leaks and make repairs. "We had many holes in the superstructure, and a lot of the deck was gone," Killin recalled.

As for the rescue vessel, the *Pigeon* became the first ship of the US Navy to be awarded the Presidential Unit Citation, given for heroism in action, in recognition of the brave actions of her crew that day.

• • •

On patrol with the *Seawolf*, which had completed her duties as a convoy escort, Mel Eckberg and his crewmates listened with horror to the familiar voice of respected radio commentator Don Bell describe the Cavite attack.

"'Right now Cavite is a mass of smoke and flame,'" Bell reported from the roof of the Manila Hotel. "'There has been no opposition in the air. . . . I have seen wave after wave of heavy bombers and dive bombers concentrate on Cavite . . . So far they are leaving the ships in the harbor alone. They are probably waiting, knowing they will have plenty of time for that.'"

After a brief pause, Bell went on, "'Ladies and gentlemen, I don't know when I shall be back on the air, but I shall be back, God willing.'"

Don Bell's real name was Clarence Beliel. He was later captured by the Japanese and interned in a camp with his family. In

Fires from the Japanese attack on Cavite Navy Yard, December 10, 1941.

camp, he survived by using Beliel as his name in order to keep his radio identity a secret from his captors.

• • •

The Japanese attack at Cavite killed nearly one thousand people, mostly civilian workers. It was also a military disaster: The *Sealion* was lost, the submarine repair facilities destroyed, and more than two hundred costly, much-needed torpedoes were lost.

Cavite had been the best-equipped naval base in the Far East. Now it was virtually unusable. It was abundantly clear that Pearl Harbor was merely the first target in the Japanese plan to seize territories throughout the Pacific.

Elsewhere in Asia, the news was equally grim as Japan continued to unleash its military power. "The British had failed to repel

Japanese landings in Malaya. British troops were retreating to Singapore. Hong Kong was under siege. Wake Island had been overrun," said historian Clay Blair.

With the battleships of the Pacific Fleet lying smoldering and broken at Pearl Harbor, there would be no swift victory against the Japanese in the Pacific. If the United States wanted to stop Japan, it would need its submarines. Most of the submarines in the Asiatic Fleet were now silently on patrol around the Philippine archipelago.

The *Seawolf* was one of them.

While the USS *Perch* escaped destruction at Cavite, her war service was cut short just a few months later. On March 1, 1942, *Perch*'s skipper, Dave Hurt, and his crew were patrolling near the island of Java when the submarine was attacked by two destroyers, which dropped depth charges, damaging the boat severely.

On March 3, as crew members tried to repair the submarine, they came under fire from five Japanese ships. They had no choice but to abandon ship and scuttle the submarine. The crew was picked up by a Japanese destroyer and transported to a POW (prisoner of war) camp on the island of Celebes (now Sulawesi) in Indonesia. Electrician's Mate Ernie Plantz, who'd transferred to the submarine force because of the better food, ended up spending the war fighting to stay alive on starvation rations.

The rice was old and full of worms. Sometimes, recalled Plantz, it was no more than " 'half a cup of rice and a half a cup of worms.' " Plantz and his fellow prisoners tried to pick them out at first. Then they figured that the worms, after all, were protein, so they began to eat them along with the rice.

Ernie Plantz survived the POW camp. When he returned to his hometown, he found his name listed among the dead on a war memorial at his high school. *Perch* had been presumed lost in March 1942 and no one knew he had survived.

His mother told him she had never given up hope.

6 THE OVERWHELMING FORCES OF THE UNKNOWN

Mel Eckberg fell into his bunk to try to get some rest, *Seawolf*'s close call at Cavite still on his mind. "We had missed being caught by less than forty-eight hours."

Eck had a hard time settling down. "I was too geared up. The *Wolf*'s powerful electric motors kept up a steady, high-pitched whine, and I thought of Marjorie and Spike, and how worried Marjorie must be, and how I could get word to her that I was all right."

No sooner had Eck dozed off than he was being shaken awake. "'Eck! Eck! They want you in sound.'"

Eck jumped out of his bunk. In the sound shack, a crewmate handed him the earphones. "'I can't figure it out, Eck. I got something here, and I don't know what.'"

Eck took over, listening hard. He caught a soft chattering. Could this be *Seawolf*'s first enemy contact? Over the intercom, Eck reported to Captain Frederick Warder that he was picking up noises, which might be two Japanese submarines communicating with each other.

"'Give me a bearing, Eckberg,' came back Captain Warder's voice."

Eck concentrated. "I turned my wheel carefully, trying to find the point on my 360-degree dial where the chatter was loudest. I tried to pin it down to a definite spot in a definite direction from the *Wolf*, but I couldn't.

Sleeping quarters on a submarine.

" 'They're all over the dial,' " Eck told the captain. " 'I get them everywhere.' "

Eck knew Japanese submarines could pose a real threat to the *Seawolf.* "Submarines can ram each other underwater, and if one locates the other by sound, it can even send a torpedo after it. . . . But if the sound did come from another submarine, the bearings must show a change over a period of time, and these did not.

"Since it was impossible for another submarine to be gliding alongside of us, at the same speed, at the same distance, never varying in angle, the noise must be coming from something else."

What could it be? Eck continued to listen. "I racked my brains . . . Suddenly I had it. *Reef fish!* Small, green-bellied 'croakers' which emit a blubbering, bullfrog like grunter under water that can deceive the most expert ear. . . . I reported to the Captain, feeling a little sheepish.

" 'Fish, Eckberg?' Over the intercom came a chuckle. 'Better go back and finish your sleep. You need it.' "

• • •

It was natural to question any unusual sound. The men of the *Seawolf* had been training for years, yet were still untested in battle. And while normal routines continued, danger could now be stalking them from any direction—a Japanese submarine below, a plane high above, or an enemy destroyer on the surface of the sea.

To add to the tension, the *Seawolf,* like other submarines on these first patrols, some of which lasted forty to fifty-five days, was sailing blind. Later in the war, code breaking would provide valuable intelligence to help guide a submarine's movements and identify the location of Japanese ships.

Yet just days into the conflict, submarine skippers possessed scant data about Japanese forces, making these early patrols even more perilous. It was unclear how many destroyers the enemy possessed, or what weapons the Japanese might have been developing in secrecy in the prewar years. Often, submarine captains like Frederick Warder were gathering valuable information about Japan's naval strength just by gazing through their periscopes.

The submarines leaving from Manila in early December were a little like cats walking softly in the dark, observed naval historian Theodore Roscoe. "Foraying in this fortnight before Christmas were boats that would carve famous names across the oceanic reaches of the Pacific, and captains and crews who would be remembered for waging some of the greatest sea-fights in history."

In these early days of the war, skippers like Frederick Warder were leading their men to do battle with what Roscoe called "the overwhelming forces of the Unknown." In doing so they "set patterns in courage and resourcefulness to be followed throughout the war and remain as an inspiration to the service."

The Asiatic Fleet submarines also faced another challenge: Their home base at Cavite had been destroyed, though it was still possible for submarines to enter Manila Bay, where the submarine tender *Canopus* was anchored.

Navy officials were taking precautions to protect this important service vessel. The *Canopus* had been camouflaged with netting and painted to look like a dock to help hide her from marauding Japanese planes. Submarines were serviced as quickly as possible, and the men stood ready to suspend operations and submerge if an air attack began. With the Japanese aerial onslaught continuing day after day, it was anyone's guess how long this arrangement could continue—or how long the *Canopus* would stay lucky.

• • •

At sea in treacherous waters, Mel Eckberg and his crewmates looked forward to nightfall, when the *Seawolf* could surface in the relative safety of darkness.

"As soon as the hatch was opened, we started our Diesels to recharge batteries. Captain Warder, always the first man on the bridge when we surfaced, climbed up, and after him the Officer of the Deck, a duty taken in rotation by the officers.

"Then came the night lookouts; then the signalmen; later the mess cooks with the garbage of the last twenty-four hours, which they cast overboard. Of the sixty-five men in the *Wolf*, these were the only ones who went topside day or night without special permission. If more were permitted, a crash dive would catch them like rats."

Even if the men couldn't stand out in the open, they tried to take advantage of the submarine being above the water in other ways, recalled Eck. "Groups of men below crowded about the ladder, breathing deep gulps of the fresh air coming down from the bridge and sucked aft by the Diesels. The cooks had begun their 'hot cooking'—meats and fish and baking—because the odors could escape now, and the blowers were wafting these tantalizing smells into every compartment."

• • •

The *Seawolf* was now moving cautiously through the waters off the northeastern coast of Luzon, the main island in the Philippines archipelago. Word had reached the *Seawolf*'s crew that on

December 10 the Japanese had landed troops at Aparri, a town on the mouth of a river on the northernmost part of the island. Having seized control of the air, Japan was ready to launch a ground invasion. If the *Seawolf* could get close enough to Aparri, it could attack Japanese vessels in the harbor—if Warder and his crew could find them.

Find them they did. Frederick Warder was about to earn his nickname.

FEARLESS FREDDIE'S DARING FORAY

Once again, Mel Eckberg had been roused from sleep to go to *Seawolf*'s sound shack. This time, though, he was pretty sure he wasn't hearing reef fish.

" 'Sound has something, sir,' " Eck reported to the conning tower, which in the *Seawolf* was above the control room and was used as the attack approach area where the captain and officers could scan the sea through *Seawolf*'s periscope.

Eck heard officer Richard Holden bark three orders in quick succession: " 'Up periscope,' " followed immediately by " 'Down periscope,' " and then " 'Call the captain.' "

A moment later, Frederick Warder climbed the ladder to the conning tower, his sandals making a slapping sound. " 'What do you have, Mr. Holden?' "

It was a destroyer. The arch foes of submarines, destroyers were equipped with torpedo tubes and depth charges, antisubmarine weapons consisting of cans filled with explosives.

The skipper peered through the periscope for fifteen seconds, no more, before giving the order: " 'Battle stations.' "

Aaap! Aaap! The raucous alarm blared. The response was instantaneous.

"Half-naked, their bodies gleaming in the yellow light, the men tumbled out of their bunks," said Eck. Around him, the narrow passageways filled and then emptied as each man rushed to his position.

Through his headphones, Eck caught a distinctive *Ping! Ping!*
It reminded him of someone plucking the E string of a violin.
"This was the telltale sound of the enemy's sound-detection apparatus. He was searching for us—sending out electrical sound
waves—and we were listening for him. We waited."

• • •

The seas were rough, and through his earphones Eck could tell
that the destroyer was pitching in the high waves. Just as *Seawolf*
had served as the escort for a convoy, it was likely that this
destroyer was playing the same role, and was guarding a Japanese
oil tanker or aircraft tender at anchor in the harbor beyond.

While the *Seawolf* could go for the destroyer, there might be
other, more valuable targets close at hand. Sinking an aircraft
tender, a vessel being used to support the bombers harassing US
troops in the Philippines every day, would help to disrupt the
Japanese invasion.

Eck could sense the tension throughout the boat as the men
waited for the captain and his approach team to assess the situation. "Two full minutes dragged by. No one spoke. I heard men
coughing, clearing their throats, shuffling, making the small
noises men make under the pressure."

As he listened to the enemy propellers through his headphones,
Eck kept the skipper apprised of the destroyer's course and position. At last, Warder made his decision.

"'Secure battle stations. We will not attack. We're going to
look inside that cove,'" he ordered, releasing the men.

Every man knew entering that cove would be extremely dangerous. Launching an attack in any kind of inlet, rather than on
the open ocean, would limit the *Seawolf*'s ability to maneuver

or take evasive action. While the captain and officers looked over the charts in the control room, the men drank coffee. The day passed.

"With nightfall, the seas grew mountainous. We drew away from the bay: Captain Warder wanted his men to catch some sleep during the night. A few of us tried to doze off, but we were too tense. Some of the boys were seasick. Most of us stayed at our stations, checking and rechecking our gear," said Eck. He distinctly recalled that the torpedo crew took time to inspect their fish carefully.

"Captain Warder and Lieutenant Deragon [the executive officer] pored over their charts in the control room: slim men both, one big, the other small, both in khaki shorts and sandals, their bodies glistening with perspiration under the subdued light."

The *Seawolf* surfaced to recharge her batteries. Everyone knew what was coming next. "The *Wolf* was going into that cove."

• • •

Before dawn on December 14, the *Seawolf* dipped silently below the surface and made her way slowly into the cove near Aparri.

Warder was executing a daring move. He wanted to bring the submarine close enough to fire at any ships in the harbor, yet not venture into shallow water. If the *Seawolf* got stuck in the mud or ran aground on a reef, it would mean disaster. Maneuvering into position required caution—and extreme patience.

"The approach was a delicate matter. We spent four hours negotiating the short distance, making periscope observations every few minutes," Eck recalled. "The order would come, 'Up periscope.' The glistening metal pillar—for all the world like a huge, shining perpendicular piston—would glide up with a soft drone, up out of its well until the periscope lens was above the surface of the water, far overhead.

"Captain Warder would place both arms over the two crossbars protruding more than a foot from either side of the periscope base, and, half-hanging on them, his forehead pressed against the sponge-rubber eyepiece, he would rotate with it like some strange acrobat in slow motion."

Eck knew what it was like to get a glimpse of the world up above this way: "the sense of shock you had when you saw the brightness of daylight, the sun sparkling on the blue waters of the sea. Looking through a periscope is like looking through high-powered binoculars: almost under your nose the sea heaves and tosses, so near that you almost pull back from the spray."

The periscope allowed the captain to add a filter if the sun were too bright, or reduce the magnification to get a better field of vision. An experienced user was also able to judge how far away any target lay, and transmit the information to the TDC (torpedo data computer) to help set up the attack.

While the captain and another officer took turns looking through the periscope, Eck's job was to listen—and listen hard. Above him, the seas were "a roaring, snapping, crackling bedlam blaring through my phones like static in a terrific electrical storm."

Against this noisy backdrop, Eck concentrated on picking out the distinct sounds of a ship's corkscrew-shaped propeller, its screws. "To hear the beating of a ship's screws above this scratching inferno of sound meant listening with such intensity that often you mistook the pulsations of your own blood for the enemy."

• • •

Then Warder spotted it: a Japanese seaplane tender at anchor, with two masts and deck guns on its forward and aft decks. It was a prize, and knocking it out would hinder Japan's ability to repair and fuel planes.

Although the destroyer was still nearby, *Seawolf* managed to slip by it unnoticed and move into attack position. Once more, the men went to battle stations. Signalman Frank Franz got ready to relay the captain's orders, repeating each command precisely.

The first one came: "'Forward torpedo room, make ready the bow tubes.'"

Next: "'Open outer doors.'"

Eck described the process: "In the control room below a man worked feverishly spinning a huge control wheel by hand . . . ten

Sailors loading a torpedo.

revolutions, eleven, twelve, thirteen, fourteen . . . Far forward in the bow, two great steel doors in the *Wolf*'s hull slowly open, exposing the blunt heads of the torpedoes."

Franz reported back up to Warder. " 'Forward tubes ready, Captain . . . Outer doors open.'

" 'Up periscope!' said the Skipper. A few moments later: 'Stand by.' "

It seemed as though the *Seawolf* was in perfect position, but her captain wasn't satisfied. Peering through the periscope, Warder called for more adjustments. " 'No, no, wait a minute! Rudy, come left a little more, little more . . . there! Hold her, Rudy. . . . Fire one!' "

Firing torpedoes isn't a simple operation. "Torpedoes are fired by an impulse of compressed air. The air pressure within the boat goes up correspondingly," Eck explained.

For that reason, he and the rest of the crew could feel each torpedo as it launched. "There was a sudden *whoosh!* as though the safety valve of a radiator had blown off. Then a gentle kick-back, as though the *Wolf* coughed, suddenly alive. I felt the pressure on my eardrums."

Eck could make out the high-pitched whine of the torpedo as it shot through the water. He listened for sounds of an explosion, which would mean a hit. Every submariner was also on the alert for problems. A bad torpedo running off course could turn and cause fatal damage. As Eck explained, "An erratic fish can circle about and come back to blow you into Kingdom Come."

The captain called, " 'Stand by to fire two. . . . Fire two!' "

Eck remained glued to his headphones. Again the hiss, the jar, the kickback. "As each fish left, I picked it up on sound. The first whine died out, then the second came into my phones. It died out. I waited tensely for the explosions. The skipper kept his eyes glued to the periscope. I listened hard."

The *Seawolf* fired four torpedoes in all. Every man waited for one sound: an explosion. It didn't come. Eck had heard the fish running. He'd caught what sounded like dull thuds. Had the torpedoes missed the target, continued past, and exploded on the beach beyond? Had the magnetic exploder, designed to activate an explosion when a torpedo passes under a boat's keel, somehow malfunctioned?

Eck reported the bad news. Wanting to determine if the destroyer had detected the *Seawolf* yet, the captain asked, " 'Sound, do you hear any propellers?' "

Again Eck listened hard. " 'No screws, sir.' "

" 'Good!' said the Skipper."

Warder decided to try again—this time with the stern torpedoes. *Seawolf* was expecting company from that destroyer any minute and had to be ready to make a quick getaway. So Warder turned *Seawolf*'s head toward the mouth of the harbor and let loose two more fish.

This time, Warder spotted white water through the periscope—lots of it—yet still no explosions or smoke. Once again, there were questions: Had the torpedo hit but the magnetic exploder failed? And what about those first fish? How could they have missed a ship at anchor under such perfect conditions?

There was no time to linger to puzzle it out because the next sound they heard was a muffled boom. A depth charge! The *Seawolf* had hung around too long. The destroyer was after her.

"The *Wolf* shook. Her joints creaked. The lights flickered, went out for a moment, then on again. It was a depth charge, mild because it was some distance away. Actually no depth charge attack can be called mild, because when 700 or 800 pounds of TNT explode in your general vicinity, any number of things can happen," Eck said, adding that "a depth charge doesn't have to score a direct hit to sink you. . . .

"An explosion can write your finish if it's near enough for the concussion to place sufficient pressure on the water surrounding your boat to stave it in or crush it altogether. If you've ever heard two stones struck together under water, you know how booming and terrifying that small report can sound, intensified and expanded by the water."

Each submariner had his own way of dealing with a depth-charge attack. Jeweldeen Brown, a radioman on the USS *Trout* (SS-202), recounted how he'd learned to cope. " 'Initially, of course, I was scared like everybody else. But then I guess you get sort of battle hardened. . . . But when they got real close and they starting breaking light bulbs and glass on gages [*sic*] and things like that then that was a little worrisome.

" 'But then I woke up one morning and I thought, I'm merely being foolish. If I'm standing here, and I heard that blasted thing go off, I'm ok. It didn't kill me. . . . The one I have to worry about is the one I haven't even heard. That's the next one. So I got along pretty good that way.' "

• • •

The *Seawolf* raced out of the cove and into open water. Captain Warder and his men had wanted to claim the first sinking of an enemy ship by a submarine. It was not to be: That honor went to the *Swordfish* (SS-193).

Warder, full of questions about what had happened, sent for torpedo officer Donald Syverson. The skipper said, "'I can't understand it. . . . I don't know what was wrong with those first fish. Got any ideas about it?'"

Syverson had inspected the torpedoes himself and found no defects. Neither man could figure out how they could have missed. Eight torpedoes: zero results. What had gone wrong?

As it turned out, *Seawolf*'s experience that day would be an omen of things to come. The men in the submarine service were brave beyond measure. Yet as they would discover time and time again in the coming months, there was definitely something fishy about those torpedoes.

CHRISTMAS RETREAT  8

"There wasn't much we could do about celebrating Christmas," said Mel Eckberg. The *Seawolf* had been on patrol since December 8 with no end in sight; the men would spend their first wartime holiday at sea.

Eck felt depressed about being so far away from Marjorie and baby Spike. He would miss his son's first Christmas. Yet thanks to some of his inventive crewmates, there turned out to be some surprises. "The first inkling I had was when I strolled into the mess hall after my afternoon watch on December 24."

As Eck and a few others were leafing through magazines, John Edward Sullivan burst in, beaming and red-faced. "Sully" was the chief yeoman, serving as the clerk for the *Seawolf*, handling files and supply orders, and maintaining official records.

"'Well, boys, she's finished. Want to take a look at her?'" Sully asked.

"'What's finished?'" Eck and the others wanted to know.

"'Why, my Christmas tree.'"

Sully led the way into the yeoman's office. There, Eck laid eyes on a Christmas tree—or at least what passed as a Christmas tree on a submarine at sea. A broom handle served as the tree trunk, with tongue depressors as branches.

"He'd made tinsel by gluing tinfoil from cigarette packages to strips of paper, and decorated the branches with that. He'd painted half a dozen flashlight bulbs green and red and silver and strung them about on a dry-battery circuit, and so his Christmas tree gleamed green, red, and silver—a work of art two feet high. . . .

"We liked that little Christmas tree," Eck recalled. "The men would look at it, and someone would say, 'Jeez, isn't that a pretty little thing,' and then you'd hear someone else's voice, 'Sure wish I was home tonight.'"

That wasn't the only surprise. A while later, someone hung up some stockings bulging with what Eck considered "the wildest collection of junk I'd ever seen in my life. A bunch of garlic; a twelve-inch Stilsen wrench; a can of oil."

Eck lingered in the small messroom, unable to sleep. Just before midnight, crewmates wandered in to wish one another a merry Christmas.

"There was a lump in my throat," he said. "I had to swallow a few times, sitting there, thinking, *Here it is Christmas, and Marjorie and Spike alone at home, not knowing if I'm dead or alive, and we're off Corregidor, and men are dying in Bataan, and we don't know if we're going to be dead or alive ourselves twenty-four hours from now.*"

• • •

On Christmas Day, the *Seawolf*'s crew got one more unexpected gift—courtesy of the cook. "Gus Wright came into the mess hall [or messroom, the area where enlisted men eat and relax] and announced what we'd have for dinner that night—mince pies. He'd been up all night baking them, twenty of them. Gus was the hero of the boat that day.

"He was a thin fellow, about twenty-eight, with buck teeth and a pleasant way about him; and the fuss the crew made over

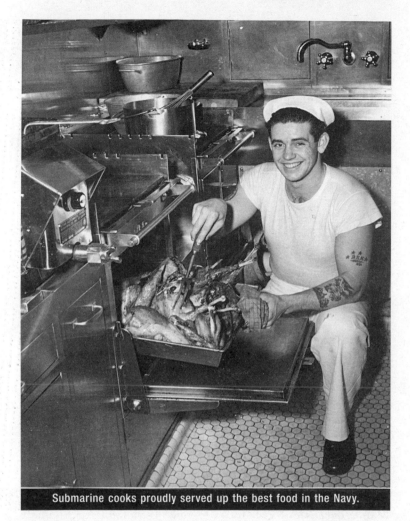

Submarine cooks proudly served up the best food in the Navy.

his surprise made him so happy that his eyes got watery, and he went back into the galley and banged his pans around until he got it out of him.

"A Christmas tree, mince pies—well, it was a better Christmas than the boys had on Bataan and Corregidor, we thought."

• • •

Bataan and Corregidor: Eck and his crewmates had been keeping up with events in the Philippines by radio. The news was not good. The United States had hoped to stand and fight, to protect the Philippines and drive the Japanese away. Instead, every sign pointed the other way: America was losing—and losing badly—in the fierce struggle to control this strategic territory.

The Japanese had landed troops on the main island of Luzon at Aparri, where the *Seawolf* had missed hitting its targets. On Christmas Eve, General Douglas MacArthur evacuated military personnel from the city of Manila, which Japan was shelling daily. MacArthur moved his ground troops to Bataan, a peninsula in Manila Bay across from the Navy base at Cavite—or what had been the base before the devastating December 10 attack.

With the Japanese controlling the air and sea around the Philippines, American and Filipino troops were effectively stranded on Bataan without hope of reinforcements or supplies (except, as we shall see, for a few things submarines could manage to sneak in).

General MacArthur himself set up headquarters in an old complex of tunnels that had been blasted out from volcanic rock on the small island of Corregidor. Nicknamed the Rock, it sits in Manila Bay about three and a half miles from Bataan. Originally intended for the storage of supplies and equipment—not to house people—the tunnels nevertheless offered a safe haven from air attacks.

Admiral Hart, who commanded both the surface ships and submarines of the Asiatic Fleet, faced some difficult decisions. Unless he abandoned the Philippines, he risked losing valuable vessels to Japanese air attacks. He determined to move the boats of the Asiatic surface fleet to the Dutch naval base at Surabaya, Java, where he would set up headquarters to direct their operation.

That left the problem of what to do about the submarines. With the loss of *Sealion*, there were now twenty-eight boats in the Asiatic Fleet. As submarine historian Clay Blair put it, Hart faced this question: "Should he abandon the Philippines as a submarine base, withdrawing the tender *Canopus* and the boats, or leave them to fight on from Bataan and Corregidor?"

At first, Hart determined that the submarines should try to hang on as long as possible. On Christmas Eve, he ordered the submarine tender *Canopus* from Manila to Corregidor, where she would be under the protection of US antiaircraft guns. It happened so quickly, there was no time to load torpedoes, supplies, or spare parts on board; equipment and weapons worth thousands of dollars were abandoned.

"*Canopus* moved in the nick of time," wrote Clay Blair. On Christmas Day, Japanese bombs blistered the Manila waterfront and fell on submarine headquarters, forcing John Wilkes, who served under Admiral Hart as the submarine boss for the fleet, along with his chief of staff, Jimmy Fife, and operations officer Stuart "Sunshine" Murray, to take cover in slit trenches. It was clear: America could no longer hold the city against Japanese invaders.

Wilkes, Fife, and Murray managed to evacuate by small boat to Corregidor. Wilkes said, "'We arrived late Christmas afternoon and set up our headquarters in a tunnel by pushing over a number of spare-part boxes to make room for a cot, a radio receiver, and one typewriter, this consisting of our sole equipment. We, by that time, were quite portable.'"

Hart himself had planned to evacuate the Philippines by naval patrol plane, but Japanese bombs eliminated that option. Instead, at two in the morning of December 26, he escaped on the submarine USS *Shark* (SS-174) headed for Java, where he would command the surface fleet.

The US Navy had now completely lost control of the waters and air surrounding Luzon. There was little fuel available; no support systems were in place. Submarines returning from patrols to Manila Bay had to stay submerged during the day and try to refit and refuel quickly at night to avoid enemy planes. Explosive mines laid in the waters of the bay made passage in and out dangerous.

By New Year's Eve, Wilkes realized the time had come to retreat. Not everyone could escape, however. There simply weren't enough submarines to evacuate the hundreds of workers— machinists, electricians, and torpedo specialists who kept the submarine fleet in operation. Many were attached to the old submarine tender *Canopus*, which, Wilkes decided, was simply too slow to make a break for it. He feared that if *Canopus* was attacked by Japanese planes while fleeing, everyone on board would be killed. The *Canopus* would remain in the Philippines until the very end.

Wilkes estimated that the submarines could rescue about 250 people; each of the ten boats then in port could accommodate about twenty-five extra men. Anyone left behind would, he knew, become a prisoner of war.

"'This was a very tough decision to make,'" Wilkes said later.

" 'I used only one guiding principle, whether officer or man. Would the men that we were to take be of value in prosecuting the war no matter where we went?' "

• • •

The *Seawolf* became part of the retreat the day after Christmas. Her passengers were members of Wilkes's staff heading to Darwin, Australia. Although 1,200 miles from Admiral Hart's new head-quarters in Java, Darwin offered the closest support facilities for the scattered submarines. While the *Canopus* remained, two other submarine tenders, *Holland* (AS-3) and *Otus* (AS-20), had already been withdrawn from the Philippines and sent to Australia.

Eck recalled the rush to ready the *Seawolf*; the crew waited until it was nearly dark because of the danger posed by Japanese aerial attacks in daylight.

"At dusk we surfaced . . . Now we set to work in earnest," Eck recalled. "There were stores to load, and we worked without rest. Apparently we were going out that same day, and we weren't going on a picnic. . . .

"By midnight oil lines had been hooked up to the *Wolf*, and hundreds of gallons were flowing into our tanks. We worked like stevedores bringing the endless stores aboard. The highly secret and confidential papers and other invaluable data were stowed in a safe position. I helped with the fuel line, and I carried boxes aboard. I looked over my radio gear, checking and rechecking it."

One incident stuck in Eck's mind. Crew member Gunner Bennett came into the sound shack, holding four yellow cans that at first looked to Eck like cans of hard candy. Far from it. It was dynamite, a somber reminder of the danger they faced.

Bennett held out the sticks to Eck. "'Here's the dope. Plant these. If we have to, before this ship is captured or abandoned, we got to destroy all gear . . . that includes your radio and sound gear.'"

Eck took the cans, then Bennett handed him four fuses, about five feet long. "'These are slow-burning,' he said. 'But if you have to set them'—he grinned—'it won't matter if you get out of here fast or not. You won't be going nowhere.'"

• • •

Shortly after midnight, *Seawolf* was ready to pull out. That's when Eck understood their mission.

"As I crossed through the control room on my way to the radio shack, I saw a man's legs coming down the conning tower," recalled Eck. "Life on a sub is so intimate that you instantly recognize your crewmates from any angle of vision you see them. . . . *These legs were strangers.*"

The legs belonged to Jimmy Fife, Wilkes's chief of staff, who greeted Eck, then strode over to study the charts.

"It seemed we were taking the U.S. Submarine High Command out from Corregidor," Eck said. "We'd have preferred action to evacuating personnel, but we realized that this was a mission comparable in importance to sinking ships. After all, ships can be replaced, but submarines officers with the training of our passengers could not.

"And we were proving once again that a surface blockade couldn't stop the *Wolf.* We were proving that the submarine has an advantage over all other craft because she could disappear from sight."

• • •

When the new year of 1942 dawned, the *Seawolf* was en route to Australia. Once they arrived, crew members would get their first chance since the war began to cable home to let loved ones know they were safe. Eck began thinking about his message to Marjorie days in advance.

"The first moment I had I sat down at my desk, trying to find words to explain all I wanted to say: how I felt when I couldn't reach her, how I knew she must have worried, how much I missed her and Spike, how I had their photographs right here in front of me when I worked and above my bunk when I slept, so that I saw them the last minute before I fell asleep and the first moment I awoke every morning.

"At last I settled on: 'Feeling fine don't worry love to all.' "

The truth was, Eck knew there was no guarantee just how long he—or any submariner—would be fine.

Submarine crews went to sea as a tight combat unit. Their ability to conduct a successful war patrol—and return to port safely—depended on many factors.

Sound military strategy and inspired leadership were essential, of course. Also important were systems to organize and supply the boats, which had to carry food, fuel, and supplies for long cruises of fifty days or more across vast stretches of ocean. And, of course, a submarine without enough torpedoes couldn't do its job. Torpedoes that malfunctioned or performed poorly were a major problem, as we shall see.

To help streamline logistics, the Asiatic and Pacific Fleet submarines were organized into divisions, usually consisting of six boats. At the start of the war in 1941, the Asiatic Fleet comprised five divisions. (Mel Eckberg's *Seawolf* was part of Division 202, which also included the *Seadragon* and *Sealion*.)

Two divisions made up a squadron. Each squadron was assigned to a submarine tender, such as the *Canopus*, or to a base. Naval expert Theodore Roscoe explained, "The functions of the tender and the base are the same—to supply office space and quarters for the squadron and division commanders and their staffs, to billet repair personnel and relief crews, to undertake all submarine repairs, short of complete overhauls.

"Everything from the replacement of a damaged propeller to the adjustment of a cranky sextant, the supplying of all necessary food, fuel, clothing, spare parts, munitions, medical stores—the care of all the material needs of the submarines and physical needs of the submariners—these are the tasks accomplished by a submarine tender or submarine base."

• • •

That crucial ability to supply submarines in the Asiatic Fleet was disrupted early in the war, when the Japanese attacked naval facilities in the Philippines. Rather than move those boats to Pearl Harbor, it was decided to base the submarines in Australia.

But Clay Blair, who wrote a comprehensive history of the Pacific submarine war, questioned the wisdom of this decision. Much of shipping to and from Japan passed through the Luzon Strait, north of the Philippines between Luzon and Formosa (now Taiwan). Blair argued that if the submarines had been moved to Pearl Harbor, boats could have patrolled the Luzon Strait more effectively, using the island of Midway as a refueling point. The consolidation of all submarines at Pearl Harbor would also have simplified the process of getting torpedoes and spare parts to the boats. And it would have allowed easier access to the Mare Island Navy Yard in California for major refitting and upgrades.

There were other factors that made Australia a less than perfect choice for a submarine base. The voyage from Freemantle, Australia, was difficult and closer to Japanese air bases, meaning that submarines had to stay submerged for safety and go more slowly. That meant the submarines couldn't stay as long in patrol areas because they had to have enough fuel for the long return trip.

Consolidation would have had another advantage: bringing all the submarines under one leadership structure. Instead, noted Blair, the Pacific and Asiatic Fleets tended to operate separately. "The two submarine commands grew into independent rival organizations, competing for Japanese shipping rather than cooperating."

ABOUT THE TIMELINES

World War II began in Europe on September 1, 1939, when Hitler invaded Poland. On September 3, 1939, Great Britain and France declared war on Germany. The timelines included in this book begin when the United States entered the war in December 1941 and cover events in the Pacific. Timelines appear at the end of each of the four sections and include some (but by no means all) of the major war events of that year.

Most battles between US and Japanese forces in the Pacific were fought using surface ships, airplanes, and ground troops, with submarines playing a supporting role at times. Please note that not every military operation included in the timelines is described in this book, which focuses on only a few of the many submarines that were active during the war in the Pacific.

DECEMBER 7: Japanese attack Pearl Harbor; Japan launches attacks in Hong Kong, Siam, Malaya, Guam, and the Philippines, where much of General Douglas MacArthur's Far East Air Force at Clark Field is destroyed.

DECEMBER 8: United States declares war on Japan.

DECEMBER 10: In the Philippines, Japanese attacks destroy the Cavite Navy Yard.

DECEMBER 21: Main Japanese invasion of Philippines begins.

DECEMBER 24: General Douglas MacArthur decides to move his Army headquarters from Manila to the island of Corregidor, "the Rock," and ground forces to the peninsula of Bataan.

DECEMBER 25: Japanese bombers attack Manila waterfront; submarine headquarters moves to Corregidor.

DECEMBER 26: Admiral Thomas Hart, commander in chief of the Asiatic Fleet (General MacArthur's Navy counterpart), leaves for Dutch naval base at Surabaya, Java, to direct overall operations from there.

DECEMBER 31: John Wilkes, commander of Asiatic Fleet submarines, decides to abandon the Philippines for Java. (Following its loss to the Japanese in February, he moves Asiatic submarine headquarters to Australia.)

PART TWO

BRAVE MEN AND TERRIBLE TORPEDOES

• 1942 •

You say I'm punchy? You'd be too,
If you'd been with me in '42,
So just sit still 'till my tale is told
of a submarine on war patrol.

—**"The First War Patrol"**
poem found on a locker on USS *Cachalot (SS-170)*

The torpedo scandal of the U.S. submarine force in World War II
was one of the worst in the history of any kind of warfare.

—*Clay Blair, Jr.*

Surrender on Corregidor.

9 THE BRAVEST STAND

January 15, 1942. Darwin, Australia. Mel Eckberg and his crew-mates on the *Seawolf* were eager to get back on war patrol. Enemy ships were out there, just waiting to be sunk. So when their skip-per, Frederick Warder, ordered some of *Seawolf*'s torpedoes removed to make room for boxes, no one could believe it.

"'Are we a sub or a transport? Now they're making a cargo carrier out of us,'" someone griped.

Then the *Seawolf*'s men got an answer that stopped all their complaints. This wasn't just any cargo, but cases and cases of ammunition—all for the relief of American soldiers still holding out against the enemy on the small fortress island of Corregidor in the Philippines.

In the past month, the situation in the Philippines had contin-ued to deteriorate. The US had pledged to defend the islands against Japan. Yet even before war broke out, military planners had questioned whether this would be feasible with the resources available. Japan had seized control of the air and seas around the islands, making it nearly impossible to send in reinforcements to aid the remaining American and Filipino forces trying to fight off the invaders on Bataan and Corregidor. In any case, President Roosevelt and his military commanders in Washington, DC, had no additional troops to send: American soldiers were needed to fight the war in Europe.

Still, the submarines were prepared to do what little they could to help. Captain Warder's order read: "You will remove all except eight (8) torpedoes and such other ammunition as may be necessary to enable you to carry up to forty (40) tons."

The *Seawolf* was about to undertake her most perilous mission yet.

• • •

"We packed ammunition until it almost oozed out," Eck said. "Ammunition piled higher and higher. It was in the forward torpedo room, the after-torpedo room. We stepped over it and we slept on it. The cases were above the level of my bunk, seven feet above the deck. That night I crawled over cases of shells to get to my bunk.

"Sleeping on that ammunition gave us a queer feeling."

Everyone knew what would happen if the *Seawolf*, packed to the gills with explosives, was blasted by a heavy depth charge. One of Eck's crewmates summed it up: " 'If they get us, they'll just blow us a little higher.' "

Carrying the perilous cargo set everyone's nerves on edge. A few days north of Australia, while the *Seawolf* was running below the surface at periscope depth, Eck heard a voice boom over the intercom: " 'Call the captain!' "

Lieutenant Richard Holden had spotted something. " 'Captain, I see something on the starboard bow. Can't make it out.'

" 'Let's take a look at it, Dick,' said Captain Warder. A thirty-second pause as he peered in the periscope. 'She's pretty far off yet . . . It could be a ship, all right . . . Down periscope.' "

The periscope sightings continued. The skipper looked again, then called Dick Holden over to see the "ship" he'd sighted. Eck could hear the surprise in the lieutenant's voice. " 'Well, I'll be. . . . A seagull floating on a log!' "

A sailor sleeps in his bunk above torpedoes.

Laughter erupted throughout the *Seawolf* as news of the false alarm spread. It was a welcome relief from the tension. For days afterward, the submariners made jokes about the missed opportunity for a target (and fresh meat). " 'How we going to attack this here seagull? Shoot torpedoes at him or get up and fire a three-inch [deck gun]? Anybody got a slingshot?' "

• • •

When not on watch or at their other duties, crew members caught up on mending, played cards in the mess hall, cleaned their clothes in "Baby," the *Seawolf*'s washing machine, or even held informal spelling bees as they lay in their bunks with their heels resting on cases of ammunition.

Seawolf had been ordered to speed to Corregidor as quickly as possible. Captain Warder knew that with a load of ammunition and only eight torpedoes (the ones in the tubes and no extras), mounting an attack on the way would be dangerous. So when a convoy of Japanese ships was sighted, Warder made no move. *Seawolf* slipped past undetected. Hours later, her luck almost ran out.

"We were gliding along the surface that night when, about 2 a.m., off the port beam and not farther away than 1,000 yards, a huge dark shape loomed up making terrific speed," Eck recalled. It was a destroyer.

"We were already starting a crash dive," he said. "Only seconds later the destroyer's propellers roared overhead . . . It was one of our narrowest escapes.

"I've often thought what would have happened had that destroyer suddenly veered hard left and headed for us. It would have been touch and go. With the ammunition aboard, that might have been *the* attack and *Seawolf*'s end."

• • •

The *Seawolf* made it safely to Corregidor on January 28, 1942, passing slowly through the treacherous minefields (areas where explosive bombs had been set) at the mouth of Manila Bay. The submarine waited out the day below the surface at 135 feet, out of sight and range of Japanese aircraft.

The next night, *Seawolf* docked and unloading began. After forty minutes, everything stopped: A raid was expected. *Seawolf* couldn't take the chance—one bomb striking the ammunition would have blasted the submarine out of the water and killed anyone nearby. Captain Warder moved *Seawolf* off a mile until seven minutes past midnight, when the all clear came, and soldiers from Corregidor could safely unload.

Eck stood on the wooden dock, glad to be breathing fresh air. Later that day, while the *Seawolf* was being reloaded with torpedoes for the next patrol, he had a chance to visit with some of the soldiers holding the Rock. He wanted to find someone in communications to see about getting some spare radio parts for *Seawolf.*

Eck made his way past antiaircraft guns camouflaged by trees into one of the Rock's tunnels. Inside it was bright—and crowded. "I saw men sleeping everywhere. They lay rolled up in blankets; dozed sitting on chairs and cases of ammunition . . . men were lining a number of hospital cots against a wall."

One soldier told Eck about the Japanese bombers that came over every day. "'You can set your watch by them. But we're knocking 'em out of the sky like clay pigeons. The other day one of our three-inch anti-aircraft set a world record. Knocked down

US military life inside Malinta Tunnel on Corregidor.

eight planes in one day. We figure more than 80 per cent of their bombs fall into the water.'"

Seawolf's dangerous mission to bring the troops more firepower had been worth it. "All I knew was, they needed ammunition and we brought it to them," said Eck.

Eck headed back to the *Seawolf* empty-handed. There were no spare parts or equipment to be had. He took one last look at Corregidor; his impressions would stay with him a long time.

"I could see searchlights playing up and down the shoreline of Mariveles, the naval base about a mile to the north. . . . Now and then, the *rat-a-tat-tat* of machine-gun fire came to my ears, and I could hear the dull thud of artillery fire from Bataan. Every few minutes, brilliant white flares split the darkness off toward

Americans fire antiaircraft guns stationed on Corregidor.

Mariveles. Searchlights continued to move their fingers across the sky. I went aboard the *Seawolf* and down where I belonged—in the sound room."

Eck reflected, "Our men were now making the bravest kind of a stand that a man can make: they were fighting off an enemy who grew stronger every hour."

Like the *Seawolf*, the *Trout* undertook a mission to help the beleaguered troops on Corregidor by delivering 3,500 rounds of antiaircraft ammunition. Skipper Frank W. Fenno and his crew arrived at the Rock on February 3, 1942.

When darkness fell, the men began the hard work of unloading the cargo. Then they loaded six 3,000-pound torpedoes from supplies still on Corregidor; these were carried by hand since there were no cranes on the dock. Crews labored until three in the morning, all the while hearing gunfire from the fighting nearby on the Bataan peninsula.

Before departing, Fenno had a problem to solve. " 'Our weight condition had been figured out on paper,' " he said. On the return trip, the *Trout* would need more weight, or ballast, so that the boat could be properly balanced; this is especially important for submarines, which move up and down in the water as they surface or dive.

" 'We requested twenty-five tons of ballast, preferably sand bags, so that we could move them around as necessary,' " Fenno said.

His request was denied: Sandbags couldn't be spared because they were being used to help fortify the island and protect soldiers from shells. The captain was offered something else instead: gold and valuables from Philippine bank vaults in Manila, which had been brought to Corregidor for safekeeping.

He agreed. The *Trout* took on two tons of gold bars, eighteen tons of silver pesos, important US State Department documents, and some bags of mail. The precious cargo was loaded by a brigade of men who passed the gleaming bars from hand to hand as gunfire lit the night sky. Captain Fenno signed a receipt and the *Trout* slipped away. Once the cargo was delivered safely, President Roosevelt was so pleased he directed that Fenno receive the Army Distinguished Service Cross.

The skipper did encounter one small snag when tallying the inventory at the end of the trip. A single bar of gold was missing. The submarine was searched top to bottom. Finally, the gold bar was discovered in the galley, where a cook had been using it as a paperweight.

USS CANOPUS (AS-9)

A less likely candidate than the Canopus *for the roll of heroine in a tale of adventure could hardly be imagined. She was no longer young, and had never been particularly dashing, but her partisans were always ready to ascribe a certain majesty of her appearance. Undeniable, she waddled like a duck, as was pointed out in many a good-natured jibe, but that was only natural in a middle-aged motherly type, and she was truly "mama-san" to her brood of submarines, which used to forage with her from the Philippines to the China coast and back again each year.*

—Captain E. L. Sackett

The submarine tender *Canopus* with her "brood" of submarines.

UNLIKELY HEROINES: LUCY WILSON AND CANOPUS

By early spring, several weeks after Mel Eckberg had ventured into the maze of tunnels on Corregidor, the plight of Filipino and American troops left on the Rock and on the nearby Bataan peninsula had become even more desperate.

Japan continued to control the air, dropping shells and bombs day after day. Japanese ground troops advanced with merciless ferocity. Allied soldiers, holed up in jungle encampments on Bataan, suffered from malaria and dysentery. The overworked nurses and doctors in one hospital struggled to care for six thousand patients.

It was now startlingly clear, if it hadn't been before, that the battle to prevent Japan from taking the Philippines could not be won. President Roosevelt himself ordered General Douglas MacArthur to evacuate on March 11, leaving General Jonathan M. Wainwright in command of Army forces. On April 6, 1942, Wainwright launched a hopeless, last-ditch attempt to staunch the invading force of Japanese troops.

"The defenders of Bataan were a scarecrow army with nothing but fire in their bellies," noted one historian. "Many who marched into battle had risen from their sickbeds as desperate officers milked the hospitals for men fit enough to carry a rifle. . . . Many advanced gripped by a mad despair, with only pride and a grim determination."

It was no longer even a contest: Japanese forces had all the advantages. American and Filipino soldiers had run out of almost everything: supplies, ammunition, food, and, ultimately, hope. Two days later, on April 8, Wainwright fled from Bataan to the tunnels on Corregidor.

The old submarine tender, *Canopus*, had somehow managed to hang on, in part thanks to a clever disguise. After she was struck in an air attack in January, Captain Earl L. Sackett and his crew set fire to oily rags to make her look like an abandoned hulk to Japanese scout planes passing overhead.

"The tough old girl was not ready for her grave yet," said her captain. What the enemy didn't know was that each night, *Canopus* became a machine and repair shop—and something else too. With functioning refrigerators and showers (and ice cream for as long as supplies lasted), *Canopus* was a temporary haven for men and women serving in primitive jungle conditions.

Army officers and nurses who could snatch a few hours leave gathered on board. "We had refrigeration, excellent cooking facilities, and decent living quarters, which seemed heaven to them compared to their hardships in the field," Sackett recalled.

One crewman later said, "'She was one fine old lady, and she went right on dishing out ice cream until the day before Bataan fell.'"

No one could deny the inevitable, though. Surrender was just days or, at the most, a week or two away. On April 8, *Canopus*—too slow to escape attacks from Japanese planes on the open ocean—was purposely sunk to prevent her use by the enemy. Scuttling her was a last resort, and the sad end of a much-loved ship.

"The *Canopus* seemed reluctant to go," said her skipper. Still, Sackett observed, her crew could take pride in the fact that the enemy had never been able to knock her out, and "she was still able to back out under her own power to deep water.

"There she was laid to her final rest by the hands of the sailors she had served so faithfully."

• • •

Canopus had been launched in 1919, two years after Army nurse Lucy Wilson was born in Big Sandy, Texas. Lucy had arrived in the Philippines in the fall of 1941, shortly after her twenty-fourth birthday. She was one of twelve female nurses on a troop ship full of male soldiers that left California in early October.

Lucy had been working in an Army hospital in Manila when the war broke out. She was napping in a room on the ward when she first heard Japanese bombs. "I tore down the mosquito net getting out of bed. I was so scared I was nauseated . . . I kept looking at the ceiling and walls to see why they didn't come tumbling down. After a few seconds I realized I would be receiving new patients and I had better get prepared."

Lucy had barely stopped to rest since. By Christmas Eve, Manila had become too dangerous. She and other nurses were evacuated by bus to Bataan; they were ordered to bring only what they could carry. Lucy stuffed a small bag with her white uniforms—uniforms that would prove useless in jungle conditions.

The young women spent that day jumping on and off the bus into muddy ditches whenever Japanese planes flew overhead. "We had nothing to eat all day and arrived at Limay [a town on the east coast of the peninsula, near Manila Bay] near midnight; and someone opened some cans of beans and remarked it was Christmas Day! We set up a hospital there. . . .

"Our white uniforms were so visible from the air that they issued size 42 olive drab coveralls to us," Lucy wrote later. "The seat came about to my knees and I weighed under 100 pounds."

On January 23, 1942, Lucy was transferred to an outdoor hospital area under the trees. The nurses' quarters consisted of cots with mosquito netting, placed inside a circle of gunny sacks tacked to trees for privacy. Lucy and the others bathed in a nearby stream.

"Here I was put in the Operating Room which was in a tent. Sometimes when bombs and shells landed we wondered if the tent wasn't going to fall down, it shook so bad. This meant that sometimes we would work night and day for 48 hours without stopping. . . . We only ate twice a day and that consisted mostly of rice with weevils in it . . ."

In fierce skirmishes against Japanese troops, thousands of Filipino and American soldiers had been pushed back to the southern portion of the Bataan peninsula. The exhausted men suffered from dysentery, dengue fever, and malnutrition. There was little protection against insects, rain, cold nights, or the incessant shelling from Japanese planes.

Many soldiers, Lucy remembered, "drank unboiled water, ate roots, lizards, snakes, snails, and any other thing they could find; and due to unknown things being poisonous, some died with food poisoning before reaching hospitals. . . . By the end of March, I think 75 to 80% of the front line had malaria."

Lucy herself fell so ill with malaria that she could barely stand. She was given quinine for her symptoms, and took only a couple of days off before soldiering on. By early April, hunger and disease were ravaging more men than the dropping bombs.

On April 8, General Jonathan Wainwright ordered the nurses to evacuate to Corregidor immediately. Lucy and her colleagues had to leave in the midst of their duties, shedding gowns and gloves.

"Walking out in the middle of an operation with hundreds lined up under the trees waiting for surgery was devastating to me," said Lucy. "This I have to live with for the rest of my life."

The nurses did not want to go, yet there was nothing they could say or do. Around them, wounded soldiers lay on bamboo beds and on the ground. "'Those eyes just followed us,'" recalled one nurse.

• • •

Lucy served the wounded on Corregidor until May 3. Conditions were slightly better than on Bataan: Although the tunnels were

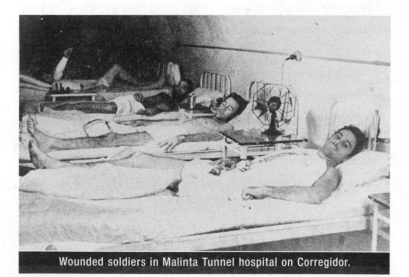

Wounded soldiers in Malinta Tunnel hospital on Corregidor.

smoky, dusty, and damp, at least she had solid rock over her head to keep out the rain. It was so crowded that nurses were assigned to sleep two to a bed. It was dangerous here too, though. Lucy barely escaped being struck when a shell landed close to the mouth of a tunnel where she stood outside eating supper.

"At times we would be in total darkness, and there was a constant water shortage because bombing and shelling interfered with the power plant as well as the ventilation system," said Lucy. "Heat and the odor of the hospital and bodies, and flies and insects added to the discomfort."

One afternoon, Lucy was called into the office of the chief nurse and told that she would be evacuated again. She was ordered to be ready to leave that night. "I was so sick and tired of retreating I thought to myself that I wouldn't do it."

Lucy walked out of the office and into the hospital ward area, where she stopped by the bed of Louis Lutich, who'd had a leg blown off by a shell (Lutich survived the war in a POW camp). When she mentioned her conversation with the chief nurse, his response was fierce and instantaneous: "'Get up and get out of here, *now!*'"

Lutich realized that Corregidor couldn't hold out much longer. When it fell, everyone, male or female, would face certain capture by the Japanese. He was right. General Wainwright made an attempt to evacuate some nurses, especially older or sick women, but seventy-seven American nurses, the largest group of US women to become POWs, were held in camps as prisoners until the end of the war.

• • •

That night, Lucy became part of the last group to escape the Rock by submarine. Twenty-five people, including thirteen

US Army nurses on Corregidor after its capture by the Japanese.

women and Earl L. Sackett, skipper of the *Canopus*, put off in a small boat into Manila Bay for the dangerous rendezvous. (Two additional men scrambled onto the submarine as stowaways during the transfer.)

Out on the water, remembered Lucy, "the world was bright with moonlight, shellfire, and bombs. Suddenly a big dark object rose up out of the water in front of us."

Captain Sackett recalled thinking, "Suppose something had happened to keep the submarine from reaching the appointed spot? Could she get through the cordon of enemy destroyers searching only a few miles outside?

"What a wonderful relief was the sight of that low black hull looming through the darkness, waiting exactly on her station!"

It was the USS *Spearfish* (SS-190), the last submarine to evacuate Americans from the Rock. As the boat surfaced, Sackett remembered, "the dark bulk of Corregidor suddenly blazed with fires and bursting shells."

The men from the submarine began hurrying the passengers aboard. Lucy had no time to look back at the horror from which she'd escaped. Weak and exhausted, she had to climb into this strange, dark boat. For a moment, she wasn't sure she could do it.

USS SPEARFISH (SS-190)

War Patrol Report
Sunday, May 3, 1942
Corregidor, the Philippines

19:40 Surfaced in position 3.5 miles bearing (220T) from Corregidor light. From 19:40 to 20:10 lay to in awash position awaiting arrival passenger boat.

20:10 Commenced battery charge.

20:25 Sighted and exchanged recognition signals with USS *Perry*. Guns on Bataan open fired on Corregidor.

20:35 Received . . . 27 passengers with baggage, files, mail and miscellaneous gear . . .

20:50 Passengers and baggage on board. Observed moonrise. Heavy shelling of Corregidor continued. Decided to lie to charging batteries until moonlight visibility increased.

21:52 Set course (270T), speed 5 knots to escape illumination caused by explosion of ammunition dump on Corregidor. Determined to run away from moon, to continue battery charge for as long as possible, and to submerge if patrolling DDs [destroyers] were sighted.

11 ANGELS ON BOARD

"The hatch was such a small opening," said Lucy Wilson. "Even with my weight only being 70 pounds after the starving, diarrhea, and vomiting over the past five months on Bataan and Corregidor, I didn't think I would be able to get into it, but I saw other people getting down it, so I did too."

On the *Spearfish*, Lucy got a surprise right away. The cook wasn't about to let down his submarine's reputation for hospitality and good food. He'd baked a treat to welcome them. "They had a single-layer chocolate cake ready to serve us," said Lucy. "We couldn't believe our eyes! It was so delicious.

"Of all the people I have ever known, those submariners were absolute tops and as each day went by, I knew they could not be beat."

• • •

The addition of twenty-seven people created even more crowded conditions than usual on the *Spearfish*. There wasn't a bit of extra space.

Lucy remembered that "later one of the crew members told me that while all this gang was coming aboard, he was wondering where they would find a place for all of us to sleep." He didn't worry about Lucy, though: She was so skinny he mistook her for the child of one of the officers who could bunk with her dad.

" 'Almost immediately after our boarding, we submerged and traveled for twenty-two hours without coming up,' said Lucy.

'That first twenty-two hours seemed like it would never end. They warned us not to talk or move about, but they didn't have to do that, we couldn't. Because of so many people on board, the oxygen supply was insufficient and we struggled just to breathe. Many passed out from the lack of oxygen and I am sure the starvation contributed to that.'"

Finding space to sleep wasn't easy. The *Spearfish* crew draped some sheets around four bunks so that the female nurses could have some privacy. Still, they had to use the "hot bunk" system, where people took turns sleeping every eight hours. Lucy was so exhausted she slept for hours.

When she woke, the news everyone had been dreading came: General Jonathan Wainwright had surrendered Corregidor. *Spearfish* had picked up a radio message from the Rock as it was about to fall to the Japanese on May 6:

> *One hundred and seventy-three officers and twenty-three hundred and seventeen men of the Navy reaffirm their loyalty and devotion to country, families, and friends.*

There had been no rescue, no victory. Japan now had occupied the Philippines. There could only be, as General Douglas MacArthur had vowed, the promise of a later return to recapture the islands.

Yet for thousands of Filipino and American soldiers stranded in Bataan and Corregidor and forced to surrender to the Japanese, there would be no return, only death. While it's difficult to know exact numbers, it's estimated that more than 70,000 men (including perhaps 12,000 Americans) were captured. They were

American prisoners of war under guard by
Japanese troops after the surrender of Bataan.

marched sixty or so miles to an internment camp, subjected along the way to heinous physical abuse and atrocities. That journey would become known to history as the Bataan Death March.

The Japanese victory in the Philippines had more far-reaching consequences and a higher death toll than the surprise attack at Pearl Harbor. With the Philippines under its control, Japan was positioned to put into play its aggressive plan to dominate the Pacific region, seizing other territories including Guam, Hong Kong, Thailand, North Borneo, Singapore, and the Netherlands East Indies.

"Our inability to defend the Philippines in 1941–1942 cost us tens of thousands of lives, and uncounted billions of dollars," concluded historian Samuel Morison.

Fortunately, the seventy-seven American nurses taken prisoner by the Japanese all survived the war. At a 1945 welcome-home ceremony for the women in Hawai'i, Brigadier General Raymond W. Bliss, assistant surgeon general of the Army, declared, " 'Your self-sacrifice has demonstrated that the high standards of the nursing profession are something real. . . . Your courage is an inspiration to the women of our country and in history you will take your place with the pioneer women who have helped establish the ideals on which we live.' "

Each nurse also received an envelope that contained a letter from President Franklin D. Roosevelt, stating in part: " 'You have served valiantly in foreign lands and have suffered greatly. As your Commander in Chief, I take pride in your past accomplishments and express the thanks of a grateful Nation for your services in combat and your steadfastness while a prisoner of war.' "

• • •

On the *Spearfish*, news of the loss was felt by the evacuees and submariners alike. "Everyone was very quiet. It was so depressing," said Lucy.

Exhausted by months of sickness and work, Lucy was still trying to recover her strength. She could fall asleep just about anywhere—even on top of full garbage bags stacked in the radio room. Many of the evacuees had trouble with seasickness, especially when the submarine surfaced at night, but Lucy wasn't bothered. As for showers, it wasn't until near the end of the seventeen-day trip that the women got a half bucket of water with which to wash.

In addition to getting used to "hot bunks" and no showers, the nurses also had to master the tricky apparatus of *Spearfish*'s toilets. It didn't go well.

" 'There were three heads [toilets] in the submarine and we were assigned one,' " Lucy said. " 'The instructions to flush it was about half a page long and so complicated that they quickly decided to have one of the submariners do it for us after a couple of disasters. It was so embarrassing!' "

• • •

"The submariners were so good to us," Lucy remembered. "They gave some of their clothing since we had lost everything we owned. In particular I remember the cut-off dungarees, which I had never seen before, and T-shirts."

The journey was not without danger. Once, when the *Spearfish* was on the surface to charge batteries, the boat sighted an enemy contact. The diving alarm "sounded like a Model T Ford car horn to me, and we went almost straight down," Lucy recalled. "This happened several times during the 3,000 mile

Nurse Lucy Wilson and the other evacuated nurses had a difficult time operating the *Spearfish*'s head, or toilet. And who can blame them? Take a look at these instructions for flushing an expulsion-type head from a 1946 US Navy training manual entitled *The Fleet Type Submarine*:

"The water closet installation consists of a toilet bowl over an expulsion chamber with a lever and pedal controlled flapper valve between, which is weighted to hold water in the toilet bowl and seats with pressure of the expulsion chamber. . . .

"Before using a water closet, first inspect the installation. All valves should have been left shut. Operate the bowl flapper valve to ascertain that the expulsion chamber is empty.

"Shut the bowl flapper valve, flood the bowl with sea water through the sea and stop valves, and then shut both valves. After using the toilet, operate the flapper valve to empty the contents of the bowl into the expulsion chamber, then shut the flapper valve. Charge the volume tank until the pressure is 10 pounds higher than the sea pressure. Open the gate and plug valves on the discharge line and operate the rocker valve to discharge the contents of the expulsion chamber overboard.

"Shut the discharge line valves and leave the bowl flapper valve seated. For pump expulsion, proceed as previously stated except that the contents of the waste receiver are to be pumped out after the gate and plug valves on the discharge line have been opened.

"If upon first inspection, the expulsion chamber is found flooded, discharge the contents overboard before using the toilet. Improper operation of toilet valves should be corrected and leaky valves overhauled at the first opportunity."

SKIPPER'S RECOMMENDATION: *Be thankful for our convenient, easy-flush toilets.*

trip, which took us 17 days, with no daylight for we only surfaced at night.

"They had a small square hand-cranked Victrola [record player] and a few records. Whenever we crash dived, everyone would grab the Victrola and records to keep them from falling because we plunged almost straight down. That was our only entertainment other than talking and singing, including our own made-up verses."

Passing the island of Bali, the captain let Lucy and the others have a look through the periscope. It was Lucy's only glimpse of daylight during the entire trip. "All we saw was a dark blob on the horizon, but I saw it!"

There was some fun too. The crew wasn't about to let their passengers cross the equator without partaking in the Ancient Order of the Deep (or line crossing ceremony), an old maritime tradition. Those who have never crossed before, "Pollywogs," become initiated as "Shellbacks" at the Royal Court of King Neptune. The submariners put a lot of effort into lifting the spirits of their guests.

"The crew was very ingenious in fixing funny and remarkable costumes for the Royal Court: King Neptune, Davy Jones, The Royal Baby, and others," said Lucy. "The fun and mystery during the preparations, plus the forewarnings we got of the awful things to come, made the hot monotonous trip more intriguing."

The event began when the *Spearfish* arrived at the equator; each passenger received a summons to appear before King Neptune and his court. The *Spearfish*'s charges against Lucy were typed up by the yeoman, and included tongue-in-cheek complaints against the young nurse for such things as:

1. *Working on the sympathies of the crew and thereby talking them out of their clothes, seats, food, and even in some cases, their hearts.*
2. *Being a cowgirl from Texas.*
3. *Always pouting.*
4. *Being hot tempered.*
5. *Telling tall tales about Texas.*
6. *Beating new born infants around while a nurse in training.*
7. *Having been fortunate enough to get away from Texas, desiring to go back.*
8. *Asking if there were a beauty parlor on board.*
9. *Making insulting remarks concerning the persons of the Royal Shellbacks.*

Lucy credited the ceremony with helping her and the other nurses begin to heal from their ordeal. In a way, it made everyone seem like a family—a family "who had just, and was still, going through some of the most horrible experiences the human body and mind can go through and come out alive, still fairly well balanced mentally and physically. Usually in one group there is at least one who is grouchy or touchy in some fashion, but I have absolutely no memory of any such person aboard at all. . . .

"I do not know how to adequately express my gratitude to the submariners for all they did for us and for making such an impossible trip so tolerable and enjoyable," she wrote later. "Had it not been for that seventeen days of good food and quiet relaxation, comradery and kind consideration, I do not know if I could have survived.

"Of course we knew of the danger we were going through

daily, at least it did not have the horrors of working 24 to 48 hours continuously, trying to sew bodies back together and wondering just how long they would last amid the constant bombing and shelling.

"A submariner not only has to perform his job perfectly, but must be able to get along with other people in extremely close quarters without very much else to do but work and sleep in unpleasant surroundings. They are the world's best to me!"

• • •

On May 20, 1942, the *Spearfish* arrived in Freemantle, Australia, where she was greeted by Charles A. Lockwood, Jr., recently promoted to rear admiral and commander of the Asiatic Fleet submarines.

While Lockwood doesn't mention the young nurse by name, from his description it seems likely that he met Lucy on the dock. "One pint-sized girl in a makeshift costume of mixed slacks and uniform, came up the submarine's hatch and onto the dock where she quietly walked from one end of the submarine to the other, looking over it carefully.

"Noticing that I was regarding her quizzically, she came up and said, 'I just wanted to see what the darned thing looks like. I've been inside it, like Jonah in the whale . . . but have never seen the outside.'"

• • •

Lucy went home to Big Sandy, Texas, where friends and neighbors celebrated her safe return and provided her with new clothes. Lucy felt so grateful for everyone's support she wore everything given to her, even dresses way too large.

Lucy did not rest for long. After training to become an Army flight nurse, she served in New Caledonia, Guadalcanal, and other Pacific islands, flying in hazardous conditions to care for and evacuate wounded soldiers.

While on Bataan, Lucy had fallen in love with a soldier named Dan Jopling, who had been captured by the Japanese. Later in the war, whenever she helped fly out prisoners from a liberated POW camp, she would ask if anyone knew what had become of him. She never heard, and assumed he was dead.

Lucy left the Army in August 1945 as the war was ending. That November, she discovered that Dan had survived the Bataan Death March. They married on December 5, 1945, and lived happily with their four children, although Dan continued to suffer from the physical and emotional aftereffects of his POW ordeal. Dan died in 1985, and Lucy passed away in 2000.

" 'We spent our lives helping people,' " said another of the Bataan nurses, " 'and we did it with honor and love and never looked back.' "

She might well have been describing the life of Lucy Wilson.

SUBMARINE SCHOOL
WOMEN CAN NOW SERVE ON US SUBMARINES

In 2012, Jennifer Noonan became one of the first three women officers to qualify in submarines.

In 1942, Lucy Wilson was a passenger on a submarine. It wasn't until the twenty-first century that women were allowed to become submariners themselves. The first women officers qualified to serve on submarines in 2012. On January 21, 2015, a Navy press release announced that the Submarine Force would be opening to enlisted female sailors as well.

"'We are the most capable submarine force in the world,'" said Vice Admiral Michael Connor, Commander, Submarine Forces. "'While we have superb technology, the ultimate key to our success is our people. In order to continue to improve and adapt in a rapidly changing world, we need to ensure that we continue to recruit and retain the most talented Sailors.

"'Today, many of the people who have the technical and leadership skills to succeed in the Submarine Force are women. We will need them. Integrating female officers into the Submarine Force has increased our talent pool and subsequently the force's overall readiness, ensuring that we will remain the world's most capable force for ensuing decades. Following our successful and smooth integration of women officers into the Submarine Force, the Navy's plan to integrate female enlisted is a natural next step.'"

12 SINK 'EM ALL!

One rain-swept evening in May of 1942, Admiral Charles A. Lockwood, Jr., hopped out of his jeep and walked into a hotel in a harbor town in Western Australia to have dinner.

In the lobby he caught a burst of noise from the lounge, where a dozen submariners on leave were gathered around a piano, belting out an improvised song: *"'Sink 'em all, sink 'em all . . . Sink all their cruisers and carriers too!'"*

Lockwood stopped short, inspired by the men's spirit (later, he used the phrase *"Sink 'Em All"* as the title for his book about the war). "These fighting words were destined to keynote our entire submarine campaign in the Pacific and their defiant ring bolstered many a man's courage in the dark days that were to come."

"Uncle Charlie," as he was known affectionately, was no armchair submariner, having skippered his first sub in World War I. The fifty-two-year-old was taking on his highest command

Admiral Charles A. Lockwood.

yet when he arrived in Australia to replace John Wilkes as head of the SubsAsiatic Force, the Asiatic Fleet submarines, which included the *Seawolf* and *Spearfish*.

Lockwood was a logical choice for the job: He was a respected leader with deep experience and the ability to hit the ground running. It didn't take him long to size up the problems that had dogged the Asiatic Fleet submarines in the first months of the war.

Lockwood believed that military strategy needed to be sharpened in the light of Japanese advances in the Pacific. While some skippers like Frederick "Fearless Freddie" Warder had distinguished themselves, other captains relied on prewar textbook strategies. Their tentative, cautious approach had led to disappointing results.

In the months to come, Lockwood would be on the lookout for young, aggressive skippers willing to take risks to help achieve the goal of destroying Japanese merchant shipping. In addition to the "skipper problem," Lockwood had to deal with a shortage of torpedoes—and worrying reports of unreliable fish.

Finally, Lockwood sensed exhaustion and low morale in both officers and men. " 'The boys here have had a tough row to hoe in the last four months,' " he wrote to a friend. As a submariner himself, Lockwood understood how essential rest could be, and so he tackled this last issue first.

Despite the fighting words in the song he'd heard, Lockwood understood what the men suffered at sea and the toll it took on sailors. "The thin faces of the officers and men, their unnaturally bright eyes, told of the tension on their nerves and the drain on their vitality produced by those long weeks submerged in tropical waters—weeks of peering into the sun glare or into the darkness for enemy targets, of sweating out depth charge attacks."

Lockwood reflected, "Beyond a doubt, their stouthearted front and resolute faces concealed many secret, questioning thoughts as to their chances of returning from these 50-day patrols into badly charted waters. . . . Not once throughout the war, was I able to watch a submarine shove off for patrol without a twinge of sorrow and a period of soul searching as to whether or not I and my Staff had done everything humanly possible to insure the accomplishment of its mission and its safe return."

One of Lockwood's first acts was to lease four small hotels in Australia as recovery spots for sailors on leave. "The submariners needed complete rest, as much as we could give them, between patrols. They must go back fit, mentally and physically, to stand the strain of 50-day patrols in enemy-controlled waters where every man's hand was against them."

The next issue, however, would take a lot longer to resolve: bad torpedoes.

• • •

Since the first patrols of the war, skippers like *Seawolf*'s Frederick Warder had raised concerns about the Mark XIV (Mark 14) torpedoes, the model most submarines used.

Back in December of 1941, when the *Seawolf* attacked a Japanese seaplane tender anchored at Aparri, Warder had set the fish to pass under the target's keel. This should have activated the magnetic exploder each torpedo carried. Yet it hadn't. Had the torpedoes missed the mark, had the exploder simply failed, or had the torpedoes been running too deep to activate the exploder? No one knew.

Nor, as it turned out, was this an isolated incident. After *Seawolf*'s lack of success on several other occasions, Warder wrote, " 'The . . . torpedoes were no . . . good. That was the problem.' "

Warder wasn't the only frustrated submarine commander. During a December 1941 patrol, Tyrell Dwight Jacobs, skipper of the USS *Sargo* (SS-188), had launched eight separate attacks, firing thirteen torpedoes without a hit.

Jacobs, who had an engineering background, set up each shot carefully, hoping to convince officials to acknowledge the problem. His report of one attempt reflects his exasperation. "During the thirty five minutes of this approach, seventeen periscope observations were made, and as it was dusk when torpedo was fired, almost continuous periscope observation was utilized during the last ten minutes. . . . No reason can be offered for this miss, since the entire torpedo had been previously checked." Jacobs concluded that in his opinion the torpedoes were faulty in two respects: the magnetic exploder and the depth settings.

In June 1942, soon after Lockwood assumed his post in Australia, James Coe, skipper of the USS *Skipjack* (SS-184), also voiced his concerns, penning a scathing, four-page analysis of the issues he encountered with poor torpedo performance during a fifty-day patrol.

"To make round trips of 8500 miles into enemy waters to gain attack position undetected within 800 yards of enemy ships only to find that the torpedoes run deep and over half the time will fail to explode, seems to me to be an undesirable manner of gaining information which might be determined any morning within a few miles of a torpedo station in the presence of comparatively few hazards," he wrote.

"The above statements may seem extreme and rabid; they represent my honest opinion and explain why 'sure hits' resulted in misses in this patrol," Coe declared. "I believe that many of the wartime misses of the other submarines of this squadron are also explained by the same discussion. If it can be shown that this explanation is wrong, I shall be the first to acknowledge it.

"What we on the submarine firing line need is a dependable torpedo; and at least the knowledge of what the fish will and will not do; when we have this, some of those . . . ships which 'got away' will start going to the bottom."

• • •

Angry complaints weren't limited to commanders of boats in the Asiatic Fleet. Skippers in Pacific Fleet submarines based at Pearl Harbor were voicing similar concerns. Even so, officials in the Bureau of Ordnance, the section at Navy headquarters that dealt with technical issues, continued to dismiss the criticisms as mere excuses for misses.

Although Lockwood wished to avoid a bureaucratic tussle, he could no longer ignore the impassioned pleas of skippers whose judgment he trusted. "So much evidence was piling up and our submariners were becoming so discouraged by repeated misses which should have been hits, we decided to do a little torpedo testing on our own."

As one submariner commented later: " 'It took Charlie Lockwood . . . to take that bull by the horns.' "

After the war, submariner Edward L. Beach—whom we'll soon meet—wasn't shy about expressing his opinion of the men running the Bureau of Ordnance. He called them "incompetent dunderheads."

• • •

Lockwood wrote to the Bureau of Ordnance, asking about any new information or tests on the torpedoes. (There weren't any.) Then he and staff member James "Jimmy" Fife (who'd been evacuated from the Philippines by the *Seawolf*) set up their own experiment, recruiting James Coe from the *Skipjack* to help out.

First, they bought a net and moored it outside the harbor in King George Sound near Albany, in Western Australia, to conduct what was, in effect, the first controlled test of the Mark XIV torpedoes. Next, they fired several of *Skipjack*'s remaining torpedoes with an exercise (not explosive head) at a normal attack range of one thousand yards.

The torpedoes were set to run at a depth of ten feet. When divers examined the net, the evidence was indisputable: The torpedoes had broken through the netting eleven feet *deeper* than the depth at which they'd been set to run.

Lockwood sent the test results to the Navy's Bureau of Ordnance, which concluded that his tests had been inaccurate. Undeterred, Lockwood and Fife conducted more tests in July. This time, in addition to sending the results through official channels, Lockwood contacted a high-ranking Navy official and asked him to help behind the scenes.

It worked. Lockwood got a policy change issued: Every skipper was informed that, officially, the torpedoes ran eleven feet deeper and adjustments should be made accordingly. Future torpedoes would get a new, improved depth-control mechanism.

Unfortunately, that wasn't the end of torpedo troubles. Solving one issue managed to cause others. Lockwood explained, "Bringing our torpedo runs closer to the surface seemed to

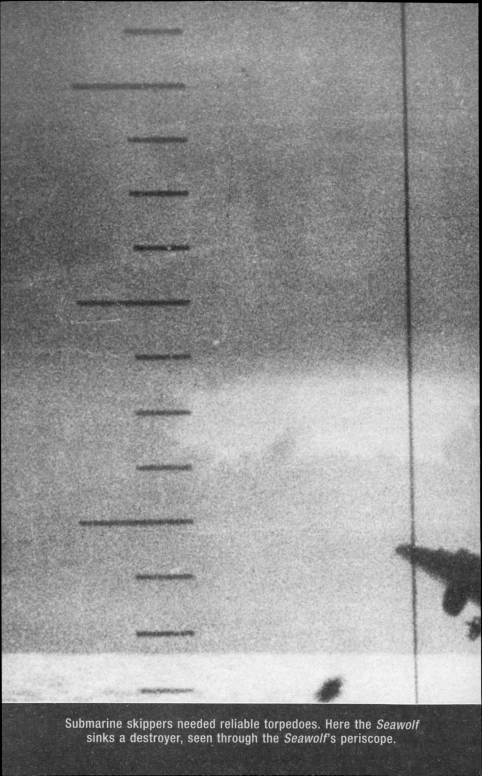

Submarine skippers needed reliable torpedoes. Here the *Seawolf* sinks a destroyer, seen through the *Seawolf*'s periscope.

multiply the number of premature explosions of war heads as well as the number of times in which torpedoes could be heard to thud against the side of a target without exploding."

In fact, it would take two more years to completely debug all the problems with torpedoes, but at least a start had been made.

• • •

The challenges facing the silent service in 1942 seemed, at times, nearly insurmountable. The Submarine Force was spread very thinly to meet its goal of eliminating Japanese shipping from more than eight million square miles of ocean.

It took time for a submarine to reach a designated patrol area; submarines also required regular upkeep and repairs. Crews needed breaks from the stress and tension caused by long patrols. Added to this was a sometimes disappointing performance from submarine commanders.

For all these reasons, it was urgent to get new boats—and officers—into action as soon as possible. One of these men and his boat would become an unforgettable team, even though Edward "Ned" Beach had never wanted to be a submariner in the first place.

And, unlike Mel Eckberg and his beloved *Seawolf*, Ned didn't think much of *Trigger* when he first set eyes on her.

USS TRIGGER (SS-237)

A fantastically colored and dangerous fish is the trigger, and like the fish after which she was named, the USS Trigger *had a fantastically colorful career and a dangerous one for the Japanese.... From the very beginning* Trigger *had a spirit of go-ahead built into her trim lines.*

—Office of Naval Records and History
Ships' Histories Section
Navy Department

NED BEACH: RELUCTANT SUBMARINER ⊕ 13

At the beginning of 1942, Edward L. "Ned" Beach Jr. reported to Mare Island Navy Yard in California for his first submarine assignment as communications officer on a brand-new *Gato* class boat called the *Trigger*. Ned drove to the docks to get his first look at her.

"There she was, a great black conning tower sticking up over the edge of the dock, with a huge white 237 painted on her side," he said. He remembered thinking: "'There's my new home . . . wonder if I'm looking at my coffin.'"

• • •

The son of a dedicated Navy officer, Ned had the sea in his blood. He'd entered the Naval Academy in 1935 at just seventeen, graduating in 1939 with honors. Ned hadn't started out as a sub-mariner. In fact, he wasn't sure he even wanted to become one. After all, his dad's advice had been, "'Stay in the big ships, that's where the real navy is.'"

Ned's previous post was on a "tin can," an old destroyer named the *Lea* (DD-118), which he'd grown to love in the two years he served on her. (Ned called her the "leaning, leaking, lopsided *Lea*.") New submarines were being built every day, though, and there was a dire need for talented officers to serve on them. Despite his best efforts to avoid the assignment, Ned had been tapped to take part. For his introduction to the silent service, he'd been sent to an intensive three-month course at the Naval

Submarine School in Groton, Connecticut, graduating at the top of his class just weeks after the war began.

Ned wasn't exactly bowled over by his first glimpse of the *Trigger* that January day. "To me, she certainly wasn't impressive, beautiful, or anything at all but an ugly chunk of steel."

What he couldn't know then was that "two and a half of the most crowded and thrilling years of my life were to be spent with her. She was to become the ruler of my life, and the most beautiful and responsive creature I had ever known: a hard, exacting mistress, but loyal, generous, and courageous."

Ned already knew that the experience and attitude of the crew was an important part of the equation for success. "If they lack judgment and initiative, so does the ship. If they lack the indomitable spirit, the absolute determination to succeed, so will the inanimate steel. But if they possess these attributes, they and their ship are unbeatable."

"All ships have souls, and all sailors know it, but it takes a while to learn to commune with one," he later wrote. "It took me a long time, for *Trigger* had to find her own soul, too."

• • •

Just as Frederick Warder, Mel Eckberg, and everyone on the *Seawolf* had done, *Trigger*'s crew put the new submarine through the shakedown process—numerous tests, dives, and training exercises—before leaving California in the spring of 1942 for Pearl Harbor.

Ned described the final preparations: "Fill her up with torpedoes, diesel oil, food, and spare parts. Make any necessary repairs and take care of the many last-minute items which always come up. Then, one May afternoon about two o'clock, good-by—this

is it! The Admiral comes down to the dock, shakes hands with the skipper, wishes him good luck and good hunting. The ship backs into the Mare Island Slough, twists gracefully, and is gone, through Carquinez Strait, past Alcatraz, and under the Golden Gate Bridge.

"*Trigger* probably had a soul already," Ned reflected later, "but we were too new to each other, too much taken up with the details of operating her complicated mechanism, to appreciate it."

• • •

"Our chance came suddenly," Ned said. He'd expected that once at Pearl Harbor, the crew would receive more training as part of the normal routine. A major battle looming on the horizon changed all that. *Trigger*'s first assignment was not a full-fledged war patrol, but an urgent dispatch for action.

Thanks to intelligence obtained by code breakers, the US learned that Japan was preparing an early June attack on Midway, the closest island atoll to Hawai'i. Midway held significant strategic importance. If Japan gained control of Midway, the island could be used as a base to launch air raids on Pearl Harbor itself.

Japan's Isoroku Yamamoto, architect of the December 7 attack, saw this as a way to finish the job begun then, and completely annihilate the US Pacific Fleet. "The success of this battle was central to the entire Japanese strategic concept of the war," observed historian Samuel Morison.

For America, it was do or die. After what happened at Pearl Harbor—and the recent, heartbreaking loss of the Philippines after the surrender of Bataan and Corregidor—letting Hawai'i fall to the Japanese was unthinkable. Admiral Chester Nimitz (who had replaced Husband Kimmel as commander in chief of the Pacific Fleet) was not about to be caught unprepared.

Advance knowledge of the attack was one of Admiral Nimitz's greatest assets as he developed a battle strategy in May, especially since the US fleet wasn't back at full strength. Japan's forces included more than 162 ships. The US could scrape together about 76 vessels, not counting Navy, Marine, and Army Air Force planes.

As for submarines, Robert "Bob" English, Charles Lockwood's counterpart in charge of the Pacific Fleet boats stationed at Pearl Harbor, set about mustering every sub he had available for one of the most crucial encounters of the Pacific war.

Even new, untried boats like *Trigger*.

• • •

By June 3, *Trigger* was in her patrol area, some twenty miles east of Midway. That night, the submarine got orders to move in to within two miles of the island. Ned knew the Japanese fleet was expected the next morning, "and maybe—*maybe*—we'd get a shot at it!"

"All night long we raced through the darkness," said Ned, "and shortly before dawn sighted the lights of Midway, dead ahead."

Then the lookout shouted a warning. Midway wasn't just dead ahead—*Trigger* was plowing right into it.

Jack Hayden Lewis, the skipper, had either miscalculated the location of the atoll's reefs or missed them entirely on the charts. The error was compounded by poor communication between the captain and officers. And what a mistake it was.

Said Ned, "There were great black rocks dead ahead, waves

splashing violently upon them! The captain and navigator dashed up on the bridge beside me.

" 'All back full!' roared the captain."

Ned could feel the boat respond as the propellers stopped and began to reverse.

Next the captain shouted, " 'Sound the collision alarm!' "

Ned heard not just one, but *all* the alarms: collision alarm, general alarm, even the diving alarm. Later he learned that the chief of the watch had been so startled he'd rung every alarm in sight.

"Disaster was on us. The rocks were huge, and so were the waves splashing over them," Ned said. "Helpless, having totally lost control, we on the bridge saw our boat drive full speed onto the rocks. We struck with a horrendous clang.

"I was looking dead ahead, right over the bow, and saw it rise irresistibly out of the water, reaching heavenward in a desperate, agonized leap. I actually thought that, somewhere behind me, we must have broken in half. I saw our bow slammed sideways to starboard, and then several more diminishing bumps as we slid forward.

"Finally, and very quickly, all forward motion stopped. The ship lay half out of the water at an improbable angle. . . . We had driven our ship aground at full power, and *Trigger* was stuck fair. . . . There was nothing we could do to help ourselves, let alone fight them."

• • •

Crew members rushed to assess the situation, taking soundings to determine the shape of the coral mass. The reef was steep, a good sign. They might be able to reverse and get the boat cleanly off without scraping her too much against the coral.

It didn't work.

"We backed . . . no luck. We were much too firmly aground," said Ned, after the first attempt failed. "Only one thing to do: lighten ship, and this task we feverishly began."

Trigger sent out an emergency call to submarine headquarters at Pearl Harbor and to US forces based on Midway. There was no way to know if rescue would come in time. If the Japanese arrived first, *Trigger* would be an easy target.

"And then came dawn . . . and here poor *Trigger* lay, bruised, battered. . . . At any moment we expected to see the enemy fleet, and high and dry as we were, our complete destruction was inevitable," Ned wrote later.

• • •

When help did arrive, it wasn't quite what Ned and the others expected. "We hoped for a regular Navy tug, a big seagoing ship with powerful engines. Instead, a tiny tug appeared, so small it resembled a toy."

Men on the rescue vessel connected a hawser (a thick rope or cable used for towing) to the stern of the submarine and began to pull. No luck. *Trigger* didn't move. Then the hawser broke.

"At this point," said Ned, "I felt sure our brand-new *Trigger* was doomed to spend the rest of her days on the reef."

Nerves frayed. Then it seemed as if maybe the tug's efforts, along with a rising tide, had helped. Suddenly, a lookout shouted, " 'She's moving!' "

Ned described what happened next. "Incredulously we look over the bow at the reef, and if you look hard enough, the slightest movement is discernible. No time to figure it out.

"All back emergency! Maneuvering, make maximum power! The four faithful diesels roar. Clouds of smoke pour out of the exhaust trunks. The reduction gears whine in a rising crescendo and the propellers throw a boiling flood of white foam over our nearly submerged stern.

"Line up your eye with the bow and the reef. She trembles. The water foams along her sides and up past her bow. Her stern is now completely submerged. She feels alive! Is that a slight change? Yes—yes—she moves! She bounces once and is off the reef. She is free!"

Trigger had been luckier than Ned could have imagined. Although damaged, the submarine was able to return under her own steam to Pearl Harbor for repairs. That wasn't all: Ned and the others had not, after all, been in imminent danger from the enemy. The Battle of Midway had taken place hundreds of miles away from where *Trigger* ran aground. Moreover, it had resulted in a decisive victory for American forces.

Ned had been worried about the consequences he and other officers could face for this terrible error. After all, he had been OOD (officer of the deck) at the time. He soon found that the euphoria everyone felt about the glorious and much-needed US victory was in their favor.

"When our skipper reported to headquarters to take his medicine and find out his fate, he was greeted with the jovial instruction to forget it. 'We just won the Battle of Midway! Haven't you heard?'"

Trigger and Ned Beach would soon get a chance to redeem their tarnished reputations.

TRIGGER TURNS IT AROUND

"It took *Trigger* a long time to develop her personality," reflected Ned Beach.

It also took a new skipper, who came on board in September 1942, to Ned's relief. *Trigger*'s near-disaster at Midway in June had been followed by an unsuccessful war patrol around Alaska and the Aleutian Islands. That dreary, cautious outing had been what Ned called an absolute zero, with no enemy contacts and no attacks made.

Skipper Roy Benson (who bore the irreverent nickname Pigboat Benny) lost no time in making his mark. He threw a party for everyone to raise morale. Benson's wit, humor, and competence, along with his "upbeat, 'let-me-at-'em' attitude" were infectious. "With his arrival aboard the *Trigger*, night turned into day," said Ned.

Ned got a taste of Benson's leadership style during *Trigger*'s second patrol (September 23–November 8, 1942), when Ned himself was at the center of his submarine's first contact with an enemy ship.

It almost turned out to be the last.

• • •

The encounter began shortly before dawn, not far off the eastern coast of Kyushu, Japan. Ned's first inkling of a ship in the vicinity was the appearance of a large dark shadow in the distance. The shadow moved. *Trigger* was running on the surface, and

Ned, who once again was OOD, soon realized he was looking at a freighter, just the sort of target they were after.

"He was steaming along steadily, purring out a fair-sized cloud of dense black smoke, with not so much as a hint of a zigzag," said Ned. Since the freighter wasn't taking evasive action, Ned assumed *Trigger* hadn't been spotted.

A close-up of *Trigger*'s bridge from the port lookout platform.

As OOD, Ned had control of the ship; his new captain stood beside him. With everyone called to battle stations, *Trigger* began pursuit, maneuvering into firing position.

" 'Get right astern of him,' " Benson told Ned, who was delighted that the captain was showing such confidence in him. The skipper could easily have decided to take "the conn" (a term meaning to control the movements of the boat) himself.

• • •

Daylight found *Trigger* still chasing her target, aiming to attack from the rear. "It would soon be time to make ready the bow torpedoes for firing," said Ned.

Yet as he stared intently through the binoculars, Ned suddenly grasped what he should have been seeing all along. " 'Captain!' I yelled. 'That's not his stern! It's his bow! He's coming right at us!' "

Ned hollered, " 'Collision Alarm! He's trying to ram!' "

The high-pitched screech of the collision alarm put Ned in mind of a ship screaming in fright. Walter Pye Wilson, the chief wardroom steward when the submariners weren't at battle stations, confirmed Ned's orders. " 'Watertight doors shut below! Boat's secured for collision!' "

Wilson was one of the few African Americans on submarines during World War II. At the time, the Navy's discriminatory practices placed severe limitations on black sailors. They were allowed to qualify only as stewards, working in food service or serving the captain and officers. But since in submarines each sailor learned every job, Wilson knew his boat inside and out. Whenever *Trigger* was in battle station conditions, he took over steering.

Wilson, said Ned, was "one of the steadiest men aboard as well as one of the most popular. . . . He had always been the proverbial tower of strength at his multitudinous duties; from wardroom to galley to handling mooring lines to battle station helmsman, he was never at [a] loss, his cool voice under stress helping to keep the rest of us cool too."

Ned sent the lookouts below. That left Ned and Captain Benson alone on the bridge, with the bow of the Japanese ship only one or two hundred yards away. *Trigger* had survived being run aground on her first outing—this could be her last patrol if Ned didn't act quickly to evade the freighter barreling toward them.

He yelled an order to Wilson. " 'Right full rudder!' "

A clear protocol for control of the boat was essential.

If you've watched a submarine film, you've probably heard the expression "I have the conn." (Sometimes *conn* is also used as a verb, as in "conn" the boat.)

Control of a ship follows a strict procedure. Only one officer at a time can conn or control the motions of the boat. Ned Beach described the protocol used to help avoid accidents such as running aground.

"Navy doctrine prescribes that, in emergency, either the captain or the navigator (but only these two) may arbitrarily take maneuvering control of the ship, 'the conn,' at any time. . . . The regular OOD [officer of the deck], and all others on watch, continue to be responsible for normal routine, but the OOD's authority to handle the ship's maneuvers has been supplanted. It remains so until the captain (or the navigator) returns it to him. . . .

"If no emergency exists, however, normal procedure is to say formally, as in relieving the watch, 'I have the conn,' or 'I relieve you of the conn.' In any case, whoever has or takes the conn, even the captain, must keep it until he has been formally relieved, for by definition only one officer can 'drive' or 'conn' the ship."

Seconds later, Ned could feel *Trigger*'s bow swerving. Wilson confirmed: " 'Rudder is right full!' "

Ned kept his focus on dodging the oncoming attacker. "It was like driving a car in heavy traffic, with two big differences. Ships are a lot longer than cars, and they steer from the stern, not the bow."

By now the ships were only fifty yards apart, with the freighter still coming full speed ahead, its single smokestack puffing out smoke. Ned called for Wilson to shift *Trigger*'s rudder to left full, hoping to squeak by the freighter charging toward them. Instantly, Wilson carried out the order.

"If Wilson's muscles had bulged at the first command, they must have gone into hard knots at this second one," said Ned. "We could see the rudder angle indicator on the bridge spin to the full left position, moving even faster than before. *Trigger* obediently stopped her swing to starboard, began to curve rapidly to the left."

It worked!

"We would pass clear," Ned realized with a sense of relief. "I felt a quick sense of satisfaction that I had successfully dodged his assault."

The danger wasn't over yet, though. Benson turned to him. " 'Ned, are you a hero?'

" 'Nossir!'

" 'Neither am I! Let's get out of sight.' The two of us dived for the hatch. As OOD I was the last man through it, and as I jumped below a rifle bullet zinged through the bridge side plating, making a neat hole a foot or two above my head.

" 'Take her down!' " Captain Benson ordered.

The crew carried out their diving routine, and *Trigger* slipped beneath the waves. The immediate danger was over.

Ned, however, was in for some good-natured ribbing about his rapidfire commands during the incident. Wilson teased, " 'If we're going to have a collision, can't you at least make up your mind where you want me to put the rudder?' "

For the first time, Ned realized what those tense moments must have been like from below, where Wilson couldn't see the danger they'd been in. But thanks to quick thinking and seamless teamwork, they'd avoided disaster.

Over the next few days, Ned was the brunt of a few more friendly jabs about his having a hard time making up his mind, but "behind the wisecracks I sensed also a hint of approving respect. Among the crew of a submarine at war, a great deal is never put into words.

"And as for Wilson and me, nothing can ever take the place of that delicious moment."

African Americans faced discrimination in all branches of the military during World War II. In the Navy, African Americans were initially restricted to positions related to service—usually working as cooks or stewards (often called mess attendants) who served food to the officers. Yet, they faced the same dangers as their fellow crewmen.

This restriction didn't keep African Americans from serving valiantly in combat. During the attack on Pearl Harbor in December 1941, mess attendant Doris "Dorie" Miller on the battleship USS *West Virginia* (BB-48) became the first African American to earn the prestigious Naval Cross in the war after he rescued several sailors, including the captain of the ship, then went on deck to fire a .50 caliber antiaircraft gun at the attacking Japanese planes.

• • •

In June 1942, the Navy began to actively recruit African Americans, who were allowed to qualify for technical specialist positions at bases, though not in combat. (Yet even training for these positions was conducted in segregated conditions until the end of 1945.) While becoming a technical specialist offered more opportunities for new recruits, men who'd joined the Navy before 1942 found themselves "frozen" in the category of stewards, and were not allowed to change their rating status until several years after the war. Many did so, despite the obstacles put in their way.

Doris "Dorie" Miller, the first African American to receive the Naval Cross in WWII.

Although official policy during World War II excluded African Americans from combat positions, actual practice was often different—especially on submarines. All submariners, no matter what rating, could earn their dolphins and "qualify" by learning all systems on board. Yet even though African Americans clearly demonstrated their mastery, becoming a torpedoman or electrician's mate was still closed off to them.

On submarines, stewards were often assigned to key roles, such as being part of gun crews during battle stations. Walter Pye Wilson routinely maneuvered *Trigger* during her encounters with enemy ships. In 1944, when the USS *Dragonet* (SS-293) ran aground and the forward torpedo compartment flooded, African American submariner Anderson Peter "A. P." Royal helped to seal off the compartment, enabling the submarine to make it safely

Retired Navy Captain C. A. "Pete" Tzomes became the first African American to command a nuclear submarine in 1983.

back to Midway. Other examples of heroism abound throughout the war years.

In 1983, C. A. "Pete" Tzomes became the first African American to command a nuclear submarine when he assumed command of the USS *Houston* (SSN-713). Read more about him here: http://www.navy.mil/ah_online/deptStory.asp?dep=8&id=72627.

SKIPPER'S RECOMMENDATIONS:

- *Read about Doris "Dorie" Miller, the first African American to be awarded the Navy Cross for his heroism at Pearl Harbor: http://www.pearlharbor.org/dorie-miller .asp. In 1973, a Navy frigate was named in his memory.*

- *An excellent book on African American submariners is* Black Submariners in the United States Navy, 1940–1975 *(2005) by Glenn A. Knoblock, who loved reading about submarines as a boy. He first encountered A.P. Royal in one of his favorite books,* Silversides, *by Robert Trumbull, published in 1945.*

  Years later, Knoblock rediscovered a copy of Silversides *in a used bookstore and became so curious about Royal's career and the experiences of other African American submariners that he researched and wrote a book. He also got to meet his childhood hero: "Few thrills could match that experience when I found that A.P. Royal was alive and well and was happy to have his entire story be a part of this book."*

SURROUNDED!

Over the next two years, Ned made eight patrols on *Trigger*, serving under several captains and receiving a promotion to executive officer (second-in-command). Ned's ninth, and last, patrol on his beloved boat went down in history, when *Trigger* and her crew endured one of the worst depth-charge attacks experienced by any submarine during the war. Even years later, some of Ned's recollections were so vivid he described the horrific experience in present tense.

To tell this story, we need to fast-forward to April of 1944, when the United States was eager to wrest the Mariana Islands, which include Saipan and Guam, away from Japan, which had controlled the archipelago in the western Pacific since World War I. (The islands were strategically important to the United States because of their proximity to Japan.)

Slade Cutter, commanding the USS *Seahorse* (SS-304), had spotted Japanese vessels in the vicinity of the Marianas, carrying troops and supplies for their defense. Sinking enemy ships in this area would support American efforts to capture the islands. One Japanese convoy headed for Saipan got past Cutter, but he soon found another and sank two ships. Admiral Charles Lockwood ordered *Trigger*'s new skipper, Fritz Harlfinger, to detour from his original route to help *Seahorse*.

Ned was at the periscope when the encounter began. "About four hours before dawn we picked up a convoy, tracked it a bit, and prepared to 'pull the *Trigger*' on it."

At first, all went well. *Trigger* got past the two lead escort ships undetected (or so Ned thought). Then, even before the main group of ships came into sight, Ned spotted a second ring of protection: five destroyers, maybe even more. Why so many escorts?

By now, it was clear that the first two destroyers had detected *Trigger*'s presence. *Trigger*'s sound man was picking up constant pinging as the two ships zigzagged on the seas above them, hunting for the submarine's exact position.

Ned and Harlfinger had planned to surface and make a night attack under the cover of darkness. They quickly abandoned that idea. Ned recalled thinking, "We'll be lucky even to get in a submerged ship before the beating [the depth charges] lying in wait for us catches up to us."

When the main convoy came into view at last, its size took Ned's breath away. "*My God!* We see through the periscope four columns of ships, five or more ships in each column. Tankers, freights, transports, and auxiliaries, all steaming toward Saipan. And closely spaced around the mass of merchant vessels is yet a third ring of at least ten, probably more, escorts.

"No time to surface and send a message [back to headquarters to alert other US submarines in the vicinity]—even if we could, with those hounds on our tail. No time even to prepare a message. No time to do anything except shoot."

• • •

Trigger's crew had to act quickly. There would barely be time for one swift, sudden attack. And it wouldn't be possible to stick around to confirm results.

A big tanker up ahead seemed the most likely target. Captain Harlfinger took the periscope from Ned for a quick look around. When he did, he happened to catch sight of a light signal from one of the destroyers to other ships in the convoy. Harlfinger understood the message: It meant the destroyer was about to discharge explosives.

There wasn't a second to spare. Ned took the periscope for the attack. "Our tanker should be about in the spot now. *Standby forward!* I turn *Trigger*'s periscope back to give the firing bearings. We're going to catch it, but we're going to dish it out too.

"But the periscope can see nothing. Helplessly I turn it back and forth in high power. . . . I flip the periscope into low power, which gives greater field with less magnification."

Ned burst out, "'Wow! It's a destroyer! He's trying to ram! He's just barely missed us—within twenty-five yards! He's firing a machine gun through his bridge windows! They're dropping depth charges!'"

The destroyer slid by, so close that through the periscope Ned could see Japanese sailors on deck readying the depth charges for release. They weren't quick enough, though. *Trigger* let off four fish. The captain ordered a deep dive. (Although *Trigger*'s crew reported hearing hits from the torpedoes, postwar records failed to confirm damage or sinkings.)

Ned expected to feel the first shocks of the antisubmarine depth-charge explosions on the way down. At first nothing happened. Then it began.

This hound had no intention of letting the fox escape.

• • •

"We are at 300 feet, but he comes in as if he could practically see us, and drops twenty-five absolute beauties on us," Ned said. The shock waves from the explosions pounded the boat.

"How *Trigger* manages to hold together we'll never know. Her heavy steel sides buckle in and out, her cork insulation breaks off in great chunks and flies about. Lockers are shaken open and the contents spewed all over everything," said Ned.

"With each succeeding shock, gauges all over the ship jiggle violently across their dials . . . In spite of careful and thoughtful shock mounting, instruments are shattered and electric circuits thrown out of order."

When the barrage was over, it was quiet for a while. The crew's hopes rose. Then the sound man picked up pinging from five more ships. *Trigger* was surrounded, caught in a deadly circle of six menacing destroyers. When *Trigger* moved, the destroyers moved with her. Hour after hour, the submarine tried to shake off her pursuers. It didn't work.

"No matter which way we go, which way we turn, they keep up with us," Ned said. "Every half hour or so one [of the destroyers] breaks off and makes a run, dropping a few charges each time—thum, thum, thum, THUM, THUM, THUM— WHAM, WHAM! WHAM!"

• • •

The attacks continued—past dawn, past noon, past late afternoon. The submarine had submerged a little after midnight. And still *Trigger* crept along, three hundred feet below the surface in black cold water.

Silence was absolutely essential. That meant the normal submarine systems like running pumps and air-conditioning had been shut down. The temperature rose to a dangerous 135 degrees. Some sailors knotted rags around their foreheads to keep beads of perspiration from running into their eyes.

"Two or three men are near collapse from [a] combination of nervous strain, lack of sufficient oxygen, and loss of salt . . . though we all eat handfuls of salt tablets. We sweat profusely, and our clothes are drenched, our socks soggy, and our shoes soaked," said Ned.

Ned Beach and his crewmates became known for "pulling the *Trigger*" on enemy ships.

The pattern continued, with each destroyer taking its turn to mount a depth-charge attack. Whenever *Trigger* tried to slip through a gap in the circle, the ships above closed ranks.

"We wonder why the six escorts do not make a single coordinated attack on us. They have us so well boxed in that such an attack really would be a lulu!" Ned wrote later. "The thought grows that possibly they expect us to surface and surrender. If they keep up these tactics, and don't sink us with a lucky depth charge, eventually we will run out of oxygen or battery power and be forced to surface. . . .

"*Trigger* will never surrender. We'll come up in the darkest hour of the night, at full speed, all hands at gun stations, and twenty torpedoes ready. It will be mighty dangerous for anything but a full-fledged destroyer to get in our way."

• • •

Finally, skipper Fritz Harlfinger reached a decision. After more than seventeen hours submerged, *Trigger* would surface—coming up after sunset and evening twilight, but before moonrise, taking a chance that the darkness would buy a little time to begin recharging the submarine's batteries.

"Our battery and oxygen would probably last us another twenty-four hours, but then we'd *have* to come up," Ned reflected.

Before that happened, though, the men on *Trigger* noticed there hadn't been a depth-charge attack in quite some time. Perhaps their stalkers had gotten careless and temporarily lost contact. It was time to make another break for it.

"We head for the biggest gap in the circle, and slowly increase speed. . . . We listen with bated breath, hardly daring to breathe," Ned said.

One set of screws was louder than the others. It was gaining, moving ahead to cut off the gap and block *Trigger*.

"All at once he stops drawing ahead," Ned recalled. "Now, as we cluster around the sound gear, we watch the telltale bearing pointer more aft, ever aft, till finally he passes across our stern! A guarded cheer breaks from the desperate men in the conning tower. We've broken through!"

It was a memorable night. "There is nothing to compare with the fresh, cool sweetness of the pure night air," Ned said, remembering the moment when *Trigger* finally broke through to the surface of the dark, quiet sea, and the hatch was opened.

"It overpowers you with its vitality, reaches deep down inside you and sweeps away every remaining vestige of tiredness, fear, or unhappiness. It is frank, pure, undiluted Joy."

• • •

That was Ned Beach's final patrol on *Trigger*, which was so damaged by the extended depth-charge encounter she required a thorough overhaul.

Except for Walter Pye Wilson, Ned was the last of *Trigger*'s original crew to depart. Wilson managed to outlast him. Ned, who'd been assigned to a new boat, the USS *Tirante* (SS-420), wrote out orders transferring Wilson to a relief crew so that his friend could get some rest. However, Wilson wasn't ready to leave *Trigger* just yet. Once Ned had gone, he asked the new exec to tear up his transfer orders.

"Wilson served two more patrols in *Trigger*, then after 12 runs in all, called it a day," said Ned. "By this time he could have had anything he wanted. He had become a legend in the submarine force, and maybe he had a premonition, for that was the patrol from which our ship did not return."

• • •

Ned was close by when the submarine he had come to love was lost almost a year later, in March of 1945. Orders called for Ned's boat, the *Tirante*, to rendezvous with *Trigger* and conduct a coordinated patrol in an area south and west of Kyushu, Japan's southernmost island.

"Since there would be some planning necessary, there would have to be discussion between the ships," Ned recalled. He was delighted to be chosen as *Tirante*'s emissary, and went about recruiting anyone who had ever served on *Trigger* to man the tiny rubber boat they would take from one sub to the other for the visit at sea.

Tirante tried to make contact with *Trigger* for three nights to finalize the arrangements. "The third night was a repetition of the second, except I spent nearly the whole time in the radio room," said Ned. "At irregular intervals Ed Secard [the radioman] tapped out the unrequited call. His face was inscrutable, his manner natural and precise. But Secard had made many patrols in *Trigger*, and when the time came for him to be relieved, he waved the man away. . . .

"A spare set of earphones on my head, I watched the silent instruments as if by sheer concentration I might drag a response from them. Every time I glanced up to the open door of the radio room, there were intent faces staring at me—worried faces, belonging to men I knew well, who said nothing, and did not need to. Once someone handed in two cups of coffee."

"Three days we waited for her, searching the radio waves, patrolling ceaselessly back and forth in the area . . . but she never answered any of our messages, never appeared. . . .

"The *Trigger* was gone, and with her many of my old friends," said Ned. "My feeling was deep. . . . When I think of our old boat, and the men still serving in her, the emotion is still there."

Ned thought about the profound difference between a lost surface ship and a lost submarine. When a surface ship is sunk, some evidence usually remains: a survivor, pieces of wreckage, nearby ships to report what has happened.

"With submarines there is just the deep, unfathomable silence."

• • •

Ned Beach went on to a distinguished postwar career in the Navy, retiring in 1966. He was also a popular author. His bestselling 1955 novel, *Run Silent, Run Deep*, was adapted into a 1958 film of the same name, starring Clark Gable and Burt Lancaster.

Walter Pye Wilson also continued to serve in submarines until 1954, when he transferred to shore duty to spend more time with his wife, Viola. He died in 1978.

When, in 1952, a new submarine named USS *Trigger* (SS-564) was commissioned in honor of Ned's old boat, Ned became her first skipper, serving with Walter Pye Wilson once again. But "nothing in her worked the way it should," Ned said later. In his eyes, *Trigger* II never had the heart of the valiant submarine after which she was named.

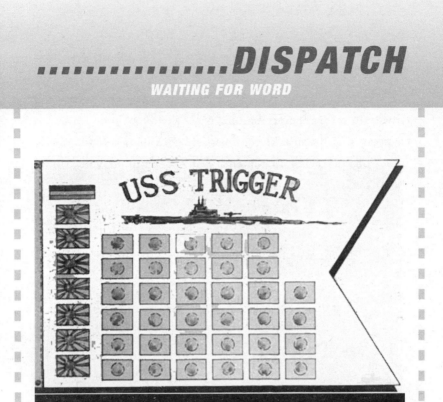

Trigger's record of ships sunk during her twelve patrols.

Edward L. Beach wrote that the men of the Submarine Force usually grieved silently when word came that a boat was lost.

The news, Ned Beach said, "is not the sudden realization that it is a day or two since a certain ship should have reported in from patrol. It is the intensified waiting, hoping against hope that some inconsequential matter, such as a broken-down radio transmitter, might prove to be the cause of the silence.

"You hear the chatter of messages from boats on patrol, going out, or coming back, reporting contacts, requesting rendezvous, or reporting results to date, but never do you hear the faint, clipped call from the vessel you listen for—never the *right* message comes in . . .

"Then an escort vessel is sent out, to wait—and wait—and finally to return, empty handed. And then you know what has happened, and you take the missing boat's name off the operations board, trying to pretend that the lump in your throat doesn't exist."

A Long, Hard Year for Seawolf

In the fall of 1942, Frederick Warder was about to make his seventh, and last, war patrol as commander of the *Seawolf*. It had been a long year, and the fearless skipper "might have chosen to take it easy," remarked historian Clay Blair. "But Warder was Warder."

The *Seawolf* left her base at Freemantle, Australia, on October 7 and, by November 2, was entering the broad mouth of Davao Gulf, a large body of water near Mindanao Island, the southernmost major island of the Philippines. Since the Japanese now controlled all of the Philippines, Warder was heading straight into enemy territory. Almost immediately, Warder sighted a freighter, the *Gifu Maru,* and sank it. Just as he had nearly a year before on *Seawolf*'s first patrol near Aparri, Warder then drew closer to shore to search for targets.

"It was a ticklish business," seaman Mel Eckberg said. "We couldn't afford to make a mistake. . . . But the Skipper brought the *Wolf* into that harbor as daintily as a ballet dancer." The submarine snuck right into Davao Harbor—near enough that through the periscope, Warder spotted houses, a church steeple, and the masts of boats at anchor.

Over the next few days, *Seawolf* explored the large gulf, managing to sink a camouflaged transport ship and diving out of range just as Japanese planes began to mount a counterattack. The enemy was on the alert for the marauding raider.

Frederick "Fearless Freddie" Warder didn't rest on his success on his last patrol on *Seawolf*.

As Warder turned *Seawolf* seaward, Japanese ships gave chase, "throwing out depth charges right and left. They were missing completely," said Eck. "The *Wolf* headed out for the mouth of the Gulf. We had to get out of here fast. It was now late afternoon. We raced under a flat sea, with a bright sun in the sky. It was risky periscope weather."

They weren't out of the gulf when Warder's voice broke over his headphones. He'd sighted a target. "'Oh, here's another one. . . . We'll take her,'" said Warder. "'Sound, this will have to be your approach.'"

Eck picked up the sound of a zigzagging freighter, alert that a submarine was on its trail. This one, though, got away. The captain went to rest. Eck tried to sleep as well, his nerves frayed from long stretches of constant alertness.

Captain Warder wasn't done with Davao Gulf, however. "It seemed as if [I] had closed my eyes for only a few minutes when the alarm went. When I hit the deck seven feet below my bunk, it jarred me awake," Eck said. He rushed through the narrow passageways to take over sound again.

No one spoke. At the periscope, Warder reported, "'He apparently doesn't see us, he's not zigging at all. This will be a big day if we can get him. Sound, can we pick him up yet?'"

Eck could. "'Yes, Captain, I have him now.'"

"'This is a 5,000 to 7,000 ton freighter,'" said Warder. "'The decks are loaded with what looks like invasion barges. We'll plunk him.'"

And so they did. As the fish left *Seawolf,* Eck heard the captain call out: "'I can see them . . . One's going to hit . . . !'"

There was a terrific blast. *Seawolf* went deep. Sinking three ships on his last patrol, Fearless Freddie Warder had once again earned his nickname.

• • •

Not long after, the submarine changed course, heading east. Immediately, Eck noticed the shift. "It suddenly dawned on me: home was in that direction," said Eck.

"I got so excited I left my station for the first time in my navy career and rushed out into the control room. The first man I saw was Lieutenant Deragon [the executive officer].

"'Where are we going, Mr. Deragon?' I asked him.

"'You're overdue, Eck,' he said with a grin, 'I knew as soon as we changed course you'd be out here. We expect to go home. How's that?'"

It was all right with Eck. He'd been dreaming about home for months. In their letters, he and his wife, Marjorie, had been planning his first night back. "We'd settled on dinner in some quiet little restaurant, candles on the table, a full-course meal, topped off by a bottle of expensive wine that had to rest in a bucket of ice.

"We wouldn't discuss the war. Marjorie wouldn't talk to me about the *Wolf.* No questions about the ships we sunk, or the escapes we had. We would talk about ourselves and about Spike, and about the home we intended to build after the war. . . . The last time I saw Spike he was twenty-six days old."

• • •

Seawolf hadn't been back at Pearl Harbor since the attack nearly a year before. Nor had her weary crew gotten much rest since the first day of the war. They'd endured seven and a half hours of depth charges at a time and pursued the enemy into tight harbors. They had patrolled vast stretches of the Pacific, sinking ships and carrying out dangerous special missions such as ferrying ammunition through enemy waters for the relief of beleaguered troops on Corregidor.

"For many weeks I hadn't seen sunlight or tasted fresh air," said Eck. "I knew I had lost weight. My pants hung so loosely. I had to use new holes in my belt to keep them up. . . . We weren't the same men who had left Cavite a year ago."

Now these veterans of successful torpedo attacks, long submerged cruises, and depth-charge beatings were about to get their first look at postattack Pearl Harbor.

"I climbed topside, emerged from the conning tower, and stood transfixed," said Eck. "The *Seawolf* was slowly gliding into

Pearl Harbor. But what a different spectacle than when we had last been here."

The destruction from the battle was visible everywhere, but so were the efforts to rebuild and repair. "The harbor on both sides of us was a staggering scene of destruction, as though a tornado had twisted across it, overturning ships, snapping crane booms like matchsticks, splitting buildings in half," said Eck.

"We passed piled-up fragments of planes, their wings jutting out grotesquely; ships splotched with huge holes, keels and hulls of nameless vessels. There was the screeching of moving derricks, the scream of air hammers, a bedlam of engines roaring, machines pounding, men at work."

Seawolf's stay at Pearl Harbor would be brief—she would head to Mare Island in California for several weeks of overhaul and repairs before her next patrol in the spring of 1943. Eck wouldn't be on her. Like some of the other old-timers, he was due for some rest. He would leave *Seawolf* after this patrol to brush up on new radio skills. Captain Frederick Warder was leaving for a new assignment too. It felt like the end of an era— and it was.

"When it came time for me to open my locker and take my personal belongings on shore, I knew I was saying good-by to the *Wolf*," Eck said. "It had been more than just a steel structure to me. I'd lived and died a thousand times on this ship. Men whom I admired more than any others I know, had lived and worked with me on this ship. I knew every bulkhead, every odor. She held no secrets from me.

"I walked through her before I took off my stuff, letting my mind wander over all the *Wolf* had done: the evacuations of men and material; the High Command, the aviators, ammunition, depth charges . . . a thousand places, a thousand thrills."

Eck and the crew gathered for the final farewell to present their skipper with a watch. " 'I have been very fortunate,' " Eck remembered him saying. " 'Here, I believe, is the best submarine crew ever gathered together. . . . Now I'm going to shake hands with every one of you.' "

When it was his turn, Eck managed to choke out, " 'Good-by, Captain, I hope I can serve with you again someday.'

"He gripped my hand hard. 'Nothing would please me more, Eckberg.' "

• • •

Neither Mel Eckberg nor Frederick Warder ever returned to the *Seawolf*. Eck's adjustment to the world outside the hull of a submarine wasn't easy at first. "The tension of these last twelve months was to stay with me for a long time after I came home.

"Marjorie was to be unhappy, Spike afraid to talk to me, because I was so irritable," he said. "For weeks, after, I'd wake up at two and three in the morning, walk around, smoke half a dozen cigarettes, and try to fall asleep again. For a long time I couldn't sleep more than three hours at a time."

The family held together. Some months later, in August 1943, war correspondents Gerold Frank and James D. Horan were on their way by train to the submarine base in New London, Connecticut. They were on assignment to write a story about submarines, when they happened to meet Mel Eckberg on the train. "He was big and brawny, his giant frame squeezed into a coach seat; he had the clear blue eyes, the hawklike gaze of a Viking; and he was the most beribboned figure we had ever seen in a navy uniform."

The journalists asked him to share his story. A week or so later, once official clearance had been given for Eck to relate details of a submariner's life, Eck invited the men home to look at his *Seawolf* scrapbook. Marjorie was busy in the kitchen, and toddler Spike sat playing on the floor. His toy: a paperweight made of teakwood, just like the deck of the *Seawolf.*

The photos and scrapbook clippings, Eck said, didn't tell the whole story. And so he told the tale from the beginning, from the first moment he clapped eyes on the *Seawolf,* until that last, bittersweet moment of parting.

• • •

The *Seawolf* went on to fight for two more years. In October 1944, on her fifteenth patrol, she was lost with all hands in a tragic case of mistaken identity.

The submarine was first bombed by a plane, and then attacked by depth charges dropped by a US destroyer. *Seawolf*'s attempts to communicate by radio were either not picked up or were not understood as the proper recognition signal.

The loss was a grim reminder of the threats facing every man aboard a submarine in a battle zone. The *Seawolf* tragedy was, fortunately, rare: She was the only Pacific submarine lost in this way.

Seawolf had amassed a proud record. "By the autumn of 1944 she had sunk 71,609 tons of enemy shipping. Few submarines had downed as many ships and as much tonnage," wrote historian Theodore Roscoe. "Fourteen patrols and 56 torpedo battles had

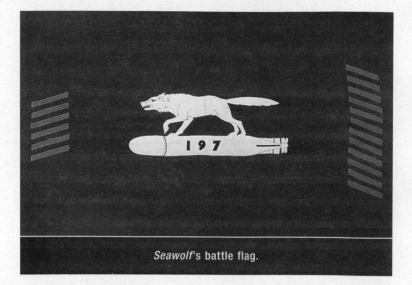

Seawolf's battle flag.

gone into her record since that long-ago day when Lieutenant Commander Warder took her around to Davao Gulf and poked her periscope into the vortex of the Tojo-Yamamoto offensive.

"No submarine in the Pacific had fought harder in the war than *Seawolf*, pioneer veteran of the Asiatic fleet."

Mel Eckberg, who loved the ship and gave her his all, would have agreed.

Submariners quoted in this book sometimes refer to tons and tonnage when speaking of their targets. Just what is tonnage?

Tonnage is a maritime term. There are different methods of measuring it (and even international conventions and agreements about it). For merchant ships like a cargo ship carrying equipment, food, or supplies, tonnage is a measurement of volume. In other words, tonnage is an estimate of how much a ship can carry, with one ton equal to 100 cubic feet of carrying capacity. Tonnage is calculated in a different way for a ship like an oil tanker or an ore carrier. In those cases, tonnage refers to the maximum weight of cargo that can be carried safely.

Warships, of course, don't carry cargo, and are measured in terms of their weight. But since it's not easy to weigh a ship, a method called displacement tons is used to describe a ship's mass. Think of a ship at sea. It takes up space and displaces a certain amount of water. One expert explains it this way: "Displacement is calculated according to the volume of water displaced, using a standard value of 35 cubic feet of sea water per long ton (2,240 pounds)."

Throughout the war, tonnage estimates of ships sunk by submarines were always approximations. And while the subject of tonnage may be complex, it's fairly easy to understand the basic principle: The larger the ship and the more it could carry, the better target it made for submarine skippers.

As one submarine historian commented, "A Japanese freighter

of 5,000 tons was more valuable, and added more to the scorecard than a military patrol craft of 500 tons; though in each case the submarine sank one ship. The displacement or tonnage also provided a guideline to determine whether or not a target was worth expending one or more of their expensive, and in the early days of the war, scarce, torpedoes."

SKIPPER'S RECOMMENDATION: *Ask your math teacher or a boat expert for more information. For educators, the Great Lakes Maritime Transportation Education Center website has a number of lesson plans relating to maritime commerce, calculating tonnage and ballast, and other STEM connections: http://wupcenter.mtu.edu/education /great_lakes_maritime/.*

USS WAHOO (SS-238)

The ship was called the one-sub wolf pack . . . she was called
WAHOO! *No one knows where she is now. Perhaps there is some*
Valhalla for submariners; some happy hunting ground for the men
who found such good hunting under the seas.

—Office of Naval Records and History
Ships' Histories Section
Navy Department

USS *Wahoo.*

WAHOO: AN UNPROMISING START

In the fall of 1942, as the war-weary *Seawolf* limped into Pearl Harbor, another submarine was just getting her start. The USS *Wahoo* (SS-238) was built just after *Trigger* (SS-237). And like *Trigger*, which had accomplished nothing in her first outing except to run aground on the rocks of Midway, *Wahoo's* first excursions gave no hint that she was destined to become a submarine legend.

In fact, it was just the opposite.

Wahoo was not a happy boat on her first patrol from August to October of 1942. The atmosphere under her cautious, perfectionist captain, Marvin "Pinky" Kennedy, was strained, with frequent drills and little time for the crew to rest. There were also personal tensions, and a lack of trust between the skipper and his second-in-command, executive officer Richard "Dick" O'Kane.

Dick O'Kane had graduated from the Naval Academy in 1936. By the time war broke out, he was a husband and father as well as an experienced, hard-charging submariner on track to command his own ship—if he could keep his temper in check, that is. That wasn't proving to be easy on the *Wahoo*.

Dick bristled over the skipper's insistence that two officers be on watch at all times, which limited the time Dick had available for troubleshooting problems that arose. Furthermore, he chafed under Kennedy's hesitant approach to attacking enemy ships. Dick, who'd served on the submarine minelayer USS *Argonaut*

(SM-1) for nearly four years, had more actual experience in boats than Kennedy, who relied on prewar, textbook strategies—strategies that seemed overly conservative to his eager executive officer.

Wahoo's third officer, George Grider, felt much the same. "After exhausting months of drills, after the build-up of tension within each man as to how he would conduct himself in danger, it was demoralizing to creep away submerged from that first target."

Dick was furious when the captain let two significant targets—a Japanese aircraft tender and an aircraft carrier—get away. He assumed the captain would be relieved of duty after that, but Kennedy was given another chance. Something did change, though.

A brash, charismatic officer named Dudley "Mush" Morton was assigned to ride along on *Wahoo*'s second patrol as prospective commanding officer (PCO), a dry run before being given his own command.

"Dudley greeted each of us with a friendly smile and a hand twice the size of ours," recalled Dick O'Kane. "His genial personality seemed contagious. . . . Hope replaced apprehensions concerning our coming patrol before I hit my bunk."

Forest J. Sterling was also new to *Wahoo*, coming aboard as yeoman with responsibility for the boat's paperwork. Sterling, nicknamed Yeo on account of his job duties, remembered Dudley Morton vividly.

When Yeo addressed the new officer formally, Mush told him, " 'Don't call me Mister Morton, call me "Mush." That's my nickname for "Mushmouth." It's the name they gave me at the Naval Academy—I like it.' "

The *Wahoo* left Pearl Harbor on November 8, 1942, on her second war patrol. Like her first outing, it was a discouraging experience for Dick. After Kennedy called off an attack on a tanker, Dick could stand it no longer. In an act of subtle defiance, he pulled out his copy of *Navy Regulations* to review the section on taking over command from a captain.

It was a risky page to leave open. Yet that's exactly what happened when Dick was called away to make a periscope search. Dick didn't expect Kennedy to appear just then, but he did. Not only that, Kennedy idly picked up the book, still open to the section about removing the captain.

Dick said nothing. "It was one of life's touchy moments," he reflected later. "No words were exchanged, but now each knew exactly where he stood with the other."

Wahoo's skipper did manage to sink two enemy ships during the patrol, which helped the crew's morale. Still, Dick had some soul-searching to do when they put into harbor in Australia. "I loved this ship and the challenge of her full potential, but could not go to sea again with my present captain when a blowup would be inevitable."

He needn't have worried. When the patrol ended, Kennedy was transferred out of submarines. The coming year would bring a new skipper for *Wahoo*. Dudley "Mush" Morton would step into the role. Mush Morton and Dick O'Kane were about to make submarine history.

JANUARY 2: Japanese forces enter the city of Manila, Philippines.

JANUARY 23: Just north of Australia, the Japanese capture the city of Rabaul on the island of New Britain in what is now Papua New Guinea, and develop a military base there.

FEBRUARY 15: Singapore surrenders to the Japanese.

FEBRUARY 27: Japan wins the Battle of the Java Sea; prior to the battle, US submarines had been unable to make successful torpedo attacks in defense of the island (in part because of defective torpedoes and also ineffective skippers); submarines do not take part; US Asiatic Fleet submarines withdraw to Western Australia.

MAY 3: Japanese occupy the island of Tulagi in the Solomon Islands.

MAY 4–8: For the first time, US forces check the Japanese advance, in the Battle of the Coral Sea (north of Australia), a battle led by carrier-based aircraft; four submarines participate with one confirmed sinking of a minelayer. Parts of Papua New Guinea remain contested territory.

MAY 14: Charles Lockwood relieves John Wilkes to command submarines in Freemantle, Australia; at Pearl Harbor, Bob English assumes command of the submarines in the Pacific Fleet.

JUNE 4–7: US hands Japan a major strategic defeat at the Battle of Midway; although several submarines of the Pacific Fleet are deployed by Bob English, none score a hit.

JUNE 20: Lockwood arranges first test of Mark XIV torpedoes, revealing that they are running about ten to eleven feet deeper than set.

JULY 5: US establishes a submarine base at Midway.

AUGUST 7–FEBRUARY 9: US and Japanese forces begin prolonged surface ship and ground conflict in the Solomon Islands, including the Naval Battle of Guadalcanal (November 12–15), which ends with Allied victory on February 9, 1943.

NOVEMBER: Following defeat at the Naval Battle of Guadalcanal, Japan goes on the defense in the Pacific, trying to hold territory gained in its offensive actions begun in December 1941.

PART THREE

HERE COMES THE WAHOO

• 1943 •

Mush was in his element. He was in danger, and he was hot on the trail of the enemy, so he was happy.

—George Grider

Morton feared nothing on or under the sea.

—Theodore Roscoe

The *Wahoo*.

18 MUSH THE MAGNIFICENT

Dudley "Mush" Morton, sometimes affectionately known as Mush the Magnificent, was built like a bear but had the playful nature of a young cub.

"Everybody liked Mush," said *Wahoo*'s third officer George Grider. "He was always roaming the narrow quarters, his big hands reaching out to examine equipment, his wide-set eyes missing nothing. . . . The tiny wardroom always brightened when Mush squeezed his massive shoulders through one of the two narrow doorways and found a place to sit."

Unlike *Trigger*'s Ned Beach, Dudley Morton didn't hail from a seafaring family. He'd been born far from the ocean, in Owensboro, Kentucky, in 1907. His mother was often ill during his childhood, so Dudley was sent to live with relatives in Miami, Florida. After high school, he entered the US Naval Academy, where he wrestled and played football, picking up his nickname along the way. His Naval Academy yearbook described his famous smile, ever-ready sense of humor, and infectious charm.

Mush brought these qualities—as well as an aggressive (and sometimes controversial) ferocity—to his leadership of the *Wahoo*. For Dick O'Kane, continuing in the role of executive officer, it was a welcome relief to serve a captain whose bold style matched his own. And unlike Dick's previous skipper, Mush had complete confidence in his executive officer.

In fact, even before they set out on their first patrol as skipper

Dick O'Kane and Dudley "Mush" Morton on the bridge of the *Wahoo*.

and exec, Mush sat down to share his innovative ideas about teamwork with Dick. In traditional submarine warfare, the captain took total charge during an attack: handling periscope sightings, positioning the sub, and gathering all the data necessary to successfully launch a torpedo at a moving target.

Mush wanted to do things differently. He believed sharing responsibilities would increase success rates. (Submarine war patrol reports were posted and discussed among officers, and the innovations developed by the two men rapidly caught on with other results-oriented submariners, becoming known as the Morton-O'Kane technique.)

"'Now, you're going to be my co-approach officer, not my assistant,'" Mush told Dick. "'You'll make all of the approach and attack periscope observations. . . . I'll conn [e.g., maneuver]

Wahoo to the best attack position, and then you'll fire the torpedoes.

"'This way I'll never get scared.'"

• • •

Even before the *Wahoo* left the dock on her third patrol, the crew sensed things were about to change. "I could feel the stirring of a strong spirit growing in her. The officers acted differently. The men felt differently," said Forest "Yeo" Sterling. "There was more of a feeling of freedom and of being trusted to get our jobs done.

"It was a feeling that *Wahoo* was not only the best . . . but that she was capable of performing miracles."

The morning of their departure, Mush called the men together to share his view of their mission: The men of the *Wahoo* would pursue every sighting possible and stay with each target until that ship was on the way to the bottom.

"'Every smoke trace on the horizon, every contact on watch will be investigated,'" Mush told the crew. "'Now, if anyone doesn't want to go along under these conditions, just see the yeoman. I am giving him verbal authority now to transfer anyone who is not a volunteer. . . . I must know within half an hour who will be leaving, so that I can get replacements.'"

After the men were dismissed, Yeo went to his small office and nursed a cup of coffee, waiting to see if anyone would show up to request a transfer. The captain soon poked his head in. "'Any customers, Yeo?'

"'Not a one, Captain,'" Yeo told him.

Mush grinned. "'That's the kind of stuff I like in a crew.'"

Yeo inserted the sailing list into his typewriter and dated it: January 15, 1943. He didn't need to make a single change to the names already on the roster. *Wahoo* got under way.

Some hours later, after waking from a nap, Yeo wandered into the messroom and settled on one of its green plastic-covered benches to read a magazine. Around him, crew members buzzed about a promise their new captain had just made: Any sailor who sighted a target while on lookout would get promoted if the *Wahoo* managed to sink the ship.

One man rose, ready to sign up for extra watches. The cook, who was puttering in the galley, called out, "'Wait a minute . . . I'm going with you.'"

The messroom of a submarine.

All the men burst out laughing. "This was the first time I had ever known of a ship's cook volunteering for watches," Yeo wrote later.

Yeo was still in the messroom a little later when all banter halted. The captain appeared. Yeo looked up, startled. "The thing that caught our attention and made us speechless was the way he was dressed. He had on an old red bathrobe and go-ahead slippers [rubber slippers or flip-flops with no heel support so you can't back up]. He also had a navigational chart under one arm and a bucket of soapy water in the other hand."

Mush greeted the men and asked if he could join them. He set his pail down, then thumbtacked a navigational chart of the islands of New Guinea onto the bulletin board. This strategic area just a few hundred miles north of Australia had been contested territory since January 1942, when the Japanese established a military base on the island of New Britain. (Today the western half of New Guinea Island is part of Indonesia, while the eastern half and nearby islands make up the independent country of Papua New Guinea.)

Making himself comfortable at the end of a bench, Mush began to wash a khaki shirt in his pail, kneading it with his large hands. Nodding at the chart, he asked, "'Any of you men ever operate in this area before?'"

No one had. Mush went on. "'We have a special mission to try and locate a harbor along this coast that the Japanese seem to be using pretty heavily. Some of the army planes out of Australia have reported a lot of shipping.'"

He added, "'Would you guys like to go in and look around? Maybe we will find a submarine tender with a lot of submarines alongside. I sure would like that.'"

Yeo and the others agreed, catching his enthusiasm. Then Mush rose and picked up his bucket. "'Guess I'll go back and hang this shirt up in the engine room to dry out.'"

After he left, crew members looked at one another in astonishment. Someone whispered, "'Rowdydow.'"

Mush could hardly be more different from their previous, standoffish captain.

A crewmate asked Yeo, "'Do you think he's crazy?'

"'Yeah, like a fox.'"

• • •

When it was time for Yeo's next watch, he grabbed a pair of red goggles used for night vision, then climbed up to the starboard lookout station on deck.

"It was an awe-inspiring night with big bright stars overhead," he remembered. "*Wahoo* was moving through the water at a steady clip, and the only noise to disturb me was the music of the waves created by *Wahoo*'s bow pushing through the water.

"Not too far away was land. The air was musty with the rich fragrance of tropical underbrush and strange flower scents. It seemed altogether too peaceful for there to be a war in progress and death lurking someplace in those jungles and at sea also."

Yeo returned below to take his turn at the wheel, keeping the boat on her set course. It gave him a different perspective. "The whole universe, of course, was shut out to me, but it was a pleasant change watching the indirectly lighted gyrocompass. When it would start moving in a circle jerkily to the right or left, a slight twist of the wheel and a short jerk back to check the ship's swing would bring *Wahoo* back on the course."

After a break for coffee, apple pie, and cheese, Yeo was back on lookout duty as night turned to dawn. This time, while topside, he happened to notice the "Mae West" life jacket strapped to the periscope. It was a flat belt that could be inflated into a tube. "This was another innovation of Captain Morton's, a safety precaution that might save someone's life if they did not clear the bridge on diving."

At that moment, Ensign George Misch shouted, "'Clear the bridge.'" As the diving siren bellowed, the bow instantly dipped below the waves.

Tired as he was, Yeo sprang into action for *Wahoo*'s standard morning dive, which was usually done at dawn to check the trim, or buoyancy status, of the submarine and make any necessary corrections to the weight in the various compartments and ballast tanks.

He dropped his binoculars, letting them hang loosely from the strap around his neck. Swinging down from the lookout platform to the deck ten feet below, he raced past Misch to the hatch. Although Yeo was quick, David Veder, the other lookout, got there first.

Yeo leaped, mostly ignoring the ladder and letting gravity take him through the hatch to the deck of the conning tower below. Halfway down, Misch, "all two thousand pounds of him," or so it seemed to Yeo, landed on his shoulders and "rode me the rest of the way piggyback. How he managed to close the hatch after him was a trade secret."

From the conning tower, Yeo then dropped down onto the floor of the control room and bent to catch his breath, bracing himself against the steep angle of the submarine's dive. When

A sailor peers down the hatch of a submarine.

finally able to speak, he told David Veder, "'I bet you don't beat me to that hatch next time.'"

Captain Morton was standing nearby, stopwatch in hand. "'Attaboy, Yeo, but you'll have to get the lead out of your pants.'"

Turning to Dick O'Kane, Mush added, "'We clipped three seconds off our diving time. . . . We're making progress.'"

Everyone on board knew his life might one day depend on just how fast *Wahoo* could disappear beneath the sea.

• • •

Each day of *Wahoo*'s third patrol brought more changes. "Most of them could be traced back to Captain Morton's stateroom," reflected Yeo, "but the initiative fever was catching and we all began to have ideas. Communication between officers and men became increasingly easier."

Yeo still couldn't quite manage to beat crewmate David Veder to the hatch during the early morning trim dives. A few days later, bruised from having Misch ride his back again, Yeo found the other lookout smugly eating a platter of scrambled eggs in the messroom. All Yeo could do was glower at Veder and sit down at another table, rubbing his sore muscles before turning in for a nap.

When he next woke, Yeo sensed something was different. It took him awhile to figure out what it was. *Wahoo* had been gliding on the surface of the sea. Now, deeper into enemy territory, the submarine was running submerged toward an unknown, uncharted harbor in the distance.

How Mush Morton found that harbor was quite a story.

SUBMARINE SCHOOL
DIVE!

As air fills ballast tanks, water is forced out when a submarine surfaces.

Just how do submarines dive?

Journalist Martin Sheridan provided a layperson's account when he wrote about his experiences in March of 1945 as the only war correspondent given permission to make a war patrol on a US submarine in the Pacific.

Sheridan joined Lieutenant Commander Walter T. Griffith and his crew during the first patrol of the USS *Bullhead* (SS-332), which in August of that year tragically became the last submarine lost in the war. Sheridan's lively account of life on a submarine, *Overdue and Presumed Lost*, was first published in 1947. Sheridan described a submarine's dive for readers eager to know more about the silent service.

"There's no such command as 'Crash dive,' as the motion picture studios would have us believe. Every dive is made as quickly as possible. That's the only way to achieve speed and perfection. All you have to do is kick out the corks, let in the water, and down you go.

"Technically, here's what really happens. Even before the conning tower hatch is shut, water is admitted into the main ballast tanks by opening a series of vents. Diesel engines are shut down and men in the maneuvering room cut over for propulsion to the electric motors fed by tons of huge battery cells.

"Air pressure is built up within the boat to test her airtightness, and the main induction, which provides fresh air from the engines and the rest of the submarine, is shut. When the proper vents are closed a 'green board' shows up on the 'Christmas tree' panel in the control room. This consists of a series of small lights—green denoting closed and red for open—which automatically show the condition of valves, vents, and hatches. It's one of the greatest safety factors aboard.

"Bow and stern planes resembling fins are always rigged for diving while the boat is underway. These regulate the depth and the angle of dive, just as the elevators of an airplane regulate its altitude and angle of climb.

"When the captain decides just how deep he wants to go, the diving officer levels off by using the auxiliary tanks amidships, the regular trimming tanks, and the bow and stern tanks to adjust his trim. Our main ballast tanks are located outside the pressure hull, as are the negative and safety tanks, used to speed surfacing or diving."

Sheridan also described what a dive felt and sounded like. "It's an uncomfortable feeling to lie in your sack during a dive, especially if you sleep, as I do, with your head toward the bow [front]. When the boat noses down rapidly you can hear water gurgling in the flooding tanks. There's an eerie crackling and creaking throughout the boat as both the depth and pressure increase. Your head is lower than your feet, and you experience a sensation of falling.

"You begin to wonder, 'When the devil are they going to level off?' Also, 'How many fathoms have we below us?' And, 'Are there any uncharted pinnacles in this area?' Then comes the reassuring hissing of the flooding after tanks. You come out of the dive, and soon your body is level again. Everyone breathes a sigh of relief."

19 OFF THE MAP: THE UNKNOWN WATERS OF WEWAK

Captain Dudley "Mush" Morton had informed his crew that the *Wahoo*'s orders included a request from headquarters to conduct reconnaissance in the vicinity of Wewak Harbor, New Guinea, the possible site of a Japanese supply base. The problem? No one had a clue exactly where Wewak was located.

"Our charts simply showed a somewhat ragged coastline, with bays, islands, and reefs, without even the name Wewak appearing," executive officer Dick O'Kane recalled.

George Grider put it this way: "How could we reconnoiter a harbor whose location we didn't know?"

George assumed the most they could—or would—do was patrol the general vicinity and then be on their way. But one night when the captain and officers were in the wardroom studying charts, Mush Morton asked the men what they thought the word *reconnoiter* meant.

George offered, "'It means we take a cautious look at the area, from far out at sea, through the periscope, submerged.'"

Mush grinned. That wasn't quite what he had in mind. "'The only way you can reconnoiter a harbor is to go right into it and see what's there.'"

George and the others exchanged glances. "Now it was clear that our captain had advanced from mere rashness to outright foolhardiness," he wrote later. "Harbors are often treacherous at best. . . . It would be madness for the *Wahoo* to submerge and

Two sailors study a chart.

enter an enemy harbor whose very location on the map we
didn't know. . . .

"Yet here was this skipper of ours, grinning at us under his
jutting nose as if he had just told a funny story, assuring us we
were going to do it and we'd darned well better find out
which harbor was Wewak or he'd just pick the most likely one
and go in."

Madness, it seemed, was exactly what the *Wahoo* was now
all about.

• • •

Help in pinpointing the exact location of the mysterious harbor came from an unexpected source. As George Grider was passing through the engine room one night, he noticed a machinist's mate named Dalton "Bird Dog" Keeter looking at a book.

" 'Hey, Mr. Grider, is this the Wewak we're going to?' " Keeter asked. He showed George a school atlas he'd bought for his kids while on leave in Australia. Though the print was tiny, the name Wewak definitely appeared on the map of New Guinea.

"A couple of months before, the idea of entering an enemy harbor with the help of a high-school geography [book] would have struck me as too ridiculous even to be funny," said George. "Now I almost hugged the book and charged forward to the wardroom with it as if it were the key to the destruction of the entire Japanese Navy.

"Mush took one look at it and reached for our charts. The wardroom began to hum with activity."

Dick O'Kane said, "The outline of Wewak was much too small. But if we could draw an accurate enlargement, we might find where it fitted on our chart."

So that's what they did, making an outline of the harbor on tracing paper (George recalled that they used toilet paper), then rigging up George's old Graflex (a brand of camera) as a make-shift enlarger so they could match the shape of the harbor to their navigational chart. The camera had been used by George's father, a flier in World War I. After George's father was killed, a fellow pilot had saved the camera and brought it home for his friend's son. It was one of George's most prized possessions.

"When I thought that a chart fashioned with the help of an ancient camera used by my father more than a quarter of a century before on the other side of the world in another war would lead us into Wewak harbor, I . . . began to believe there was some kind of guiding destiny behind the *Wahoo*'s third patrol," George said.

As they examined the enlargement, the men discovered that the cove itself appeared to be a good size—perhaps nine miles long, with a width of about two miles across in some places. From the information they compiled, George and the others also guessed the water might be two hundred feet deep in many areas, making the harbor feasible to penetrate. They were also able to identify some distinguishing geographic features to help guide them. One nearby island was named Mushu, which, of course, everyone immediately abbreviated to Mush. It seemed a good omen.

"Mush was delighted," George recalled. "He ignored the uncertainties and concentrated on the fact that we would have deep water, if we stayed where it was, and unmistakable landmarks, if we could spot them in time to use them."

• • •

Time was short, however. Morton and his crew were now heading north from Brisbane, Australia, approaching Vitiaz Strait between the islands of New Guinea and New Britain. But they had orders to head north and be in the area of Palau on January 30, nearly a thousand miles and a week's travel away. To have enough time to explore Wewak Harbor before their next assignment, Mush and his crew needed to arrive by dawn the next morning.

Submarines can go faster when not submerged. There was only one problem with *Wahoo* continuing to speed along the surface of the sea: The presence of a Japanese airfield based on New

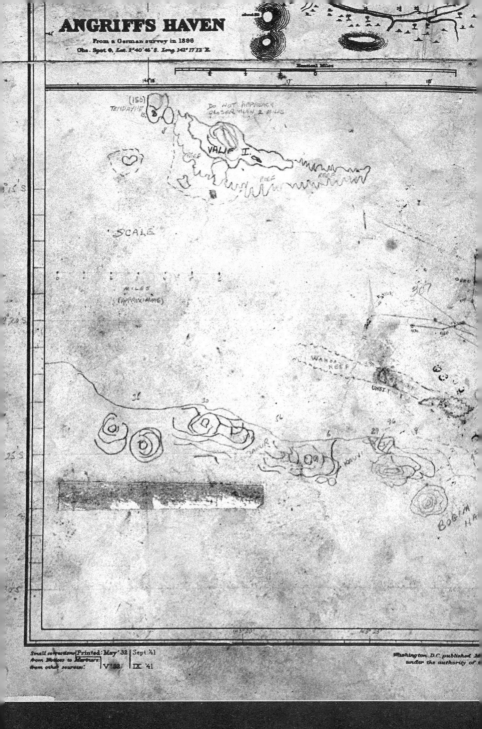

The map of Wewak Harbor hand-drawn aboard the *Wahoo*.

KAIRIRU
ISLAND
(FLAT TOPO
SUMMIT)

KAIRIRU STRAIT

MUSHU
ISLAND

MUSHU

DALLMAN
HARB.

2d. EDITION Dec. 1920

No. 2976

Britain. *Wahoo* would probably be able to dive out of danger in time if spotted from the air, but being sighted at all would ruin the element of surprise. And surprise was crucial to Mush's plan to sneak into Wewak Harbor and attack whatever enemy warships or supply vessels happened to be there.

"Normal prudence called for submerged cruising," Dick O'Kane observed. "But the situation was not normal."

Mush's solution was to post extra lookouts using binoculars fitted with protective lenses in the glare of the sun. As they moved along the New Guinea coast, George Grider was on watch. George couldn't help compare what *Wahoo* was doing now with her first lackluster patrols.

"It was a strange and unfamiliar experience to see enemy land lying black and sinister on the port hand, to feel the enemy planes always near us, and yet it was invigorating," he said. "Contrary to all tradition on the *Wahoo*, we kept to the surface during daylight hours . . . though we were never out of sight of land and often within close range of enemy airports."

George knew Mush was willing to take risks—now he discovered exactly how far the skipper would go. "He wandered up for a bit of conversation when I was on the bridge, and suddenly as we talked we sighted a plane about eight miles away. About the same time, the radar picked it up and confirmed the range," said George. "We had always dived when we sighted a plane in the past, so I turned for the hatch. Mush's big hand landed on the back of my collar just as I reached the ladder.

" 'Let's wait till he gets in to six miles,' he said softly.

"I turned and went back. Great Lord, I thought, we're under the command of a madman. We stood and watched as the plane

Dudley Morton (left) in the conning tower of the *Wahoo*.

closed the range. At six and a half miles his course began to take him away from us, and in a few minutes he had faded from sight.

"By gambling that he hadn't seen us, Mush had saved us hours of submerged travel, but even though it had worked, I wasn't sure I was in favor of it."

George stayed on the bridge. Another hour passed. He sent down for his sunglasses, then sunscreen lotion. They were within twenty miles of the enemy airfields when Mush finally gave the order. "'All right, George, you can go ahead and take her down now.'

"Two blasts practically punctuated the captain's statement," recalled Dick, "and *Wahoo* slipped quietly under the sea."

• • •

Submarine sailor on the lookout.

When Yeo Sterling had awakened to realize that *Wahoo* was now running submerged, he went into the messroom to ask cook John Rowls what was going on.

" 'We've been laying off an unknown harbor and looking it over. The Old Man thinks it might be Wewak Harbor—the one we've been hunting for,' " Rowls told him.

A little later, seaman Delville "Moose" Hunter appeared, poured himself some coffee, and sat down to relay the latest from the conning tower. " 'The Old Man spotted the masts of something on the other side of the peninsula. He's all excited. It might be that submarine tender he's been dreaming about. We're going in to find out.' "

Yeo wished he could be closer to the action. Wistfully he asked, " 'How's things up there?' "

" 'Different, lot's different, now that Mush has taken over. Why, for one thing, he lets O'Kane handle the 'scope and he stands around directing everything. I think he does the mathematics in his head,' " Hunter told him.

Yeo's next words broke the tension. " 'I guess he's like me,' I said. 'I got a photographic memory, too.'

" 'Huh?' " His crewmates gazed at him skeptically.

" 'The only thing is my film never seems to develop.' "

The men chuckled, but soon returned to waiting tensely, ears alert to any new sound. "The atmosphere was heavy with danger all about us," Yeo said. "Our heightened senses were quick to interpret the slightest *Wahoo* change or noise. An outburst of excitement in the conning tower carried down to us and we listened until it subsided."

Yeo suddenly remembered something a teacher had once told

him: " 'Every person is the center of his own universe. If a straight line were drawn from the center of the moon to the center of the earth, it would have to pass through the person drawing the line.'

"I thought about that and about myself. That meant the imaginary line was passing right through the crew's mess on the *Wahoo*. If I were the center of the universe, then everything radiated away from me in circles."

And right now he was in the center of danger, hidden under a vast, treacherous sea, and very far from home. Yeo tried to imagine the circles that spread out from the familiar world of the messroom, where he sat on the green plastic cushion of the bench, to the unknown threats above him in a placid island harbor.

"*Wahoo* was my cocoon, which, in turn, was wrapped in a body of water. I tried to visualize the water, and my picture of clear tropical waters with a sandy bottom was not reassuring. Surrounding this body of water must be beaches with straw-thatched huts and maybe Japanese installations with natives and soldiers, and perhaps native boats drawn up on the beach or in the water."

Yeo couldn't help asking himself: "What kind of Japanese warships were anchored here?"

All at once, the answer to that question spread like wildfire throughout the submarine.

THE APPROACH

The *Wahoo* had submerged two and a half miles off the mouth of the uncharted waters of Wewak Harbor at about three thirty in the morning of January 24, 1943, just as the first hints of gray smudged the dark horizon to the east.

"We spent the entire morning nosing around that harbor, trying to find out what was in it and where the safe water was," said George Grider. "As Dick spotted light patches of water in the scope, he called off their locations and we noted them on our chart as shallows. From time to time we could pencil in landmarks. One of these we called Coast Watcher Point."

That landmark got its impromptu name when the current swept *Wahoo* so close to land that "all of us in the conning tower, taking turns at the periscope, could see a Japanese lookout, wearing a white shirt, sitting under a coconut tree right on the point," George said. "We saw him so clearly, in fact, that I am sure I would recognize him if I passed him on the street."

Unlike Yeo Sterling in the messroom, George had a front-row seat in the conning tower as assistant approach officer. He was about to witness the first instance of Mush's unique attack strategy, with executive officer Dick O'Kane handling the periscope during the approach. George thought that "few captains other than Mush ever had such serene faith in a subordinate that they could resist grabbing the scope in moments of crisis."

Right now, Mush didn't seem worried—far from it. His

The *Wahoo* control room.

confidence was infectious. "For all the tension within us, we managed to reflect his mood . . . Mush even kept up his joking when we almost ran aground," said George.

The near-accident happened when Dick reported that they were getting too close to shore. Dick said, " 'I have the periscope in high power, and all I can see is one coconut tree.' "

George thought they would be dangerously close if one tree, even magnified six times, filled the scope. Then Mush spoke up. " 'Dick . . . you're in low power.' "

Instantly, Dick flipped the handle to high power and cried, " 'Down periscope! . . . All back emergency! My God, all I can see is one coconut!' "

The *Wahoo* backed away in record time.

• • •

Mush had kept his cool then, but by early afternoon, even the skipper's nerves began to fray. The crew had spent tense, dangerous hours creeping below the surface, seeking a target—with no results. Then, at last, Dick spotted something in his periscope lens that appeared to be the bridge of a ship. It might, he reported, be a freighter or a tender of some sort at anchor.

" 'Well, Captain,' somebody in the conning tower said, 'we've reconnoitered Wewak harbor now. Let's get cracking out of here and report there's a ship in there.'

"We all knew it was a joke, however much we wished it weren't," recalled George.

" 'Good grief, no,' said Mush, coming to life. 'We're going to go in and torpedo him.' "

• • •

The harbor was calm and smooth as glass. *Wahoo's* periscope would be easy to spot against that mirrored surface. Periscope sightings had to be quick and precise.

"We would not leave a telltale periscope feather at our approach speed of 3 knots, but on each observation, water was lapping the lens of the scope," said Dick. Seconds later, the enemy ship took on a distinct shape. Dick asked Mush to have a look.

"The two of them stood there like a couple of schoolboys," said George, "peering through the scope each time it was raised, trying to decide what kind of vessel lay ahead. At last they agreed, and Mush looked happily around the conning tower.

" 'It's a destroyer,' he said."

CHAPTER TWENTY

The skipper got a fierce, excited look in his eyes George would never forget. " 'We'll take him by complete surprise,' he assured us. 'He won't be expecting an enemy submarine in here.'

"Mush was right about that," George thought. "Nobody in his right mind would have expected us."

Down the Throat

In the crowded conning tower of the *Wahoo*, voices dropped to whispers. The temperature was now close to a hundred degrees. To avoid detection, sound was kept to a minimum. All auxiliary motors, including the air-conditioning, had been turned off. Perspiration dripped from the men's faces.

"We had the element of surprise on our side, and nothing else," said George Grider, who had turned over his diving officer duties to Hank Henderson for the approach phase. "We were now six miles inside an uncharted harbor, with land on three sides of us, and in a minute or so the whole harbor would know we were there."

Mush had decided on an attack range of about three thousand yards. The outer doors of the six forward torpedo tubes were opened. An instant later, everything changed. Through the periscope, Dick O'Kane saw that the destroyer had left anchor and was under way.

"Now our plan to catch this sitting duck was gone," said George. "Later, perhaps, we could get a shot at her in deep water. But Mush was in no mood to be reasonable."

Yeo Sterling and a few other crew members were getting a play-by-play from radioman James Edward Carter, who was in touch with the conning tower through headphones. Carter reported, "'She's up-anchored and heading toward us, all fifteen hundred tons of her.'"

Yeo felt his heart beginning to pound; his mouth got dry. He waited, knowing exactly what it would feel like in the *Wahoo* when a torpedo left the tube.

In the conning tower, with his eyes glued to the periscope, Dick had a clear view of the destroyer. Mush hadn't moved to take over the periscope sightings. "I believed it was his way of showing confidence in me," said Dick, "and I would not let him down."

Dick was lining up the torpedo shots using the TDC (torpedo data computer). Shooting a torpedo at a moving ship is not like shooting an arrow at a still target. Dick had a lot to take into account: the speed and angle of *Wahoo* relative to the target, the speed and course of the target, and, of course, the motion of the torpedo through water.

Beside Dick, Mush stood with his finger on the firing plunger, cool and confident. As soon as Dick called out the command to fire, the first torpedo was on its way with a shudder and zing. It was quickly followed by two more. Everyone in the boat could feel what was happening.

"*Wahoo*'s hull bucked as a torpedo shot out to try and intercept this terrible menace to her safety. Another left its tube at a slightly different angle, followed shortly afterward by a third torpedo. *Wahoo* settled down to a brief agonizing wait to learn the results," said Yeo. "Without realizing it, our eyes were glued to the second hand of the clock."

"'All hot, straight and normal,'" reported Jim Buckley, on sound.

Seconds passed. No explosions. The first three fish—then the fourth—missed. Only two more remained in the forward torpedo tubes. Dick would have to make them count. There wouldn't be time to reload the forward tubes or swing the boat around to fire the four torpedoes in the stern tubes.

Wahoo had lost the advantage of secrecy. Like a beast in the wild, the destroyer wheeled toward them, heading into the fan-like pattern in the water created by the wakes of the torpedoes.

"The situation had changed drastically," recalled George. "A destroyer is named for its ability to destroy submarines, and this one was coming at us now with a deck full of depth charges."

" 'All right,' said Mush. 'Get set for a down-the-throat shot.' "

• • •

"We had talked about down-the-throats in wardroom bull sessions, but I doubt if any of us had ever seriously expected to be involved in such a shot," said George.

"It is what the name implies, a shot fired at the target while he is coming directly toward you. No one knew for sure how effective it would be, because as far as I know there was then no case in our submarine records of anyone's having tried it.

"But it had one obvious virtue, and two staggering disadvantages. On the one hand, you didn't have to know the target's speed if the angle was zero [in other words, straight on]; on the other hand, the target would be at its narrowest, and if you missed, it would be too late to plan anything else. In this particular case, we would be shooting a two-ton torpedo at a craft no more than twenty feet wide, coming toward us at a speed of about thirty knots."

Moments before, George had been thinking what a fine story about their success in locating Wewak Harbor he'd have to tell his wife, Ann, and son, Billy, when he got home. "Now I remembered with relief that I had left my will ashore at the beginning of the patrol."

It was hard for George to imagine getting out of this fix, especially since his fate was in the hands of someone undertaking his first submarine combat attack: Dick O'Kane.

"For a fleeting moment," recalled Dick, "I thought of the prewar orders covering like situations. At this range . . . we went deep and fired on sound information."

That was then.

Now Dick calmly went about lining up the last shots. He knew that if *Wahoo* was more than 1,200 yards away from the target, the destroyer would have time to maneuver out of the way. As soon as the Japanese captain spied the next torpedo's wake, he would begin to take evasive action. Yet if *Wahoo* got *too* close—within 700 yards—the exploding mechanism on the torpedo wouldn't have enough time to arm.

Dick had a window: a 500-yard "hitting space." Taking into account his estimate that the destroyer's speed was thirty knots, Dick figured he'd have thirty seconds—and only thirty seconds—to launch torpedoes five and six.

"'Stand by to fire,'" called Dick. "'Fire five!'"

Suddenly, there was confusion: Dick couldn't see above the water. The boat had dipped below periscope depth. Hank Henderson, George realized, had momentarily lost steering control. Mush called down the hatch to the control room, "'Bring her up, Hank, boy, bring her up.'"

Dick clung to the periscope. Seconds later, *Wahoo* was back in position. The destroyer was still barreling down on them. They'd missed.

Dick told them what he saw. "'He's still coming. Getting close.'"

• • •

From his seat in the messroom, Yeo broke out in a cold sweat and decided that Mush must have nerves of steel. Yeo tried to keep track of each torpedo as it left the tube. He remembered wondering, "How many were left? Only one left in the sixth tube. Would we have time to use it?" A certainty that he was about to die swept over him.

Up in the conning tower, George was impressed at how calm and "utterly cool" Dick seemed. He marveled at the change in his fellow officer. Dick had been frustrated and unhappy under their previous captain. It seemed, George thought, as if Dick "had been lost, seeking his true element, and now it was found. My opinion of him underwent a permanent change.

"It was not the first time I had observed that the conduct of men under fire cannot be predicted accurately from their everyday actions, but it was the most dramatic example I was ever to see of a man transformed under pressure from what seemed almost adolescent petulance to a prime fighting machine."

For his part, Dick was determined not to miss the final shot. He wanted to wait until the last moment, when the narrow destroyer would present the widest target possible.

Dick kept the periscope's wire bisecting the destroyer's bow. His target was dead ahead. "I watched her come, already showing a white 'V' bow wake. . . . Her image filled my lens," Dick recalled. He shifted the periscope lens to lower power. This setting meant the destroyer's image looked smaller, and "much less disturbing."

CHAPTER TWENTY-ONE

Dick asked Mush, " 'When shall I fire, Captain?'

" 'Wait till she fills four divisions in low power.'

" 'She already fills eight.' "

Even Mush became impatient then. " 'Well, for heaven's sake . . . fire!' "

Dick called, " 'Fire six!' "

Mush echoed him with " 'Take her deep!' "

Instantly, George sprang down the ladder to the control room to take over as diving officer. "I couldn't take her really deep, because we had no idea what the depth of the water there was, and it wouldn't help to strike an uncharted reef. But I took her as far down as I dared, to ninety feet, and we rigged for depth-charge attack.

"We were no longer the aggressor. Now our time as well as our torpedoes had run out, and we were helpless to fight back. All we could do was grab on to something and stand by for the final depth-charging of the USS *Wahoo*. Our time had come, and we waited for the end almost calmly," said George.

"The first explosion was loud and close," he remembered. "A couple of light bulbs broke, as they always do on a close explosion. . . . We waited for the second blast, each man lost within himself, looking at objects rather than at other men, no eyes meeting, as is appropriate for the final moments of life."

The men waited. And kept waiting.

A MIGHTY ROAR 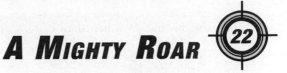 22

George Grider found himself counting: "Ten, twenty, thirty seconds." They should be feeling the destroyer's next depth charge by now. Still the silence continued. George looked up, and saw the faces around him take on expressions full of disbelief and wonder.

Someone in the pump room broke the spell, exclaiming, "'Jeez . . . Maybe we hit *him*!'"

At that, George heard Mush laugh and holler, "'Well, by God, maybe we did.'"

They had. All at once, the *Wahoo* was shaken not by depth charges but by "a mighty roar and cracking, as if we were in the very middle of a lightning storm," said Dick O'Kane. "The great cracking became crackling, and every old salt aboard knew the sound—that of steam heating a bucket of water, but here amplified a million times. The destroyer's boilers were belching steam into the sea."

From where Yeo sat, he could hear shouts erupt from the conning tower and control room. Someone burst out, "'It's a hit!'"

Mush Morton ordered, "'Bring her back up to periscope depth, George.'"

Once again, Mush let executive officer Dick O'Kane do the honors. Dick took a long look through the periscope. "'There she is. Broken in two.'"

"Bedlam broke loose on the *Wahoo*," said George. "I waved to Hank to take over in the control room, grabbed my Graflex

Photograph of the Japanese destroyer *Harusame* in Wewak Harbor taken through *Wahoo*'s periscope.

[camera], and shot up the ladder. Mush had named me ship's photographer, and I was going to get a shot of that target one way or another.

"It wasn't easy. Even Mush wanted to take a look at this, and every man in the crowded conning tower was fighting for a turn by the time the skipper turned aside. But at last my chance came. Somehow I got a few pictures and moved out of the way.

"And now Mush, who was almost a tyrant when it came to imposing his will on us in emergencies, returned to the democratic spirit he always showed when something good happened.

"'Let everybody come up and take a look,' he called."

When the loudspeaker crackled with the invitation to head to the conning tower on the double, Yeo Sterling sprang to his feet and followed the crowd into the control room.

"A line had formed at the foot of the ladder [to the conning tower] and I crowded in," said Yeo. "My turn came and I looked quickly, seeing the blur of broken destroyer hull and its slighted slanted deck near the water line. Black and white smoke was pouring from amidships, and the rigging was polka-dotted with white uniforms."

Someone yanked the periscope handles away and Yeo stepped back. He saw Mush grinning and thought Dick was having a hard time concealing his triumphant mood.

The only one not caught up in the glory of the moment seemed to be the cook, John Rowls, who complained to Yeo that the excitement was wreaking havoc with getting out the next meal. " 'Chow will be spoiled by the time anyone's ready to eat.' "

For once, no one seemed to care about food as the crew absorbed the impact of *Wahoo*'s daring attack and their narrow escape. " 'The war is one Japanese destroyer shorter,' " someone said.

In fact, although the men on the *Wahoo* believed they'd sunk the destroyer, later found to be the *Harusame*, it had only been damaged. If the attack had been at sea in deep open water, perhaps the *Harusame* wouldn't have survived. But since the ship had been struck close to land, the Japanese were able to beach it and make repairs. The destroyer returned to action by the end of 1943. Not for long, though. The *Harusame* was sunk by US planes eighteen months later.

• • •

After a little while, Mush Morton appeared in the crew's mess-room, a wet towel pressed to the back of his neck. "'All my nerves are tied up into a knot at the back of my neck.'"

Mush asked pharmacist's mate Leslie Lindhe to pass out what he called the depth-charge medicine.

Lindhe brought out a large carton with a lid on it. "'Get your depth-charge medicine here,' he announced. 'Anybody don't want theirs, let me know.'"

Depth-charge medicine? Yeo had a sneaking suspicion what that might be. Peering inside the carton, his eyes widened as he spotted several dozen miniature bottles of brandy.

It was another of Mush's new (and popular) ideas.

• • •

It had been a long day for everyone. But it wasn't over yet. *Wahoo* still needed to backtrack nine miles to open sea.

"We were still celebrating when a bomb went off close," said George. "Down we went again to ninety feet, realizing there was an airplane up there on lookout for us."

The *Wahoo* made her way cautiously out of the harbor. Mush ordered the sub to run submerged half an hour past the point when the sound man could pick up any beach or surf noises. By then, it was after seven and growing dark.

"Three blasts sent us to the surface into God's clean air. It has a fragrance, but it takes a day submerged in a submarine before that can be appreciated," said Dick. "Four engines were rumbling and in minutes would take over the load from our battery, which was driving *Wahoo* to the north. Back on our port quarter were huge fires above the harbor, probably lighted to silhouette that submarine [*Wahoo*], should she try to escape."

Dick was about to lay out their next course, when Mush intervened, "'George, you take over navigation for a day, and, Dick, you hit your bunk.'

"It was an order, but I offered two modifications," Dick recalled, "a game of cribbage first, and that Krause [signalman Fertig Krause] be relieved of duties too. In the excitement we had not particularly noticed it, but we had not turned in for 35 hours."

Later, in his war patrol report, Mush Morton noted, "The conduct and discipline of the officers and men of this ship while under fire were superb. . . . I commend them all for a job well-done, especially Lieutenant R. H. O'Kane the Executive Officer, who is cool and deliberate under fire."

As for Yeo Sterling, he was treated to a magnificent tropical sunset and an equally glorious moonrise when he took the first watch. "When the sun balanced itself precariously on the earth's horizon . . . it presented an enlarged blood-red, slightly distorted orb that could be viewed with the naked eye," he wrote later.

"In the east, a darkening band of gray widened, getting ready to push the colors out of the sky as soon as the sun would be swallowed up. A dim moon took shape, becoming a brighter silver in proportion to the evening's waning."

Yeo pulled himself out of his reverie, knowing the safety of each man on board depended on his being alert. Still, that feeling of oneness stayed with him. "I came below decks with a deep feeling of serenity upon me."

Why was there such a difference between the cautious attack strategies of skippers like Marvin "Pinky" Kennedy, who had been trained in the prewar era, and the new breed of leaders like Dudley "Mush" Morton and Richard "Dick" O'Kane, who embraced more aggressive tactics?

George Grider, who served with both Mush and Dick and went on to command the USS *Flasher* (SS-249), explained it this way: "Ideas about what a submarine should do on a war patrol had changed drastically since the bombing of Pearl Harbor. Most of our prewar training had been conducted with the idea that a sub would be a scouting vessel proceeding ahead of the fleet. . . . It was thought that a submarine's major function was to proceed a day or so ahead of the fleet, make the initial contact with the enemy, maintain that contact, send back reports, and conduct attacks in conjunction with our own forces.

"After the bulk of our Pacific Fleet was either sunk or disabled at Pearl, however, it became evident that this sort of strategy would not be feasible. We *had* no fleet. . . . Our mission, then, was to proceed to our assigned area . . . to patrol it and to sink any and all Japanese naval or merchant ships we encountered."

Finding qualified captains to execute that strategy remained a challenge throughout the war. Historian Clay Blair noted that in 1943 and 1944, approximately 14 percent of skippers were relieved for not producing results; the figure was higher in

1942, when 30 percent were reassigned for being unproductive. "The 'skipper problem' in the U.S. submarine force remained constant," he wrote. "There was always a shortage and always nonproductivity."

23 WAHOO ON THE ATTACK

The next morning, as *Wahoo* headed north in the open seas toward Palau, the submarine encountered a small Malaysian fishing boat fleeing the Japanese. Adrift after its engine failed, the vessel had six fishermen on board; three others had perished from starvation and lack of water.

"Our crew pitched up oranges, fresh and canned fruit, part of our day's supply of bread, and filled their water breakers," said

Wahoo assists sailors on a fishing boat.

Dick O'Kane. "Just in time came Krause's penciled chart to go with a can opener, and we sent them on their way with a wave and a prayer."

Mush Morton's *Wahoo* would not always extend mercy to individuals caught at sea in the midst of war. A few days later, Mush was at the center of the most controversial action by a US submarine commander during World War II.

• • •

Wahoo continued on its northern course toward Palau. George Grider was on the bridge on the morning of January 26, sweeping the seas with his binoculars, when he spotted smoke on the horizon.

"The great weakness of the Japanese merchant marine," he commented later, "was that its ships could never stop making smoke. Almost every time we sighted them it was from the smoke they made—a tremendous advantage, for it meant that a ship completely out of sight over the horizon and traveling a course that would not have brought it closer could be spotted, hunted down and sunk."

And that was exactly what *Wahoo*'s skipper had in mind.

Forty-five minutes later, the crew spotted the masts of two ships, which appeared to be freighters without a military escort ship. Since it was daylight, the submarine submerged and prepared to attack. With Dick manning the periscope once again, *Wahoo* fired two torpedoes at the leading ship, and two more at the other. Three out of the four fish hit their targets. One vessel had begun to sink; the other, a damaged freighter, started toward the submarine. Then, as Dick looked through the periscope, he reported a third ship on the scene, possibly a troop transport.

"We were entering the sort of situation in which Mush was at his absolute best—a cloudy and confused situation," George reflected later. "Here was an injured ship headed directly at us, evidently intent on ramming us, while astern of him and still on the original course was yet another—a big one."

Wahoo fired three torpedoes at the transport, and then two more direct, "down the throat" shots at the freighter still barreling toward them. Noted George, "Before the day ended, I was to have a higher regard for the captain of that freighter than for any other enemy skipper we ever fought."

Wahoo dived deeper just before the freighter hit its conning tower, and turned hard to the left to avoid being rammed. Explosions sounded above them. When Mush brought the submarine up to periscope depth a few minutes later, the officers could see that the transport they'd struck had stopped dead in the water.

"'Let's finish him off,'" George remembered Mush saying. Two torpedoes later, *Wahoo* scored a direct hit and the ship began to sink rapidly, with soldiers jumping from her into the water.

At first, *Wahoo* turned away from the troop ship toward the damaged freighter, which was now trying to escape the scene of destruction. As *Wahoo* followed, Dick spotted the masts of a fourth ship on the horizon, which appeared to be a tanker.

And at that moment, Mush Morton made a fateful decision.

• • •

"Our battery was getting dangerously low," George recalled. "We had been down [submerged] since eight o'clock, most of the time running at high speed, and it was now a little past eleven-thirty."

So, rather than immediately pursuing the new target, a tanker, and the damaged freighter, Mush ordered *Wahoo* to surface to recharge batteries. When the *Wahoo* surfaced, Mush drew closer to the floating wreckage of the troop transport ship, later identified as the *Buyo Maru*, and ordered his men to demolish the small lifeboats and rafts now bobbing in the water.

The *Buyo Maru*, sunk by *Wahoo* on January 26, 1943.

Those boats, and the waters, were filled with enemy soldiers, or so *Wahoo*'s captain thought.

Accounts differ as to what happened next. According to executive officer Dick O'Kane, the captain's goal was to destroy the boats to prevent enemy soldiers from getting ashore. Dick recalls Mush told him, "'Every one who does can mean an American life.'"

Dick remained steadfast in his defense of his skipper, claiming, "Some Japanese troops were undoubtedly hit during this action, but no individual was deliberately shot in the boats or in the sea." Other eyewitnesses disagree, reporting that Mush ordered the deck gun crew to fire at survivors. Estimates vary as to how many men died or how long the attack continued.

But there was a tragic aspect to this incident. No one on the *Wahoo* realized that not all the survivors were enemy soldiers.

In fact, the troopship had been carrying an estimated five hundred Indian prisoners of war, who were engaged in deadly struggles with their Japanese captors as they tried to cling to floating debris.

Yeo Sterling saw one man waving a piece of canvas and remarked on it as unusual, since he knew that normally the Japanese did not surrender. In the heat of battle, no one stopped long enough to analyze what that might mean: The man was indeed attempting to wave a white flag. Some Indian survivors later said they shouted and tried to identify themselves as captured POWs to no avail.

It's difficult to know how many people died. One modern researcher estimates the death toll at nearly three hundred Indian prisoners of war, and eighty-seven Japanese soldiers. Whatever actually occurred, Mush Morton, motivated by an intense desire to defeat the enemy, never had regrets. He was not censured by superiors, nor was any policy issued at the time.

Still, not every skipper followed this lead. Submarines, of course, could not carry prisoners of war the way larger ships could. But most submarine captains targeted the ships, not the men on them.

In his 1975 chronicle of WWII submarine warfare, Clay Blair observed, "To some submariners, this was cold-blooded murder and repugnant. However, no question was raised about it in the glowing patrol report endorsements. . . . Whether other skippers should follow Morton's example was left up to the individual. Few did."

Perhaps another reason the *Buyo Maru* incident received little attention at the time was that it was lost amid the other spectacular successes of Mush Morton's first patrol as skipper—successes that came as a breath of fresh air after the disappointments of the first thirteen months of the submarine war.

After leaving the wreckage of the *Buyo Maru*, *Wahoo* pursued the other two ships and launched attacks, expending its last two torpedoes. While Mush thought he'd sunk both, for a "clean sweep" of the sea, postwar reports revealed that the last ship on the scene, the tanker, was only damaged. At the time, though, *Wahoo*'s victories made the submarine and her charismatic captain instant celebrities.

When she arrived triumphantly at Pearl Harbor on February 7, 1943, the *Wahoo* had traveled 6,554 miles and burned 92,000 gallons of diesel fuel (about fourteen gallons per mile). The submarine was met by a crowd, a band, and the press, all eager for some good news. A broom, symbolizing *Wahoo*'s apparent "clean sweep," soon became famous.

"We made quite a stir when we slid into the dock at Pearl early in February with a broom flying at the masthead to show we had swept the seas clean—and with no more than two hundred gallons of fuel left in our tanks," said George. "The war correspondents had a field day."

The broom atop *Wahoo* proclaimed her clean sweep of the seas.

The *Wahoo*, noted Dick, had "put a crack in the silence of the 'silent service.'" Mush and the submarine became front-page news across the country, with the now-famous skipper appearing in newsreels and newspapers.

Reporters tracked down Harriet Morton, the captain's wife, who was quite surprised to find her husband in the news. According to George, "Mush had talked to her by phone the day before, but all he had told her was that the *Wahoo* had done better than he expected."

For his part, Dick O'Kane would take to heart Mush Morton's comment over a cribbage game one night as they headed toward Pearl Harbor. "'Tenacity, Dick. Stay with 'em till they're on the bottom!'"

• • •

Just before the *Wahoo* docked at Pearl Harbor, Yeo Sterling had been kept busy typing up Mush Morton's first patrol report—a report that would be circulated within the Submarine Force as a teaching tool for how it should be done. Mush made recommendations for a Navy Cross for executive officer Dick O'Kane, and a promotion for Dalton Keeter, recognizing his role in locating Wewak Harbor in the atlas.

Mush also asked Yeo to complete leave orders for thirty days "Stateside" for several petty officers (though not for Yeo himself). Yeo countered that he *was* a leading petty officer.

Mush grinned. "'You're not leading enough, yet. Besides I can't spare the best . . . yeoman in the submarine Navy.'"

Yeo would remember those words.

Dick checked the final typed copy of *Wahoo's* patrol report before heading for the Royal Hawaiian Hotel to enjoy letters from home, dips in the ocean, and lots of fresh vegetables and green salads. After copies of the report were posted, Dick found himself barraged by questions from fellow officers about the attack strategies he and Mush had used, especially in Wewak Harbor.

Dick reflected on the impact that *Wahoo*'s success would have on the Submarine Force's attempts to put an end to Japanese shipping. "Morton had demonstrated, in one patrol, the very tactics some of us had been urging.

"While a few other boats had used some of these tactics, it was *Wahoo* under Morton that had turned the corner completely from the prewar submerged vessel of opportunity to an aggressive raider, even on the surface when conditions would permit," Dick later wrote.

Further, he reflected, the patrol's statistics clearly demonstrated what it took to actually sink ships. "In round figures, we had been submerged over 500 hours on the second patrol [under *Wahoo*'s previous skipper], and just under 50 hours on our third [under Mush Morton]. This would never be the norm for submarine patrolling, but it should demonstrate to any boat that at times she can surface close to the enemy for a good, high-periscope search, and then dive again."

• • •

"Only one question troubled us," recalled George. "The word had spread that we were going to lose one of our officers. New submarines were coming off the ways at a rapid rate back in the States, new submarines that required crews and experienced officers."

When the news of his transfer arrived, George was disappointed. He had been assigned to be executive officer of the USS

Pollack (SS-180). "I groaned. . . . Built in the 1930s, she certainly would be a comedown from the *Wahoo*. . . . Instead of a new boat, I would be on an old one. It was a promotion, but it wasn't worth it."

George was replacing Gus Weinel, an old classmate from the Naval Academy. As George arrived on the *Pollack*, Weinel was just leaving, holding a box with a sextant he'd won at the Academy for being first in his class in navigation. George couldn't help envying his friend, who was taking command of a new submarine, the USS *Cisco* (SS-290).

"I never saw him again," said George. The *Cisco* was lost on her first patrol.

"I left the *Wahoo* with great sadness," reflected George later. "A fighting craft becomes more than a place to live and work for the men who serve on her. She has a personality of her own, and especially in wartime her men develop attitudes toward her which are grounded far more deeply in emotion than in logic.

"To those of us who had made three patrols on her, the *Wahoo* had become part warrior comrade, part glorious Amazon . . . a burly, confident, reckless wench with a touch of coarseness and an overwhelming and often exhausting claim on our emotions."

George took some treasures with him, however, including "the homemade chart of Wewak harbor, created with such frantic zeal during the early days of the third patrol."

How did he end up with this lucky prize?

"A big controversy over who should keep the chart had arisen a few days before we returned to Pearl, and Mush, who never pulled his rank in such matters, had suggested that we deal a cold deck with the chart as a prize," George said. "I drew a flush."

(After the war, George Grider donated the map to the US Navy Submarine Force Library and Museum in Groton, Connecticut.)

• • •

Dick O'Kane and Mush Morton continued as a dynamic team on *Wahoo*'s fourth and fifth patrols, from February through May of 1943, where the submarine's successes and daring exploits became legend.

Dick himself was promoted to command his own submarine before *Wahoo*'s sixth, unsuccessful patrol in the Sea of Japan in the summer of 1943. It was a patrol that put skipper Mush Morton in a very bad mood.

"Good Hunting"

"Mush was boiling mad," reported Charles Lockwood after hearing the captain's report of his fruitless patrol in the Sea of Japan. "He had found plenty of targets but a combination of deep running and duds [torpedoes that ran too deep or did not explode] had broken him down."

Torpedo problems still plagued the older fish, but new, more reliable ones were becoming available. "All Morton wanted," recalled Lockwood, who was now commanding Pacific Fleet submarines at Pearl Harbor, "was a quick turn-around, a load of our new torpedoes, the Mark XVIII [Mark 18] electric, and an area in the Sea of Japan."

Mush wanted to go back and get another crack at all those ships he had missed. So Lockwood agreed to send *Wahoo* (now on her seventh patrol) and the USS *Sawfish* (SS-276), under Lieutenant Commander E. T. "Gene" Sands, to the Sea of Japan in September 1943.

Yeo Sterling had enjoyed his recent leave so much he was still sore from the sunburn and blisters he'd gotten at Waikiki Beach. Before their departure from Pearl Harbor, he returned early to *Wahoo* to take care of official correspondence. Among the letters that had arrived was one with his name on it: He'd been approved to attend stenography school, a step that would allow him to be promoted. The course would start in November.

Yeo was eager to go, and he also wanted a break from the long weeks of war patrols. He rushed to show the letter to Mush Morton in the wardroom. His heart sank at the captain's next words.

" 'Yeo, I'm going to ask a favor of you . . . Howsabout you making one more patrol with me? We'll be back in October. When we get in, I'll get you plane transportation back to the States.'

" 'Captain, your word is good enough for me. I'll get back to work.'

"He grinned at me. 'Thanks, Yeo, I knew you wouldn't let me down.' "

• • •

Just before *Wahoo* left Pearl Harbor on September 5, 1943, Mush Morton pulled up to the dock in a jeep, a special passenger beside him. As part of his job, Yeo started to ask the visitor for his name and address. Then he stopped and stammered, " 'Why, you're Gene Tunney—*sir!*' "

Commander Gene Tunney, heavyweight boxing champion of the world from 1926 to 1928, would be traveling as far as Midway Island on the *Wahoo*. Yeo was still on deck when he heard Tunney telling Mush his plans for improving the physical fitness of submariners, who, he said, simply didn't get enough exercise. He went on to share his recommendations, which included daily exercises and drills instead of long hours on the beach (and needless to say, no beer) when submariners were on leave.

Yeo could imagine what his crewmates would have to say about that. "I thought, Oh brother, and this is the great Gene Tunney! No wonder he became a world's champion heavyweight boxer, but he sure don't know anything about submarines."

Mush grinned at Yeo. "'The Commander has a fine idea, don't you think so, Yeo?'"

"'The men will receive it with great enthusiasm, sir,'" Yeo replied. (It's pretty safe to assume he had a hard time pulling off that response with a straight face.)

• • •

Wahoo's schedule called for less than a day spent at Midway en route to patrol the Sea of Japan. In the few hours they were there, Yeo sensed an unexpected tension in his fellow crew members. One sailor lost a good luck ring. Another, whose wife was expecting a baby, confided in Yeo that he had an attack of nerves, and feared he'd never hold his son or daughter in his arms.

At about two thirty in the afternoon, as the weather was getting drizzly, Mush stuck his head into Yeo's office on the *Wahoo*. He asked if Yeo had his orders made up to leave the submarine to attend that stenography course. Yeo hadn't, but assured the captain he could get the paperwork finalized in a hurry.

Mush announced, "'We've got an hour before we sail. Let's go up to the Squadron and get you a relief.'"

"We went topside and over the gangway together," said Yeo. "I crawled into a jeep with him, and he drove along the dock recklessly. I still thought he was joking, and that when we got there, I would find a clerical job that needed attending to."

It was not a joke. Mush had, for reasons Yeo never fathomed, changed his mind. As the paperwork was being filed, the captain remarked that he was giving up the best yeoman he'd ever had. Yeo felt himself bursting with pride. "I had been complimented by the best submarine skipper in the Submarine Fleet."

At that point, everything happened quickly, so as not to delay *Wahoo*'s departure. Once a replacement yeoman was found, Mush and Yeo returned to the *Wahoo*, where Yeo cleaned out his locker and stuffed his seabag with his belongings. Fellow crew members filled his pockets with hastily written notes and letters for loved ones back home.

Near the dock, a jeep waited to give him a ride, but Yeo said he would make his own way back to headquarters. He wanted to watch the *Wahoo* as long as he could.

"I heard the diesels come to life, and helped push the gangway in toward *Wahoo*'s deck. Then there was just the bowline left, and when the Captain ordered it thrown off, I pushed the line handlers away and pulled the bight [loop of rope] clear of the bollard [post on a wharf] and heaved it into the water. *Wahoo*'s fog horn sounded a loud parting blast and a whistle on the bridge sounded shrilly . . . *Wahoo* drifted away from the pier and began to move away slowly.

"Captain Morton's voice came across the widening water. 'Take care of yourself, Yeo.'

" 'Good hunting,' I shouted back."

Yeo waved at everyone still topside on deck as the *Wahoo* pulled away. He sat down on his seabag on the planks of the dock. And he stayed there while the *Wahoo* drew away, became smaller and smaller, a tiny silhouette on the horizon. Then she headed into a rain squall and was lost to sight.

The date was September 13, 1943. Forest "Yeo" Sterling was the last man to see her.

• • •

Mush was scheduled to make an update report to headquarters on October 26. "Days dragged by and still no word came," wrote Admiral Charles Lockwood. "It just didn't seem possible that Morton and his fighting crew could be lost.

"As time went on—Admiral Nimitz allowed me a week's margin on reporting losses—I finally had to send the dispatch which added *Wahoo*'s name to the list of 'overdue, presumed lost.' The entire Submarine Force was saddened by the news that she, one of our most valuable units, would never come steaming in again with a broom at her masthead and Mush Morton's fighting face, with its wide grin, showing above the bridge rail."

Records credit *Wahoo* with sinking four ships in the Sea of Japan on her last patrol. "This makes her final total 20 ships for a total of 60,038 tons," said Lockwood. "Postwar reports indicate she was sunk by depth charges from a plane in La Pérouse Strait [or Soya Strait, a body of water off the northern part of the Japanese island of Hokkaido] on October 11, 1943."

Lockwood immediately stopped activities in the Sea of Japan.

• • •

George Grider's last meeting with Mush Morton had taken place a few months before, in April, when his boat, the *Pollack*, had docked at Midway beside the *Wahoo*. Mush and Dick O'Kane were there to greet him.

"We had run into foul weather that delayed our arrival, and my old shipmates on the *Wahoo*, knowing I was navigator, had read the dispatch announcing the delay with great glee," recalled George. "As we pulled alongside, Mush and Dick were standing on the dock, looking up at me.

Dudley "Mush" Morton became a symbol of a new breed of submarine skipper. Pictured here is a sinking Japanese cargo ship seen from the periscope of the *Wahoo*.

" 'What happened, George?' Mush asked innocently. 'Forget about the International Date Line?'

" 'Aw, Captain,' Dick explained, loud enough for every man aboard the *Pollack* to hear, 'he just got lost again.' "

In speculating later about *Wahoo*'s final days, George felt that the loss of his most experienced officers had an impact on Mush Morton. Dick O'Kane and George himself, who had been part of Mush's team, had both been transferred to other boats. Another senior officer, Roger Paine, had gotten an attack of appendicitis the night before the *Wahoo* set off on her last patrol.

George said, "By now virtually all Mush's old associates in the conning tower were gone, replaced by men who naturally thought of their great and famous skipper as infallible. I believe that, on previous patrols, Mush had come to rely subconsciously on his officers to tell him what not to do, and with the loss of Roger this safety factor disappeared.

"Here was a man whose valor blazed up so brightly that at times he could not distinguish between the calculated risk and the foolhardy chance, and now the men who knew him well enough to insist on pointing out the difference were gone."

The *Wahoo* would not be forgotten. Ned Beach captured what many in the Submarine Force felt: "I like to think of *Wahoo* carrying the fight to the enemy, as she always did, gloriously, successfully, and furiously, up to the last catastrophic instant."

In October 2006, the US Navy reported that an international team of divers and experts had found the wreck of the *Wahoo* near the Japanese island of Hokkaido. Historical records indicate that on October 11, 1943, the *Wahoo* had been spotted by Japanese planes; it appears Mush Morton and the crew likely sank four ships before being attacked and sunk.

Sixty-four years later, the USS *Bowfin* Submarine Museum and Park in Honolulu, Hawai'i, held a memorial ceremony for the *Wahoo* on October 11, 2007. Over two hundred people attended.

> **SKIPPER'S RECOMMENDATION:** *Find out more about* Wahoo *in the Dive Deeper resources section or visit http:// www.oneternalpatrol.com/wahoo-navy-release.htm. See a photo of the 2007 memorial service at sea at http://www .oneternalpatrol.com/wahoo-ceremony-at-sea.htm.*

JANUARY 2: As part of Allied efforts to take back Papua New Guinea from Japanese control, the village of Buna is recaptured.

JANUARY 20: Bob English, commander of submarines at Pearl Harbor, is killed in a plane crash; Lockwood is named COMSUBPAC, commander of the Pacific Fleet subs, at Pearl Harbor.

FEBRUARY 7: Japanese depart Guadalcanal; Allies claim victory there on February 9.

MARCH 2–4: Japanese troopships incur heavy losses in Battle of the Bismarck Sea, in the Southwest Pacific.

APRIL 18: Pearl Harbor mastermind Isoroku Yamamoto is killed in an attack through the efforts of US code breakers.

JULY 4: Admiral Charles Lockwood sends first three submarines into the Sea of Japan but attack results are disappointing.

AUGUST–DECEMBER: US and Allied forces adopt "leapfrogging" attack strategy across Pacific islands, including the Gilbert and Marshall Islands, with the goal of reaching and invading Japan.

OCTOBER 11: *Wahoo* is lost on a patrol in the Sea of Japan.

DECEMBER: Submarines end the year with approximately 350 war patrols, about the same as in 1941–1942; subs are credited with sinking 335 ships for 1.5 million tons, a 100 percent increase over 1941–1942.

PART FOUR

THE FIGHTINGEST

• 1944–1945 •

It is one thing to be an executive officer and an entirely different thing to be the man one step higher, who must make the final decisions . . . It was a glorious feeling . . . but it was also a lonely feeling, and a disquieting one.

—George Grider

O'Kane is the fightingest naval officer I have ever seen.

—Dudley "Mush" Morton

Submariners are always asked about claustrophobia. 'How can you exist in such a small enclosed space? I'd go stark raving mad,' people invariably say. The answer is simple. Submarine sailors don't want 'a view.' They don't want to see through glass windows around them. They feel much safer inside thick, strong steel. Besides, you don't only see the stuff of the mere ship around you.

In the Navy, your mind is far away, on your job, on the condition of whatever it is you're responsible for; you feel that your hands are not attached at the ends of your arms, but out at the limits of consciousness, the perimeter of your vision, through the periscope maybe, or the throttles of a big diesel engine, reaching for the controls of your destiny.

—Edward L. Beach Jr.

USS TANG (SS-306)

USS Tang, *in her short but brilliant career identified herself as one of the U.S. Navy's most fightingest ships.*

—**Office of Naval Records and History
Ships' Histories Section
Navy Department**

Tang under construction at Mare Island Navy Yard in California.

DICK O'KANE'S ICE-CREAM MACHINE

In May 1943, after five patrols as executive officer on the *Wahoo*, Dick O'Kane got his own command. Before he left, *Wahoo*'s crew presented him with an engraved silver cigarette case. As Dick walked away, he had a lump in his throat. He would never set foot on *Wahoo* again.

Dick heard the news about *Wahoo* that fall, while he was head-long into shakedown preparations for the brand-new USS *Tang* (SS-306). "My beloved *Wahoo* was indeed 'overdue and presumed lost.' This would add an extra note of seriousness and determination to our final training."

Dick had no time to sit around and grieve—he had weighty responsibilities before him. With nine years of sea duty in various ships and three patrols with Mush Morton as his skipper fresh in his mind, Dick knew he was as prepared as he'd ever be. To Dick's relief, his new boat was in good shape as well. "*Tang* had no bugs. She performed as if she'd been at sea a year, and it was rather up to us to catch up to her."

Tang would make her first war patrol on January 22, 1944, almost a year to the day when, in an unknown harbor called Wewak, Mush and Dick had made their famous "down the throat" shot on a destroyer.

Now Dick had his chance to live up to Mush's complete confidence in him and carry on the fighting spirit of *Wahoo*. That would mean sinking every enemy ship encountered. It also meant ensuring that his crew members were happy and well fed.

That's why Dick was determined to get an ice-cream machine for his new submarine. " 'Why, only the Chief of the Bureau of Ships could authorize such an installation!' " Dick was told when he brought up the matter officially.

"It was the answer I had expected from the shipyard commander," Dick recalled.

However, a man who had faced a destroyer in a "down the throat" shot wasn't about to be stopped by a little bureaucratic red tape.

Dick knew there was an ice-cream maker available. In fact, one of his men had it on good authority that the officers' wardroom of the battleship USS *Tennessee* (BB-43) was just about to get one—unless, of course, *Tang* nabbed it first.

Dick got on the phone to the man in charge to make his case, assuring him that the installation would not at all affect the submarine's refrigeration system. Dick got his way, and the men of the *Tang* got their ice cream.

Dick had another essential improvement in mind for *Tang*: to convert a useless warming oven into a baking oven for pies and bread. "If a steward became adept at making pies and pastries he could very nearly write his own ticket in the navy, and I'd never been averse to sampling their experiments."

Dick was successful in the baking-oven mission too. Both devices became popular during *Tang*'s first patrol in warm tropical seas, though the ice cream always seemed to win out. Said the new skipper, "I had to shake my head . . . as I watched the beautiful wedges of pie being smothered with globs of ice cream, but all hands seemed to like it that way."

In his cabin during the last night at Pearl Harbor before *Tang*'s maiden patrol and his own first outing as a commanding officer, Dick reflected on how many people had helped to bring the new submarine to this point, from the many workmen who'd built her, to the friends and family who'd gathered at Golden Gate Bridge to wave the boat off with good wishes and prayers.

All that hard work had been worth it: The submarine was ready. *Tang* was, Dick reflected, "a vibrant ship, performing without flaw under the most critical eye. She surely would not be found lacking during our coming endeavors against the enemy."

Soon, Dick heard men returning from watching a movie on base. There was a quiet knock on his cabin door.

The next words he heard were: "'All hands are aboard and *Tang*'s ready for patrol, Captain.'"

It was now up to him.

Enjoying dessert on a submarine.

Dick O'Kane and the crew of the *Tang* weren't the only submariners who liked ice cream. Once, when *Trigger* was being overhauled at Pearl Harbor, Ned Beach was approached by Lieutenant John "Stinky" Sincavich, who wanted to install an ice-cream machine on board.

" 'We think we know where we can get one,' Stinky told him. 'Just think how good a big heaping bowl of cool raspberry ice or peach melba would taste.' "

Trigger got her ice-cream maker and everyone began enjoying ice cream on a daily basis. But the machine's motor was finicky.

And it burned out entirely when the ice-cream machine was on at the same time as a battery charge, which caused higher voltage.

Morale dropped. "Stinky—now known as Officer in Charge of Ice Cream—was immediately called on the carpet by the skipper," recalled Ned.

Trigger's electrical wizards came in for their share of teasing too: If these "sparktricians" could keep the main motors of a submarine running, why were they having so much trouble with a simple ice-cream machine?

Eventually, the machine was fixed, to everyone's delight. To ensure that the malfunction wouldn't occur again, Stinky left strict written orders: "Even if the Captain himself had ordered it, permission to start a battery charge had to be obtained first from the Officer in Charge of Ice Cream."

SKIPPER'S RECOMMENDATION: *To see a photo of a laughing Lieutenant John "Stinky" Sincavich, who died when* Trigger *was lost in March 1945, visit the On Eternal Patrol website: http://www.oneternalpatrol.com/sincavich-j-w.htm.*

George Grider, a plank owner on the *Wahoo* who went on to distinguish himself as captain of the *Flasher*, wrote a lively first-person memoir entitled *War Fish* in 1958. In it, he tells of an incident late in 1944 that a less forthright man might never have revealed.

Fresh off the triumph of sinking six ships on his first patrol as a skipper, George feared his cockiness might be followed by a humbling. And that's what happened one night after he gave orders for *Flasher* to outrun a Japanese patrol boat through the Lombok Strait, which connects the Java Sea and their destination, the Indian Ocean.

George sent the lookouts and the OOD down, and remained on the bridge alone. He didn't want to dive the boat unless absolutely necessary, knowing it would slow their progress.

George had worked out a plan to throw pursuing patrol boats off. "We had prepared a can filled with gunpowder and oil-soaked rags, with a fuse in it, and the idea was to light it in case of an attack by a patrol boat and throw it far overboard. It would explode and flare up, and the enemy would think it was us and chase it while we went merrily on our way."

Now, though, as he came under fire from the enemy, lighting a match didn't seem like such a good idea anymore.

"Instead," reported *Flasher*'s distinguished captain, "I dropped the can overboard and began trying to decide which portion of my anatomy I least wanted to be hit."

George ducked behind some eighteen-inch circular storage tanks.

"Too little has been written about the problem of what to expose if you have to expose something," he reflected. "At first I crouched with my head and shoulders behind the tank, thinking to guard my upper extremities. A shot whistled past, my rear end twitched, and a horrible thought occurred to me.

" 'Good lord,' I muttered. 'If I get shot in the can, it'll be awful! What will I say?'

"I turned nervously around, assumed a squat, and left my head exposed. But of what value is an unimpeached buttocks if the head be missing?"

Finally, George decided on a "desperate step." He hid halfway down the hatch, with only the tip of his head showing.

• • •

The *Flasher* outran the patrol boat. George informed the OOD it was safe for him to return to the bridge. His feelings of cockiness had vanished.

"No one on *Flasher* ever knew," said George later, who confessed what happened only when writing his memoir fourteen years later.

George Grider, who suffered a heart attack at age thirty-five, recovered to become a lawyer and serve as a US congressman before passing away in 1991 at the age of seventy-eight.

SKIPPER'S RECOMMENDATION: *We often start with the Internet when we do research, but don't neglect bibliographies. That's how I discovered George Grider's wonderful memoir,* War Fish. *I noticed that another author had included a quotation from George in his book. I looked at the source note, then the bibliography. I was able to order online a used paperback copy of* War Fish *and make the acquaintance of this amazing man.*

A sailor and his mascot.

STOWAWAYS

Ice-cream machines weren't the only unofficial additions that sometimes ended up on submarines. On July 8, 1944, the USS *Gurnard* (SS-254) was about to depart Freemantle, Australia, on her next patrol, when a little black dog ran up to crewman Bill Gleason on the gangway. He shooed it off back toward shore.

The engines started up. Feet on the rungs of the ladder, Bill was already headed down the hatch by the forward torpedo room when he paused for a quick, last look around. And there it was again! The dog was about to leap onto his shoulders.

Spontaneously, Bill grabbed the tiny creature, tucked it under his jacket, and went below to his bunk to figure out what to do next. The *Gurnard* was soon under way: no going back now.

Bill had four hours until his next watch. Before then "a name was to be had, food, water and toilet arrangements figured out. The first three were comparatively easy, but the last presented a major problem," said Bill, adding, "When one has a problem on a submarine it is best to share it with someone."

Bill decided to name the pooch Penny, since she was "small change." He settled her on his bunk and went to explain his new predicament to his friend, torpedoman Bill Parks. At first, "he was flabbergasted. . . . Finally I convinced him to help me out."

Already, things were out of control. "While we were talking, my eye caught Penny hopping through the water-tight door into forward battery, where she squatted and did her business. Both Parks and I gasped at her audacity, but she had the right instinct. If one has to go somewhere, where better than officers' quarters?"

Eventually, the two friends decided to train the dog as if the submarine were any house. Bill went to the cook and asked for extra cardboard from food cartons, and soon Penny learned to relieve herself in the forward torpedo room. When the submarine was on the surface, Bill would sneak her topside.

All went well, and the stowaway remained a secret from the captain.

Not for long.

•••

Penny on the deck of USS *Gurnard*.

It happened when Bill was on watch in the control room and (he presumed) Penny was with Parks in the forward torpedo room. Bill heard the captain holler, "'Steward, what . . . did you spill on deck?'"

The skipper had stepped barefoot out of his cabin—right into Penny's mess. The steward's mate, who'd been let in on the secret, had no choice but to spill the beans.

"'Gleason to the captain's cabin, on the double,'" blared the boat's announcement system.

Bill presented himself meekly.

"'Where is it, Gleason?'" asked the captain.

Bill admitted that the dog was with his friend, and Parks was summoned to appear carrying Penny. "The skipper's eyes never left the poor dog. I could see the twinkle begin to radiate from them, and hoped for salvation," said Bill.

The captain reminded Bill that it was against regulations to have an animal aboard a submarine on war patrol. Even to Bill's own ears, his excuse sounded a bit feeble. "'I just couldn't throw her overboard, could I, sir?'"

Then the skipper took Penny into his arms and asked what kind of dog she was.

"'I have no idea, sir. She only weighs four and a half pounds,'" Bill replied. Hoping the commander was a dog lover, he added, "'Must be a rare breed.'"

"'Although it's very unusual . . . I'm going to let you keep her aboard, but only for this patrol. . . . After all, I can't very well throw her overboard, now can I?'"

• • •

And that, pretty much, was that. Penny became the mascot of the *Gurnard*, riding along on four war patrols, standing watch with Bill Gleason, and even earning a combat pin.

However, on *Gurnard*'s eighth patrol, Bill noticed that Penny was growing weary of sea duty. During a depth-charge attack, the boat shook and the lights went out. Normally when this happened, Penny would lie still on a small blanket near the chart desk. This time, she jumped up and disappeared.

Two hours later, when the *Gurnard* was clear of danger, Bill went to look for Penny. "We finally found her in the captain's cabin, shivering and trying to hide under his desk. I knew then, Penny had had enough sea duty.

"I'm sure she went there to request a transfer, from the only one aboard who could honor that request. I swore then . . . that as soon as we were ashore, I would find a home for her and retire her from active duty in submarines."

On May 18, 1945, Bill found himself in California with thirty days' leave. Smuggling Penny into his jacket, he boarded a plane for Ohio.

Said Bill later, "When my mother saw Penny she couldn't resist her any more than Parks or the skipper. Penny was at last home, after serving honorably on the old *Gurnard*."

The submarine's beloved mascot became a local celebrity and lived to the ripe old age of seventeen. She was buried in the yard outside the bedroom Bill had slept in as a boy.

• • •

Penny was not the only canine to see service on a submarine in World War II. When William Galvani was director of the Submarine Force Library and Museum in Groton, Connecticut, he published an appeal for information about "sea dogs" in *Polaris*, which was the monthly magazine of Submarine Veterans of World War II. The response was so phenomenal the museum mounted an exhibit called Sea Dogs: Mascots of the Silent Service.

Among the submariners with four sea legs was a small mongrel named Garbo (after the famous movie star Greta Garbo), mascot of the USS *Gar* (SS-206). She was taken on about the time of the submarine's tenth patrol and stayed with the crew for the five patrols until the end of the war. Garbo gave birth to two puppies (the father was apparently the mascot of another submarine) and went home with a crew member in peacetime.

Luau, mascot of the USS *Spadefish* (SS-411), was a "plank owner," a member of the original crew. She was lured away from a group of Marines in a California restaurant by crew member "Shaky Jake" Lewis, who fed her juicy morsels of steak from his own fork. Luau appeared front and center in a photograph of the commissioning ceremony of the *Spadefish*. In the postwar years, *Spadefish* veterans kept in touch through a newsletter entitled, naturally, *Luau*.

Luau even made it into official Navy submarine war reports. In his report of *Spadefish*'s first war patrol, skipper Gordon Underwood wrote, "The dog, LUAU, contributed greatly to the morale with her ready playfulness with all hands. She was a bit perturbed by the depth charges, but soon recovered with only a slight case of 'depth charge nerves.'"

During rest and recreation in Honolulu after the submarine's first war patrol, crew members found a mate for their mascot. On December 11, 1944, while *Spadefish* was on patrol near Majuro in the Marshall Islands, Luau had puppies. "'The whole ship was awake for the birth, waiting for the results,'" remembered one crew member. As each pup was born, the news came over the ship's announcement system.

In the official time log for December 11, the captain noted: "22:48 FLASH NEWS. Ship's dog LUAU gave birth to the first of six pups."

Needless to say, Luau and her puppies appeared front and center in the group photo following the completion of their second war patrol. It wasn't possible to keep all the puppies, of course. But that wasn't a problem.

Before the *Spadefish* left Majuro in January of 1945, all the puppies had been given away—except the runt of the litter, named Seaweed, a funny-looking pup who followed his mom all around the submarine. Luau and Seaweed remained with *Spadefish* for the duration of the war.

Not all stowaways were dogs. As the USS *Pogy* (SS-266) left Pearl Harbor in April 1944 on her sixth patrol, torpedoman Bill Battenfield was certain he spied a big rat scuttling across the floor. At first he hesitated to tell anyone, afraid his crewmates would think he was seeing things.

Five days into the patrol, Bill spotted the creature again, looking even larger than before. He was "a real monster . . . I pointed and yelled, 'There's the rat!' As luck would have it, no other torpedoman saw it."

After this happened once more, Bill knew his fellow crewmates were shooting him strange looks. Bill resolved to catch the rat and "prove that I still had all my marbles. I reverted to the old bird trapping method of boyhood. I found a small square metal box, propped it upon a stick on one side and placed cheese bait underneath.

"As I stood my four-hour watches I held the cord in my hand, eyes glued on the trap, ready to yank the cord and entrap my elusive rodent. No rat showed, but plenty of crew members came to the torpedo room door to watch my fruitless efforts."

When *Pogy* took on five prisoners of war after sinking a ship, Bill found an unexpected ally in his effort to prove the rat existed. One of the Japanese POWs spotted the creature too, although because of the language barrier, the man couldn't be the witness Bill needed.

That's when Bill abandoned his efforts to capture and kill the stowaway. "I gave up. I kind of felt sorry for the little guy. After all, he was suffering depth charge attacks right along with the rest of us."

So Bill began putting out food and water for the rat. Soon after, the *Pogy* was engaged in a surface battle. Every time the deck guns fired, the rat would skittishly run to a new hiding place. Finally, someone besides Bill saw it.

Bill enjoyed a great moment of satisfaction. But when the conversation turned to how to kill the rodent, he unexpectedly found himself putting up a defense. "By now I had grown attached to him." Bill stopped telling anyone about his rat sightings.

When the patrol ended, the *Pogy* went to California for overhaul. After the rest of the crew had left, Bill returned to check on the rat but couldn't find him. Bill figured the rat had decided to take some shore leave too.

"I imagined him enjoying stateside duty after the harrowing experience on a fighting submarine," said Bill. "He was probably out there romancing some girl rat at the local garbage dump. He sure had some great sea stories to tell his girlfriend about his ride on the *Pogy*."

The *Tang* had no stowaways when she set off from Pearl Harbor in January 1944 on her maiden patrol. But she did boast a determined new commander.

It didn't take long for Dick O'Kane to prove himself. In his first outing as skipper, Dick found himself locked in a duel with a destroyer. Luckily, he'd had some past experience with destroyers, including the famous "down the throat" shot in Wewak Harbor.

On February 23, despite fierce rain squalls, *Tang* managed to spot a three-ship convoy (a tanker, a freighter, and a destroyer escort) off the coast of Saipan in the Mariana Islands. Dick feared *Tang* might have been sighted, since the ships were following a zigzag course. Visibility was low, but smoke from the coal-burning freighter helped him track his quarry.

"Sometimes the ships would emerge on the same course, sometimes on another, but more and more frequently it became necessary to go in after them and then to retire when they showed up suddenly closer than expected," said Dick.

"We had them—destroyer, tanker, and freighter, in column and heading for Saipan—and it was just a matter of how and when to shoot."

• • •

Dick assessed the situation and formulated a plan. The freighter was third in the column, and *Tang* would take on that ship first, attacking from the stern. Dick explained his reasoning: "When a person walks down a street or rides on a bus, he habitually looks where he is going. This habit is so ingrained that an after lookout tends to look where his ship is going."

In other words, unless a lookout was very well trained, there was a likely chance he might miss an approach from the rear. And that's exactly what happened: Dick brought *Tang* into firing position and sank the freighter with three quick torpedo hits. If the Japanese sailors in the convoy hadn't suspected they were being followed before, they certainly knew it now. What they didn't know, though, was *Tang*'s precise location when she made the attack. The tanker and the destroyer both shot off their deck guns, but no shots came close to the submarine.

At midnight, Dick ordered his executive officer, Murray "Fraz" Frazee, to keep following the two remaining ships. Then, Dick instructed him, an hour before first light, Fraz should maneuver *Tang* so that instead of being behind the convoy, she would be in front of them—by about ten thousand yards.

"'It's all in here, Fraz,'" Dick said on his way to his bunk, handing over the orders. "'One of us has to be bright-eyed at dawn, and that means me.'"

Come dawn, *Tang* would dive—and then launch another attack.

• • •

Dick's confidence in his new exec and the other officers proved to be sound. When Dick woke before dawn, Fraz reported that the two remaining ships were just where Dick wanted them to be. There had been some wild maneuvering in the night, but Fraz was proud that he'd been able to stick with their target. Dick ordered *Tang* to stop and let the Japanese ships come to within seven thousand yards.

"The enemy closed, and Venus, now a morning star, came up dead ahead, nearly as bright as a quarter moon. You are always in the light path of the moon or a planet when you view it from your ship, but in this case *Tang* was also on the same light streak being viewed by the enemy. He was now taking on a distinct shape as he neared.

"I had to grit my teeth and tell myself, almost audibly, that he could not see us. The slight gray of morning twilight did not help, but we were putting together the best elements of a night approach and a daylight attack.

"This was no time for wavering."

• • •

Tang slid below the sea. Then, just before six a.m. on February 24, 1944, Dick gave the order to go to battle stations.

"In a few minutes it would be light enough to see through the periscope," recalled Dick. The enemy continued on the same zig-zag course. "We dropped to 100 feet and went ahead full. . . . The high-speed run would require 20 minutes."

Counting the freighter dispatched the day before, *Tang* had already sunk four ships on this patrol. Dick had only eight torpe-does left—four forward and four aft.

No submarine on her first patrol had ever sunk five ships, and Dick wanted *Tang* to be the first. An oil tanker was a valuable target. After all, if enemy planes had no fuel, they could not shoot at American aircraft, ships—or other submarines.

• • •

Fifteen minutes later, they were getting close. It was a little after six by now. *Tang* slowed to three knots for a periscope check—a quick one. With the morning sea as smooth as a glimmering mirror, Dick let the periscope barely break the surface before bringing it under the water again.

" 'We're right on,' " Dick reported, partly to reassure all hands and partly to set his own mind at rest that his approach was correct.

For each periscope reading, Dick raised the scope inches above the sea—for just three or four seconds. Each time, he captured one small, crucial piece of information—a glance at the destroyer's mast, or a look at the top of the tanker for a bearing.

Dick wanted a clear shot at the tanker, and that wouldn't be easy. The escort destroyer was always on the move, crisscrossing back and forth across the tanker's bow to protect her from the submarine that might still be on the prowl.

On the prowl they were. This was a game that required steady nerves—and Dick O'Kane had them. A memory of Mush Morton and Wewak Harbor came to his mind.

"I had," he said later, "faced this situation before, in *Wahoo*, a much more taut one with the destroyer coming at nearly 30 knots at my raised periscope and with but one torpedo left that we could fire.

"By comparison this was nothing, except this time I was in command."

Dick ordered the doors on the torpedo tubes open.

"The destroyer had crossed the tanker's bow and was heading directly at us, about 800 yards away. I would not disrupt our setup on the tanker until the last instant, and that was approximately one minute away," said Dick.

Then, just as Dick had hoped, the destroyer turned to the right, leaving the tanker exposed in front of *Tang*. Now Dick was so close, it wouldn't matter if the tanker spotted *Tang*'s periscope—there wouldn't be time for the target to maneuver out of the way.

"If we were sighted, the tanker could not possibly do anything about it; her last hope, the destroyer, was just passing under her stern heading away."

Dick was ready.

" 'Constant bearing—mark!' " he called out.

" 'Set! . . . Fire!' Fraz hit the plunger, and the first torpedo zinged on its way," said Dick. "The next three followed, each to hit a specific point along her starboard side.

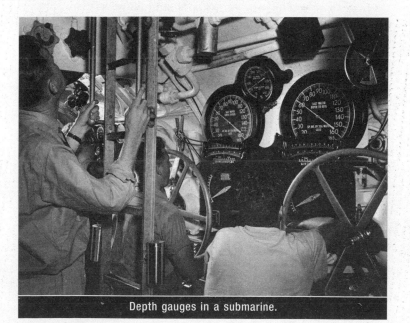

Depth gauges in a submarine.

"On the tanker, the lookouts saw the torpedo wakes and were pointing and waving right up to the explosions. I saw not one of them leave his post. It was quick; the torpedo run was only 23 seconds. Debris went into the air, and the entire ship was enveloped in a mass of billowing flame and grayish-brown smoke. She started down immediately. Fraz took the scope and watched her go in just four minutes. The time was 0643.

"*Tang* went deep, too," said her skipper, "and the depth charges started one minute later, but they were not close."

• • •

Dick ordered a deep dive: Once the destroyer figured out where *Tang* was, the depth charging would start in earnest.

" 'Level off at five hundred, Bill,' " Dick told the diving officer.

That's when the trouble started.

Instead of leveling off, *Tang* kept going down.

THE SEA WAS ALL OURS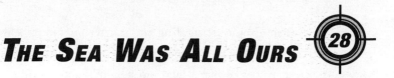

Tang passed the five-hundred-foot mark and kept going down. She was taking in water in the forward torpedo room. Dick dropped from the conning tower into the control room to assess the situation.

The boat continued to dive.

Dick gave orders to blow air pressure into the tanks to try to halt the drop. The first shot of high-pressure air wasn't enough. He ordered more air: " 'Blow safety! Blow bow buoyancy!' "

Dick checked the gauge: She should be swimming up. But the depth gauge told a different story: *Tang* had dropped 612 feet. There were other maneuvers he could try, Dick knew, but some, such as blowing air into the main ballast tank, would cause bubbles to rise to the surface—and reveal *Tang*'s position to the enemy.

"We held on, waiting and listening," said Dick. "The minutes dragged."

Then the diving officer called out good news. " 'We've got her.' "

"These had been the nine longest minutes of my life, and I daresay all hands felt the same," Dick recalled. But they had the submarine under control again.

Dick went to check on the leak in the forward torpedo room. Despite his years of experience, he let out a gasp at what he saw. "The scene was not as Hollywood would picture it, with men in water up to their armpits, struggling and sputtering. Nonetheless, Hank's [Flanagan] crew was going about its serious business knee deep in water. It looked like a lake, no less, half submerging the culprit, our leaky No. 5 torpedo tube."

The crew brought *Tang* back up to a hundred feet and leveled off. At this depth, they heard the sounds of the destroyer's screws as it searched for them. It wasn't unexpected, but it wasn't what Dick wanted to hear while he was still trying to control the leak.

"'Stop pumping,'" Dick ordered, knowing the sounds of the pumps would be a dead giveaway of the *Tang*'s position.

But he couldn't stop the pumps for long. Already the water in the torpedo room had risen another foot. Dick couldn't let much more seawater in without further damage to other equipment.

The destroyer lingered above, almost as if she was waiting for the right moment. The destroyer's captain would have extra motivation to demolish the submarine that had sunk the two ships under his charge.

And so began a tense game of cat-and-mouse. The repairmen worked desperately—the longer *Tang* could go without pumping, the more silent she could be, and the better chance the sailors had of slipping away from the destroyer's grasp.

Dick knew exactly what the destroyer's captain had in mind. "An axiom of antisubmarine warfare is to stay with the enemy, for one never knows the extent of the troubles that may exist below. The Japanese captain had read the book, and the destroyer remained on top of us throughout the afternoon."

One hour, then another, then another dragged by. But as to why the expected depth charges hadn't yet come, Dick could only hazard a guess. "Perhaps it was wishful thinking, but we concluded that the 12 depth charges where the freighter sank, the occasional drops during the night, and the numerous charges after the tanker's sinking had left her with but one good salvo, which she was saving just for us.

"The enemy's error, I believe, was to assume that we were deep, where any sane submarine ought to be. How could he guess that we were watching him so as to counter every move? It was undoubtedly baffling to hear us, start a run, and then lose contact time after time."

Sunset was coming, making it harder to see the destroyer in twilight in their brief peeks through the periscope. Then darkness fell. It was pitch-black through the periscope.

"The destroyer would be getting nervous, too, now knowing that we might be on the surface," said Dick. "We delayed pumping, hoping to add to her anxiety, and thoroughly expecting a high-speed depth-charge run."

Forty minutes later, Dick heard the sound of the destroyer's propellers, closer than ever, "their fast *swish-swish-swish* roaring through our hull. The bearing remained steady and then drifted just a hair to the right, but that was enough."

Dick showed the daring he had become known for with Mush Morton on the *Wahoo*: He set *Tang* on a course to squeak past the destroyer in the opposite direction below. Eight "tooth shakers" (slang for depth charges) shook the submarine, but soon the destroyer could be heard heading away.

It was a little like a dog slinking off with its tail between its legs. Some hands on board were convinced that the destroyer was so humiliated at having lost both her ships, she had blown herself up. In any case, reflected Dick calmly, it was "a highly agreeable parting."

Tang surfaced at last, to the cheers of her crew, who had survived a daylong duel of wills with a destroyer—all while setting a record of five sinkings on their first patrol. While they hadn't been on the original menu for the day, the cook began frying steaks in celebration. Dick thought the executive officer, Fraz, had ordered them to be thawed during those long, trying hours. Divers went overboard to try to fix leaks, working in the dark by feel.

"The sea was all ours, under a black though star-filled sky, but best of all was the aroma of God's fresh air," said the new skipper, breathing a sigh of relief. "As of this moment there was never a happier submarine crew."

• • •

When they stopped at Midway Island for a two-week break, Dick was first on the dock to greet the division commander. As he turned back to the sub, Dick got his first look at *Tang* from a distance. The last six weeks had changed her: The newness had all rubbed off.

"Gone was the former glossiness of her black paint. Salt water, wind-driven spray, and the tropic sun had bleached it to a slate gray, somewhat splotched, like the camouflaged freighters of World War I," he said. "No longer as if out of the showroom, she looked like she'd been places and done things, and indeed she had.

"I liked the way she looked and made a mental note that no one was to get loose with fresh paint."

Crew members poured onto the dock. "To a man they were grinning from ear to ear. At the moment I could not say whether the pride I felt was in our ship or these men; both, I guess, for they were inseparable."

While *Tang* underwent repairs, there was also time for some relaxation. Some of the crew went fishing, returning with enough mahi mahi for a fish fry, with beer and softball. A few days later, *Tang* set out with orders to join other submarines in support of US air strikes on Palau, which was still held by Japan. Among *Tang*'s duties would be lifeguarding: plucking downed aviators from the sea.

· · ·

By spring 1944, the Submarine Force could boast more successes than failures. Code breakers were able to provide submarine captains with the locations of possible targets. With more reliable torpedoes and with the success of aggressive skippers like Morton, O'Kane, and others, confidence that Japanese shipping could be squelched rose.

Submarines like the *Tang* took on expanded roles. Groups of boats were deployed in wolf packs while others were tapped as escorts for convoys of fleet ships. Submarines also played an important role as "lifeguards," rescuing downed aviators from the water during aircraft assaults, as the United States began to drive the enemy from islands Japan had held earlier in the war.

Some pilots, though, were a bit wary of being rescued by a submarine—even after they'd been shot out of the sky.

· · ·

"Submariners were an unknown and uncertain factor to the Army aviators," wrote Admiral Charles Lockwood. This was especially true when pilots ended up going along for longer submarine rides than they bargained for (or, as Lockwood put it, experiencing more "thrills and hazards" than expected).

Take the story of a pilot named Jack Heath, stranded when his plane went down in September 1944 in Manila Bay. With the help of Filipino fishermen, he reached the island of Mindoro. From there he was evacuated by the USS *Ray* (SS-271).

" 'I thought that I had been rescued. I say I thought that I had been rescued, but a few times later I had my doubts,' " said Heath of his submarine experience. " 'Captain [Bill] Kinsella took me out and got me bombed, depth charged, had me aboard 34 days and practically made a submariner out of me. Finally got me into Midway and I was flown back to Pearl.' "

Along the way, the *Ray* rescued another "zoomie," a fighter pilot named James Brice who had been shot down off Lingayen.

" 'We picked him up after he had been in the water about two days,' " said Heath. " 'He came aboard, so I had a little company in order to take our stand against the submariners. We both got back O.K. and we are really 100 percent for these submarine men.' "

During her second patrol, *Tang* set another record: this time as a lifeguard in the vicinity of Truk Lagoon (which today is also known as Chuuk State and is part of the Federated States of Micronesia). The US had nearly driven the Japanese from their base on Truk Island. In late April, Admiral Chester Nimitz sent Navy aircraft carriers to wipe out any remaining enemy aircraft on Truk, as well as attack ships near the many small islands in the area. *Tang* would be on hand to help support the air strikes.

• • •

"Lifeguard was our mission," said Dick. "We'd go wherever necessary and do whatever we had to in rescuing downed aviators."

Tang was the only submarine assigned to support the assault. Dick brought his boat into position early on April 30. A little after eight in the morning, Dick got the first radio call from the aircraft carrier task force commander: A bomber had been downed by enemy antiaircraft fire. *Tang* raced to the spot to pick up the plane's survivors on a raft.

"*Tang* lit out, her screws digging holes with full battery power while the diesels fired," said Dick. "The sight ahead as we closed the atoll would have brought a lump of pride to anyone's throat. Our bombers were peeling off through a hole in the clouds . . . a hole filled with flak, and diving straight through. . . . If they had that courage, we could at least get this survivor, two miles off the beach."

Two US Navy planes returning from their mission flew overhead to help guide the submarine's course. Then, from the lookout platform, *Tang*'s lookout, a sailor from Maine with a "Down East" twang, cried out, " 'Thar she blows!' "

Tang reached the raft, four miles from its reported position, in just ten minutes. The boat's crew had practiced what Dick called "an old-fashioned man-overboard drill" many times, making a "wide turn to place the raft upwind and a needle-threading, slow, straight final approach." The training paid off: They had the four airmen aboard "in three shakes."

Throughout that day and into the night, *Tang* darted here and there, responding to radio messages whenever a downed plane was reported. When darkness fell, Dick put the submarine on a zigzag course, firing a green signal light every few minutes just in case they'd missed any rafts.

On day two, *Tang* was kept even busier, speeding around the atoll to rescue airmen from the sea. Dick got a clear view of the action in the skies: "Time and time again, it seemed the [US] dive bombers would not be able to pull out, but they did, almost all that had not been hit, and some of those that had and were trailing smoke.

"The obvious devotion of these men, pushing danger aside in carrying out their task, made all of us proud to be a small part of the same navy."

• • •

Tang left the battle with twenty-two extra men on board. Dick and her crew had set a record, rescuing more aviators than any other submarine during the war.

"There had been sub-air rescues before," wrote Dick later, "but never one like this."

Just as the crew of the *Spearfish* had gone above and beyond to make evacuees like Lucy Wilson feel welcome, the sailors on *Tang* extended submarine hospitality to their aviator guests.

"*Tang* was a happy ship," said Dick. "The new members of her ship's company were not accustomed to drop-in movies, or hot, home-baked bread at midnight."

And, of course, there was that homemade ice cream.

These photographs depict the most successful rescue of American airmen by submariners in World War II, led by Dick O'Kane and the crew of the *Tang*.

Nine airmen on a plane await rescue by *Tang*.

Tang rescuing downed airmen.

Tang destroys a US plane to prevent its use by the enemy.

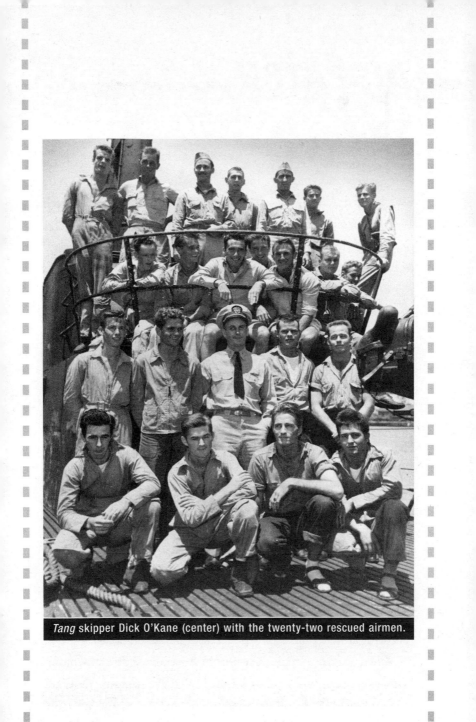
Tang skipper Dick O'Kane (center) with the twenty-two rescued airmen.

Submarines didn't carry doctors. Usually a pharmacist's mate with limited training took care of treating common ailments such as fevers, colds, athlete's foot, or rashes. In September 1942, *Seadragon*'s fourth patrol became part of submarine legend when Seaman First Class Darrell "Dean" Rector became ill. Pharmacist's Mate First Class Wheeler B. Lipes concluded that Rector had a severe case of appendicitis.

Usually, men with appendicitis were kept on a liquid diet and given ice packs. In this case, Lipes feared his crewmate would die without an operation. He told the young seaman, "'I can do it, but it's a chance. If you don't want me to go ahead . . .'"

Rector agreed; skipper Pete Ferrall gave his approval and ordered *Seadragon* to glide as smoothly as possible at a depth of 125 feet. They converted the officers' wardroom into an operating room, with the executive officer serving as assistant. "Lipes devised surgical instruments from the wardroom silverware— bent spoons for muscle retractors, for example—sterilized in torpedo alcohol." He also fashioned a mask from a tea strainer and put the patient out with ether.

What would have been a quick, simple operation with a trained physician took two and a half hours, with the "doctor" following instructions from the medical books on board.

When *Seadragon* arrived at port in Australia, Admiral Charles Lockwood went on board and heard from the captain what had taken place. Lockwood recalled, "The seaman came into the wardroom with eyes shining and proud as a peacock of being the first man ever to have an appendectomy in a submarine. He pulled up his shirt and displayed a scar about six inches long."

Lipes told Lockwood the hardest part was finding the appendix. When he found out how long the operation took, Lockwood asked Lipes, "'Good Lord . . . will a shot of ether last that long?'

"'Oh, no, sir,' he replied, 'but whenever I'd feel his muscles stiffen up, I'd know he was coming out of it and I'd give him another shot!'"

Lockwood was so impressed he decided Lipes should be promoted to chief pharmacist's mate. "His courage, resourcefulness and willingness to take responsibility certainly deserved high recognition."

The squadron medical officer was not as pleased, but, as Lockwood put it, "we got 'Doc' promoted anyhow."

Rector received the historic operation on his nineteenth birthday. Later he transferred to the *Tang* under Dick O'Kane. Sadly, he did not survive *Tang*'s loss in October 1944.

SKIPPER'S RECOMMENDATION: *View a photo of Darrell "Dean" Rector at the On Eternal Patrol website and read what World War II veteran Wheeler B. Lipes had to say about the brave young sailor at http://www.oneternalpatrol.com /rector-d-d.htm.*

29 THE LAST, TERRIBLE TORPEDO

A few months later, in September of 1944, Dick O'Kane and the crew of the *Tang* set out on their fifth patrol. This time, Dick was without his talented executive officer, Murray "Fraz" Frazee, whom he had recommended for promotion. But just as Mush Morton had nurtured Dick's career, Dick himself had developed a talented crew of officers and men, and had tremendous trust in his new exec, Frank Springer.

They set out on patrol with a determination to fire each and every one of *Tang*'s twenty-four torpedoes and make them count. All were the new, Mark XVIII Mod 1 electric torpedoes, which were increasingly replacing the unreliable Mark XIV ones.

The only mishap early in the patrol came when Dick inadvertently fell through an open hatch and broke his left foot. The pharmacist's mate did the best he could, telling the skipper, "'You've got some small broken bones—I could feel 'em, but they're pretty straight now . . . there's nothing they'd do ashore that I haven't done except to take some X rays, and I already know about what they'd look like.'"

Despite Dick's broken left foot, it looked to be another record-setting patrol. Dick had already sunk two ships when, early on October 23 near the China Coast, *Tang* encountered a large convoy of ten ships—five freighters and five escorts.

Deftly maneuvering inside the escorts, Dick fired nine torpedoes, scattering the convoy and sinking three ships. The next night, *Tang* discovered yet another convoy. Again avoiding the escorts, Dick snuck into the center, letting off ten torpedoes, which sank two large freighters and damaged another.

By this time, *Tang* had only two of the twenty-four torpedoes remaining. Dick drew the submarine away, in order to check the last two torpedoes, load them into tubes three and four, and return to finish off the last ship so it couldn't be towed away by the escorts. After this, *Tang* could head for home.

The first torpedo ran true.

Dick was on the bridge when the final fish shot through the water toward its target. "The torpedo, our very last, broached in a phosphorescent froth only yards ahead of *Tang*'s bow, turned sharply left, and commenced porpoising in an arc off our port bow."

The torpedo had popped to the surface, then had begun to circle back in a deadly arc—straight toward the submarine.

Desperate to move *Tang* out of its path, Dick yelled, "'All ahead emergency! Right full rudder!'

"It was now coming in. We had only seconds to get out of the way."

• • •

Those seconds were not enough. The submarine was too long, the torpedo too fast. It did miss amidships, but struck the aft torpedo room with a devastating explosion. The time was about two thirty a.m.

Automatically, Dick yelled an order to close the hatch, but it was already too late, and the men in the conning tower, including executive officer Frank Springer, drowned when the sea poured in.

To Dick, *Tang* seemed to be struggling like a great wounded animal. The submarine sank almost instantly from the stern.

Despite heroic struggles, only nine members of *Tang*'s crew were able to escape and make it through the night.

Five men had been in the forward torpedo room and used Momsen lungs (an underwater rebreathing mechanism) to reach the surface; one had escaped from the conning tower; and three had been on the bridge.

Dick O'Kane was one of them.

• • •

Tang and seventy-eight men who had served her so well were gone.

The next morning, the nine survivors were picked up by a Japanese destroyer escort, which was also rescuing men from the ships that *Tang* had sunk. Dick and eight other survivors were interned in a Japanese prison camp.

No one had known the fates of *Wahoo* and *Trigger* when they were lost. But with *Tang*, American code breakers were able to gather bits and pieces by monitoring Japanese radio transmissions.

"All stories seemed to agree on three particulars—great damage to the enemy, shallow water, and *Dick O'Kane in a . . . prison camp!*" recalled Ned Beach.

Tang's former exec, Fraz Frazee, heard the news when he returned to Pearl Harbor after his leave in California.

There was a catch, though. The information was extremely top secret. Any leaks could alert the Japanese that their codes had been cracked. That meant that no civilians could be told—including family members.

"'All I could do was bite my tongue,'" said Fraz, who desperately wanted to let Dick O'Kane's wife, Ernestine, know that her husband was alive. For security reasons, he couldn't. "'Ernie O'Kane . . . had to suffer.'"

Escape from the *Tang*.

WOLF PACK: AVENGING THE WAHOO

As 1945 began, Vice Admiral Charles Lockwood prepared to move his headquarters from Pearl Harbor to the submarine tender *Holland*, based in Guam, which was now in American hands. Guam would put the submarine commander closer to late-war actions in the Philippines and Japan.

American submarines had achieved remarkable success against Japanese shipping, their key objective at the start of the conflict. The tide of war in the Pacific had turned in favor of the Allied forces, and that meant a shifting role for the silent service. Submarines had rescued 144 airmen in the past two years, and would continue to support US efforts to capture islands lost to the Japanese at the beginning of the war.

There was one other mission on Charlie Lockwood's agenda for his submarines: to penetrate the minefields of the Sea of Japan and sink any vessels they found right on the enemy's doorstep. Lockwood felt sure that the area was thick with targets, driven there by the aggressive actions of submarines and carrier task forces. The plan's code name was Operation Barney, after Barney Sieglaff, a member of Lockwood's staff designated to work full-time on the effort.

• • •

"Ever since the loss of *Wahoo* in those waters in the autumn of 1943, the Sea of Japan had been 'out of bounds,'" wrote Theodore Roscoe. "Captured documents, old charts, Japanese prisoners and other sources of information had confirmed suspicions that the Japan Sea was guarded by minefields."

Submarines tried to avoid minefields as much as possible. Getting in and out of the Sea of Japan had posed the most difficult challenge. Military officials believed that the east and west straits were full of mines, as was the narrow center exit, called Tsugaru Strait. The northern exit also posed problems: Lockwood felt sure La Pérouse Strait (also known as Soya Strait), where Mush Morton's *Wahoo* had in all likelihood been lost, was still being heavily patrolled by enemy aircraft and surface ships.

Lockwood felt better prepared to deploy submarines to this treacherous area now, however. During the fall and winter of 1944–1945, American scientists had been working to develop effective mine-detecting devices, known as FM sonar gear, which would enable submarines to actually "hear" an enemy mine in the water.

Lockwood was eager to put the new devices to use and even took charge of training operators and skippers. He arranged tests of the FM sonar, equipping two submarines, USS *Tinosa* (SS-283) and *Spadefish*, and sent them out to try to detect mines.

By May of 1945, Lockwood was ready. He even asked his boss, Admiral Nimitz, for permission to lead the mission in person. It was denied.

It was time to avenge the *Wahoo*.

• • •

The nine submarines in the wolf pack had their own official code name: Hellcats. The boats were divided into three groups, the Hepcats, the Polecats, and the Bobcats. The operation launched from Pearl Harbor and Guam between May 27 and May 29 of

Two of the Hellcats—*Tinosa* arriving at Pearl Harbor, *Spadefish* in the foreground.

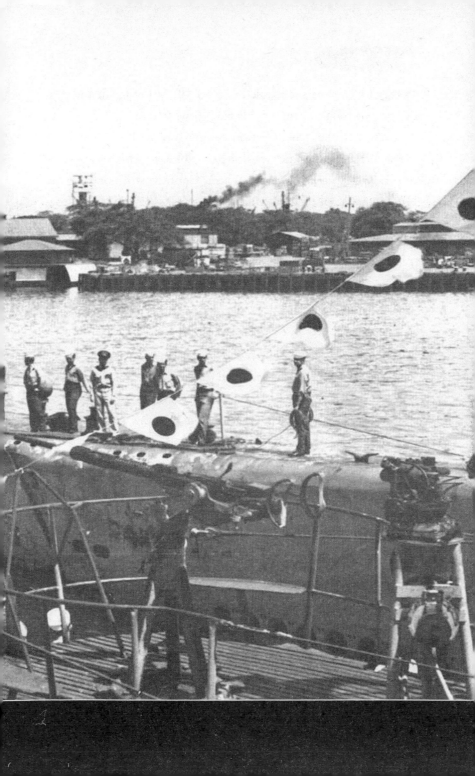

1945, with the boats scheduled to reach the Sea of Japan and pass by packs through its minefields from June 4 to 6.

Even with the new detection equipment, the boats had some close calls with the undersea lines, or cables, to which the explosive bombs (mines) were attached. Contact with one of the mines could cause it to detonate, potentially blowing a hole in a submarine's hull. Slipping submerged into the Sea of Japan on June 6, skipper Richard Latham on the *Tinosa* reported, "'There was a scraping, grinding noise as the mine cable slid down the starboard side. No one moved or spoke. Would it snag and drag the mine into us? . . . How close the mine came to us, we'll never know.'"

The captain of the *Spadefish* (whose mascot was Luau) heard loud explosions in the distance and feared for the two other boats in his Hepcats group: "'Had *Sea Dog* or *Crevalle* come to grief?'"

But both USS *Crevalle* (SS-291) and USS *Sea Dog* (SS-401), under her commander Earl Hydeman, leader of the expedition, made it safely through. Once through the minefields, Hydeman said later, "'All hands breathed a little easier.'"

The captains had been ordered to hold off on any attack actions until sunset on June 9, to ensure that all nine boats in the wolf pack were in place in their designated areas. They would then set out to do as much damage as possible.

And that's exactly what they did. "The Hell Cats turned out to be one of the most successful submarine operations of the war," historian Clay Blair wrote.

Over the next ten days, *Sea Dog* sank six enemy ships, *Spadefish* five, and the USS *Skate* (SS-305) sank four vessels, including a Japanese submarine. In all, eight of the nine Hellcats sank a total of twenty-eight ships for 54,784 tons. Only one boat, USS *Tunny* (SS-282), had no luck with its torpedo attacks.

But Operation Barney was not without a heartbreaking loss.

• • •

Born in Georgia, Lieutenant Commander Lawrence Lott Edge was a devoted husband and father when he became skipper of the USS *Bonefish* (SS-223) a year before, in June 1944. Like Dick O'Kane, Lawrence had gained valuable experience serving under other captains as executive officer, and felt ready when his orders came through.

Writing to his wife, Sarah, he said, "'When I came out here, as you know, I wasn't really sure whether I was ready for this next job . . . now I do feel sure that I'm ready for it . . . Anyhow, I pray to be truly worthy of it, because if I can be truly successful at it of all jobs, I'll be able to feel that at last I'm really doing something to hasten the end of this war, and my return to you and Boo [nickname of his daughter, also named Sarah]—which is all I really live for now.

"'Each ship we sink seems to me to cut the long wait for that great day by another hour, or perhaps day, or week or month, and I am glad (though I hate to think of what has happened to some of the poor mortals . . . who happened to be on those ships).'"

Lawrence was indeed ready and performed well as a captain. On his first patrol, he was awarded a Bronze Star for sinking two ships and damaging a third. In another letter to Sarah, he spoke of what motivated him and others to keep going despite the long, dangerous days at sea.

Lawrence wrote that he and other men were fighting for "'our country, the place where our wives and families are, the place

USS *Bonefish.*

which we want to keep safe and happy for you, so that we can eventually return to you there and live the kind of life with you that both you and we believe is the best the world has to offer.'"

A year later, Lawrence and *Bonefish* were tapped to take part in Operation Barney. The submarine arrived in Guam in early May, just as word came that Nazi Germany had surrendered. Welcome as the news was, everyone—especially the submariners about to embark on a dangerous mission in enemy waters—understood that the war in the Pacific was not yet over; Japan would not surrender easily.

Before setting off, Lawrence penned a letter to Sarah, assuring her that he loved her "'so deeply and completely . . . You'll be constantly in my thoughts as well as my heart until I can write again—and for always.'"

During Operation Barney on June 18, Lawrence, who had already sunk one ship, asked for and received the green light to penetrate Toyama Bay, on the northern shore of the Japanese main island of Honshu. There, *Bonefish* sank another target.

But when the Hellcats gathered at the designated rendezvous spot to exit the Sea of Japan on the night of June 24, only eight boats turned up. With so many submarines gathered close together, it was too dangerous to wait for *Bonefish*. The Hellcats made it out of La Pérouse Strait without incident.

• • •

On July 26, 1945, Lawrence's wife Sarah wrote to her beloved husband, whom she called Shug. She wanted to share news of their little girl Sarah "Boo" and of the new baby expected soon. Before she could mail the letter, the telegram announcing the loss of the submarine arrived.

Sarah kept her letter, in which she had written:

> *Dearest Sweetest Love,*
>
> *Only a note tonight, because it is late again. Went to Dr. Upshaw today and think I'll stick to him for the delivery. Today he listened to the heartbeat and said, "Well, I*

Bonefish skipper Lawrence Edge.

think it's a boy!"... Time will tell! About three more weeks to be exact.

Shug, you must come in before then, because you must have the news promptly... I went home after I left Dr. Upshaw and looked for one [a cable from him] stuck under the door, but no envelope! I also looked up to see the extent of your longest patrol. A few more days and this will equal it!...

Good night, dearest, and sweetest of dreams, always.

Postwar records show that after sinking its second ship, *Bonefish* was spotted in the shallow waters of Toyama Bay and destroyed by antisubmarine depth charges. All hands were lost.

On August 12, 1945, the Navy Department officially announced that the *Bonefish* was overdue and presumed lost.

On that same day, Sarah and Lawrence's son was born. Sarah named him Lawrence Lott Edge Jr.

JANUARY 29–FEBRUARY 7: US forces drive the Japanese from the Marshall Islands, securing Majuro atoll on January 31 and Kwajalein atoll by February 7; submarines support the effort by lifeguarding, reconnaissance, and efforts to intercept Japanese vessels; submarine *Skipjack* sinks a destroyer.

FEBRUARY 16–17: Americans successfully strike Japanese base on Truk; *Tang* sinks a fleeing freighter and USS *Searaven* (SS-196) rescues three airmen.

FEBRUARY 23–JUNE: US begins operations in the Marianas, which include Saipan and Guam; submarines, including USS *Sunfish* (SS-281) and *Tang*, are deployed for reconnaissance, to attack retreating Japanese ships, and for lifeguarding support.

FEBRUARY 29: US lands troops to begin takeover of Admiralty Islands, and is in control by April, enabling the Allies to use the Admiralties as a staging point for military operations in the final months of the war.

APRIL–JULY: General MacArthur nearly recaptures all of New Guinea, which will be completed by Australian forces in 1945.

JUNE 15: US forces land on Saipan in the Marianas, securing it within three weeks.

JUNE 19–21: In the Battle of the Philippine Sea, America wins a decisive victory in a clash of aircraft carriers; submarines USS *Albacore* (SS-218) and USS *Cavalla* (SS-244) sink two Japanese carriers.

JULY 21: US forces land on the island of Guam; a submarine refueling and repair base is later established there.

OCTOBER 20: General MacArthur's 6th Army lands at Leyte, beginning fulfillment of his pledge to return and liberate the Philippines from Japanese occupation.

OCTOBER 23–26: Battle of Leyte Gulf in the Philippines. In a four-part conflict, the US Navy defeats the Imperial Japanese Navy, demolishing much of the enemy's remaining power at sea; submarine USS *Darter* (SS-576) sinks the enemy's flagship cruiser and disables another; submarine USS *Dace* (SS-247) sinks a cruiser. Two submarine wolf packs chase retreating Japanese ships. In all, submarines sink or damage six cruisers and destroyers.

OCTOBER 26–DECEMBER 25: Leyte Gulf is secured, bringing the end of the war closer.

DECEMBER 15: General MacArthur's invasion forces target the Philippine island of Mindoro as a stepping-stone to the main island of Luzon; US surface ship convoy is attacked by kamikaze pilots on the way; landings on December 15 are unopposed.

DECEMBER: US submarines have the most successful year yet against Japanese shipping, mounting 520 war patrols, and sinking 603 ships for about 2.7 million tons, effectively destroying the enemy's capacity. Attacks on Japanese fleet ships also increased, with submarines sinking seventeen carriers, battleships, and cruisers. Nineteen US submarines were lost.

Looking forward, US military planners focus on an invasion of Japan by November 1945 as the only way to get Japan to agree to unconditional surrender.

PEACE BE NOW RESTORED

• 1945 •

The valiant efforts and incomparable achievements of United States Navy submariners cannot be summarized in statistics. Neither graphs nor percentages could measure the leadership of an Admiral Lockwood . . . the skill of commanders such as Morton and O'Kane, the courage of every submarine's crew . . .

From mess attendants to admirals, all were captains courageous.

—Theodore Roscoe

The long-awaited day has come and cease fire has been sounded. As Force Commander I desire to congratulate every officer and man of the Submarine Force upon a job superbly well done. My admiration for your daring, skill, initiative, determination and loyalty cannot be adequately expressed . . .

You have deserved the lasting peace which we all hope has been won for future generations . . . May God rest the gallant souls of those missing presumed lost.

—Charles A. Lockwood

Signing of surrender papers aboard USS *Missouri* on September 2, 1945.

World War II in Europe ended in May, but the war in the Pacific continued into the summer of 1945.

To force the Japanese government to surrender and avoid a prolonged invasion of Japan itself, the United States made a controversial decision to unleash the first two atomic bombs in history at Hiroshima and Nagasaki on August 6 and 9, 1945.

This action killed hundreds of thousands of civilians and ushered in the nuclear age. It also ended the war: Japan's Emperor Hirohito accepted the terms of unconditional surrender proposed by the Allies, so long as Japan could keep its emperor.

World War II was over.

• • •

Just before midnight on August 14, Admiral Chester Nimitz sent the following message to all Navy units, including submarines,

> *Cease offensive operations against Japanese forces. Continue search and patrols. Maintain defense and internal security measures at highest level and beware of treachery or last moment attacks by enemy forces or individuals.*

When word came that hostilities had ceased, Herman Kossler, skipper of the USS *Cavalla* (SS-244), was patrolling near Tokyo Bay. To celebrate, he ordered a small ration of medicinal brandy mixed with pineapple juice to be distributed to the crew.

At that moment, an airplane buzzed toward the submarine. The skipper cleared the bridge and the *Cavalla* dived. When Kossler asked the executive officer whether the brandy had been given out yet, the exec told him the crew decided it might be best to hold off.

General Douglas MacArthur and General Jonathan Wainwright in September 1945 after Wainwright's release from a POW camp.

"'Captain, I talked it over with the boys and they decided to wait until the treaty was signed.'"

• • •

In August, at the Omori prisoner of war camp in Japan, captors had put *Tang*'s captain Dick O'Kane and other POWs to work digging bomb shelters and caves in preparation for the expected invasion of Japan by Allied forces.

"Thirty of us had been detailed for this daylight-to-dark work, but by the end of the second week only ten of us could even walk the six miles to the site," Dick said. By now, something called gyp corn, normally used to feed hogs, had replaced the rice the prisoners had been given to eat.

"Just when everything seemed its darkest, Emperor Hirohito's voice went over the 1MC at the work site. We understood one key expression—'The war is over.' It was August 15, 1945."

On August 28, Captain Harold Stassen arrived at the camp to begin to make arrangements to evacuate the POWs to American ships waiting offshore. He had planned to begin the operation the following day. One look at the condition of the men spurred him to begin moving them immediately.

"We all weighed in the 90s, but my high temperature sent me to isolation. For some of us it was a long and trying voyage home, but once there our recovery was complete," said Dick.

Admiral Charles Lockwood was shocked when he saw Dick for the first time. "He was just skin and bones. His arms and legs looked no bigger than an ordinary man's wrists, his eyes were a bright yellow from jaundice (the result of rat-contaminated rice, I was told) and the dysentery from which he suffered would have killed him in a few more weeks. Dick's was the worst case I saw but many others were in pitiable condition."

Writing about Dick after the war, submarine historian Clay Blair remarked on his record: "In just over four war patrols, Dick O'Kane sank twenty-four confirmed ships for 93,824 tons, which made him the leading skipper of the submarine war in terms of ships sunk. (Slade Cutter and Mush Morton tied for second place with nineteen ships each.) In addition to the Medal of Honor, O'Kane received three Navy Crosses and three Silver Stars and a Legion of Merit."

Some of Dick's fellow prisoners and crew members from *Tang* left for civilian life, while others decided to stay in the Navy. "There was no assurance that we would return to submarines," said the brave skipper and POW survivor. "But at sea or ashore, none of us would ever take our wonderful land with all of its freedoms for granted."

• • •

On September 2, 1945, the surrender documents ending the war in the Pacific were signed on the deck of the battleship *Missouri*. During the ceremonies, General Douglas MacArthur declared:

> "*Let us pray that peace be now restored to the world, and that God will preserve it always. These proceedings are closed.*"

By spring 1945, the war in Europe is drawing to a close. Hitler commits suicide on April 30; the Germans surrender in Italy on May 2; and on May 8, Hitler's successor authorizes Germany's unconditional surrender.

JANUARY 9: US troops land on Luzon, main island of the Philippines, with support from surface ships in Lingayen Gulf.

JANUARY 13–MARCH 3: In the Philippines, General Douglas MacArthur goes ashore on Luzon on January 13, with the Army reaching Manila in early February; a fierce, destructive battle lasting several weeks takes place within the city, which is liberated by early March.

FEBRUARY–JUNE: By February 26, the United States has recaptured Corregidor, "the Rock." Efforts to fully liberate Luzon and clear Manila Harbor of mines continue until the end of June.

MARCH: In attempts to force the Japanese government to surrender, the United States begins B-29 bombing raids against major Japanese cities, including Tokyo, Kobe, Osaka, and Yokohama, killing thousands of civilians. Submarines support the raids by performing lifeguard duties for downed aviators. In 1945, eighty-six different submarines rescue 380 airmen.

APRIL 1: US forces invade the island of Okinawa, Japan, with resistance ending on June 21. Submarines play a small role in reconnaissance.

APRIL 12: President Franklin D. Roosevelt dies.

MAY 8: Germany surrenders, ending World War II in Europe.

JUNE 4: Nine submarines in three wolf packs enter the Sea of Japan. *Bonefish* is lost.

AUGUST 6: The US drops the first atom bomb, on Hiroshima, Japan.

AUGUST 9: The US drops a second atom bomb, on Nagasaki, Japan.

AUGUST 14: Japan surrenders, ending World War II.

SEPTEMBER 2: Surrender documents are signed aboard the USS *Missouri*.

AFTER
SECTION

What we saw and did during those years was much like what thousands of other submariners saw and did. . . . Although war was and is no way for human beings to live, there are times when there is no choice, for a nation and its citizens, but to fight.

—REAR ADMIRAL CORWIN MENDENHALL

STILL ON PATROL

UNITED STATES NAVY

U.S. SUBMARINE VETERANS WORLD WAR II

U. S. NAVY SUBMARINES PAID HEAVILY FOR THEIR SUCCESS IN WORLD WAR II.

A TOTAL OF 374 OFFICERS AND 3131 MEN ARE ON BOARD THESE 52 U. S. SUBMARINES STILL ON "PATROL."

ALBACORE
AMBERJACK
ARGONAUT
BARBEL
BONEFISH
BULLHEAD
CAPELIN
CISCO
CORVINA
DARTER
DORADO
ESCOLAR
FLIER
GOLET
GRAMPUS
GRAYBACK
GRAYLING
GRENADIER
GROWLER
GRUNION
GUDGEON
HARDER
HERRING
KETE
LAGARTO
PERCH

PICKEREL
POMPANO
ROBALO
RUNNER
R – 12
SCAMP
SCORPION
SCULPIN
SEALION
SEAWOLF
SHARK I
SHARK II
SNOOK
SWORDFISH
S – 26
S – 27
S – 28
S – 36
S – 39
S – 44
TANG
TRIGGER
TRITON
TROUT
TULLIBEE
WAHOO

WE SHALL NEVER FORGET THAT IT WAS OUR SUBMARINES THAT HELD THE LINES AGAINST THE ENEMY WHILE OUR FLEETS REPLACED LOSSES AND REPAIRED WOUNDS.
FLEET ADMIRAL C. W. NIMITZ, U. S. N.

I CAN ASSURE YOU THAT THEY WENT DOWN FIGHTING AND THAT THEIR BROTHERS WHO SURVIVED THEM TOOK A GRIM TOLL OF OUR SAVAGE ENEMY TO AVENGE THEIR DEATHS.
VICE ADMIRAL C. A. LOCKWOOD, JR., U. S. N.

P. F. S. 59   COMMANDER SUBMARINE FORCE 1943 – 1946

Submarines lost at sea are considered to be on "eternal patrol."

ON ETERNAL PATROL

The first confirmed sinking of a Japanese ship in the Pacific by a submarine in World War II was made by the USS *Swordfish* (SS-193) on December 9, 1941. It was recorded as attack number one. The last confirmed sinking belongs to the USS *Torsk* (SS-423) in the Sea of Japan on August 14, 1945. It is listed as attack number 4,735.

The first submarine lost in the Pacific was the *Sealion* at Cavite on December 10, 1941. The last was not Lawrence Edge's *Bonefish* but the USS *Bullhead* (SS-332), which left on her third patrol on July 31, 1945, with eighty-five on board, and most probably was sunk by Japanese aircraft.

Below are the fifty-two submarines lost in World War II in the Pacific in chronological order (read down each column):

Sealion	Grenadier	Grayback	Tang
S-36	Runner	Trout	Escolar
S-26	R-12	Tullibee	Albacore
Shark	Grayling	Gudgeon	Growler
Perch	Pompano	Herring	Scamp
S-27	Cisco	Golet	Swordfish
S-39	S-44	S-28	Barbel
Grunion	Dorado	Robalo	Kete
Argonaut	Wahoo	Flier	Trigger
Amberjack	Corvina	Harder	Snook
Grampus	Sculpin	Seawolf	Lagarto
Triton	Capelin	Darter	Bonefish
Pickerel	Scorpion	Shark II	Bullhead

FACTS AND FIGURES

Here are some facts and figures about US submarines in World War II:

- On December 7, 1941, when the Japanese attacked Pearl Harbor, the US Navy had 111 submarines; of these, 51 operated in the Pacific, with 29 attached to the Asiatic Fleet at Manila in the Philippines and 22 with the Pacific Fleet at Pearl Harbor.

- No submarines were lost in the attack on Pearl Harbor on December 7, 1941.

- During the war years, a total of 288 US submarines went to sea.

- In World War II, 52 US submarines were lost—almost one in five.

- Of the 16,000 US submariners who served in war patrols, approximately 3,500 died, giving the silent service a casualty rate of nearly 22 percent, the highest for any branch of the military.

- Submarines fired 14,748 torpedoes; 465 different skippers commanded boats in combat, and 6 received the Medal of Honor.

- Including attacks by Allied submarines, a total of 4,742 separate attacks were logged in the Pacific and Far East against the Japanese.

- Although figures have continued to be updated in the post-war years with new information from Japanese sources, it's estimated that US submarines sank 1,314 Japanese vessels—for about 5.3 million tons.

- Casualties inflicted by US submarines on the Japanese merchant marine were extremely heavy; it's estimated that more than 16,200 men were killed and another 53,400 wounded in submarine attacks.

- The US Submarine Force, including backup personnel, totaled about 50,000, representing 1.6 percent of the US Navy but accounting for 55 percent of Japan's maritime losses.

- Postwar analysis concluded that submarines contributed substantially to US victory in the Pacific. "'The war against shipping was perhaps the most decisive single factor in the collapse of the Japanese economy and logistical support of Japanese military and naval power. Submarines accounted for the majority of vessel sinkings and the great part of the reduction in tonnage.'"

- Each submarine kept a logbook. These Submarine War Reports, which have been declassified and are housed online at the Historic Naval Ships Association (HNSA) website, provide hour-by-hour accounts of events. According to the HNSA website, over 1,550 patrol reports filling approximately 63,000 pages of text were created.

ROSTERS

PEOPLE (AND DOGS)

- Captain Edward L. Beach Jr., officer on the *Trigger* and *Tirante*; named skipper of *Piper* in final months of the war; author whose books include *Run Silent, Run Deep*
- Joseph M. Eckberg, crew member on the *Seawolf*
- Lawrence Lott Edge, skipper of the *Bonefish*
- Robert "Bob" English, commander of Pacific Fleet submarines at Pearl Harbor until his death in an airplane crash in January 1943
- George Grider, third officer on the *Wahoo* who went on to command the *Flasher*
- Admiral Thomas Hart, commander in chief, Asiatic Fleet, encompassing surface ships and submarines (SubsAsiatic Force)
- Admiral Charles A. Lockwood, Jr., commanded SubsAsiatic Force in 1942; in 1943, moved to command Pacific Fleet submarines; helped solve torpedo problems
- Luau, mascot on the *Spadefish*
- General Douglas MacArthur, commander, US Army forces in the Far East, supreme commander for Allied Powers, Southwest Pacific Area
- Martin Matthews, fifteen-year-old sailor at Ford Island Naval Station at Pearl Harbor
- Dudley "Mush" Morton, *Wahoo*'s skipper
- Admiral Chester Nimitz, commander in chief, US Pacific Fleet

- Richard O'Kane, executive officer on the *Wahoo*; skipper of the *Tang*
- Penny, mascot of the *Gurnard*
- William Bernard "Barney" Sieglaff, Navy official on Admiral Lockwood's staff, for whom Operation Barney was named
- Forest Sterling, yeoman on the *Wahoo*
- Hideki Tojo, prime minister of Japan
- Frederick B. Warder, skipper of the *Seawolf*
- John Wilkes, commanded the Asiatic Fleet of submarines (SubsAsiatic Force) under Admiral Hart until replaced by Lockwood in spring 1942
- Lucy Wilson (Jopling), US Army nurse evacuated from Bataan and Corregidor on the *Spearfish*
- Walter Pye Wilson, longest-serving crew member on *Trigger*; one of the most well-known African American submariners in the war
- Isoroku Yamamoto, Fleet Admiral of the Imperial Japanese Navy

EXPERTS

This book relies on primary sources, memoirs, and works by notable historians. Here are three naval experts whose names appear frequently in these pages:

- **Clay Blair, Jr.** was a submariner, historian, and journalist whose *Silent Victory: The U.S. Submarine War against Japan* (1975) is considered the definitive history of submarines in the Pacific. At more than a thousand pages, it was informed by interviews with many people who've since passed away. Blair served on a submarine tender and two patrols of the *Guardfish* during the war.

- **Samuel Eliot Morison** was a naval historian and Pulitzer Prize–winning author who served in both world wars. Morison wrote a fifteen-volume history of US Navy operations in World War II. I relied on an abbreviated version, entitled *The Two-Ocean War: A Short History of the United States Navy in the Second World War*.

- **Theodore Roscoe** was the author of *United States Submarine Operations in World War II*, published by the Bureau of Naval Personnel in 1949 and compiled from official material. The title may sound boring, but it's a large, beautifully designed book, full of photographs, illustrations, and maps. (It's also quite hefty—it's said the first draft of the manuscript weighed ten pounds.)

NOTE FROM THE SKIPPER: Throughout this book, submarine commanders are referred to as their men would have called them, as captain or skipper, regardless of their military rank.

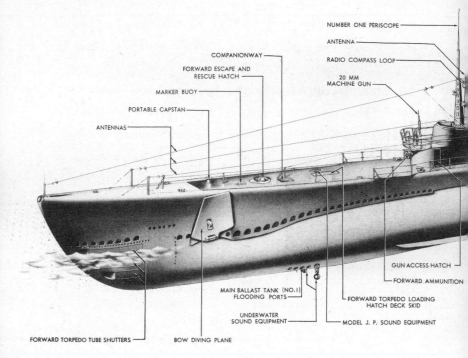

NUMBER ONE PERISCOPE

ANTENNA

RADIO COMPASS LOOP

20 MM
MACHINE GUN

COMPANIONWAY

FORWARD ESCAPE AND
RESCUE HATCH

MARKER BUOY

PORTABLE CAPSTAN

ANTENNAS

GUN ACCESS HATCH

FORWARD AMMUNITION

FORWARD TORPEDO LOADING
HATCH DECK SKID

MAIN BALLAST TANK (NO.1)
FLOODING PORTS

UNDERWATER
SOUND EQUIPMENT

MODEL J. P. SOUND EQUIPMENT

FORWARD TORPEDO TUBE SHUTTERS

BOW DIVING PLANE

DIAGRAM OF A SUBMARINE

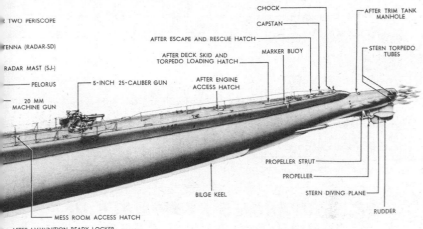

TWO PERISCOPE

TENNA (RADAR-SD)

RADAR MAST (SJ-)

PELORUS

5-INCH 25-CALIBER GUN

20 MM
MACHINE GUN

AFTER ENGINE
ACCESS HATCH

AFTER DECK SKID AND
TORPEDO LOADING HATCH

AFTER ESCAPE AND RESCUE HATCH

MARKER BUOY

CAPSTAN

CHOCK

AFTER TRIM TANK
MANHOLE

STERN TORPEDO
TUBES

PROPELLER STRUT

PROPELLER

STERN DIVING PLANE

RUDDER

BILGE KEEL

MESS ROOM ACCESS HATCH

AFTER AMMUNITION READY LOCKER

MMUNITION READY LOCKER

TOP SUBMARINES

In war patrol reports, submarine captains included the dates, times, and estimated results of their attacks on the enemy, such as whether torpedoes hit or a ship sank. But the information was incomplete: It wasn't always possible for a submarine commander to see how damaged a target was, or stay in the area long enough to see a ship sink.

After the war, teams from the Joint Army-Navy Assessment Committee (JANAC) went to Japan to attempt to compile losses from Japanese sources. Over time, more data has been added to the JANAC findings. In the postwar years, formerly secret Japanese radio messages and documents were declassified and translated, allowing researchers to more accurately confirm the outcomes of attacks.

TOP SUBMARINES BY NUMBER OF CONFIRMED SHIPS SUNK

Boat	Skippers	Ships Sunk
Tautog	Willingham, Sieglaff, Baskett	26
Tang	O'Kane	24
Silversides	Burlingame, Coye, Nichols	23
Flasher	Whitaker, Grider	21
Spadefish	Underwood, Germershausen	21
Seahorse	Cutter, Wilkins	20
Wahoo	Kennedy, Morton	20
Guardfish	Klakring, N.G. Ward	19
Rasher	Hutchinson, Laughon, Munson	18
Seawolf	Warder, Gross	18
Trigger	Benson, Dornin, Harlfinger, Connole	18

TOP SKIPPERS BY NUMBER OF CONFIRMED SHIPS SUNK

Skipper	Number of Patrols	Ships Sunk
Richard O'Kane, *Tang*	5	24
Slade Cutter, *Seahorse*	4	19
Dudley Morton, *Wahoo*	6	19
Eugene Fluckey, *Barb*	5	16
Samuel Dealey, *Harder*	6	16

BEST WAR PATROLS BY NUMBER OF CONFIRMED SHIPS SUNK

Boat and Patrol No.	Skipper	Ships Sunk
Tang - 3	Richard O'Kane	10
Wahoo - 4	Dudley W. Morton	9
Tang - 5	Richard O'Kane	7
Flasher - 5	George Grider	6
Spadefish - 1	Gordon Underwood	6

Note: Data is from *Silent Victory* by Clay Blair, Jr., as of 1975, pp. 984–990 (based on JANAC—Joint Army-Navy Assessment Committee).

GLOSSARY

- **acey-deucey** – sailors' version of backgammon
- **AO** – a ship carrying oil used to fuel other vessels
- **approach** – torpedo attack
- **archipelago** – a group of islands
- **AS** – submarine tender
- **ASR** – submarine rescue vessel
- **ballast tanks** – tanks that can be filled or emptied with water in order to submerge or surface a submarine; submarines also had fuel ballast tanks

    To see diagrams of a WWII submarine including its tanks and compartments, visit the San Francisco Maritime National Park Association and click on the appropriate diagram: http://maritime.org/doc/fleetsub/appendix/index.htm.

- **BB** – battleship
- **bow** – front, or forward, part of a ship
- **COMSUBPAC** – Commander, Submarine Force, Pacific Fleet
- **conn** – running the ship; can also refer to the conning tower
- **conning tower** – compartment above the control room used for navigating and directing attacks and using the periscope; located midship, and above it was the bridge deck, radar and radio antenna, and periscope shears (housing and support for periscopes)

    To see these above-deck features clearly (including a broom such as the one Wahoo *boasted), view the USS* Pampanito *at the San Francisco Maritime National Park Association at http://www.maritime.org/tour/pier.php.*

- **DD** – destroyer
- **depth charge** – an antisubmarine weapon consisting of explosive charges and a fuse set to detonate at a specific depth and dropped by a ship or plane into the sea. Depth charges subjected the submarine to powerful and destructive shocks; to avoid detection and damage, submarines would remain silent and dive deep.
- **exec, XO** – executive officer, second-in-command
- **fish** – torpedo
- **head** – toilet, water closet
- **Mark XIV (Mark 14) torpedoes** – two-speed, steam-powered torpedoes
- **mess, messroom** – crew's eating area, counterpart of the officers' wardroom
- **OD, OOD** – officer of the deck, who conns the ship on the surface
- **old man** – slang for captain
- **outer doors** – movable covers over the torpedo tubes
- **PCO** – prospective commanding officer
- **plank owners** – members of a crew when a ship is placed in commission
- **port** – left side of a ship
- **screws** – ship's propellers
- **skipper** – captain
- **SM** – submarine minelayer
- **SS** – submarine
- **starboard** – right side of a ship
- **stern** – the rear or aft part of a ship
- **TDC** – torpedo data computer used in setting up torpedo shots

- **tin can** – nickname for a destroyer
- **trim dive** – a dive done to adjust the weight and relative buoyancy of a submarine so that it can move up and down in the water; *trim* is a maritime term
- **True** – Abbreviated as T (as in the war patrol report on page 103); a maritime navigation term referring to True North Pole
- **wardroom** – eating area for officers

DIVE DEEPER:
LINKS TO RESOURCES

There's so much to learn about submarines and World War II. Below I've listed online resources to get you started. Site addresses can change, so please ask a librarian if you need help locating information or expanding your search.

TOP RECOMMENDATIONS

Find a Submarine or Maritime Museum Near You
Check here for a list of submarines at museums in the United States. http://www.submarinemuseums.org/

Remembering Those on Eternal Patrol
This site is dedicated to all men lost in the US Submarine Force. Photos of sailors lost on boats featured in this book, including *Tang*, *Trigger*, *Seawolf*, and *Wahoo*, can be seen by clicking on the submarine, then on the individual's name. http://www.oneternalpatrol.com/

PRIMARY SOURCE: SUBMARINE WAR REPORTS, HISTORIC NAVAL SHIPS ASSOCIATION

At the end of each war patrol, submarine commanders created a report. During WWII, over 1,550 reports—totaling some 63,000 pages—were generated. During the 1970s, these were reproduced on microfilm. In 2009, a digital version became available online.

The reports are microfilmed images, so you may want to ask a librarian for help. You can access these at: http://www.hnsa.org /resources/manuals-documents/submarine-war-reports/

OTHER RESOURCES FOR THE US NAVY, SUBMARINES, AND SUBMARINE HISTORY

African American Submariners in the US Navy
http://www.history.navy.mil/browse-by-topic/diversity/african -americans-in-the-navy/african-american-submariners -in-the-us-navy.html

Descriptions of Submarine Classes
http://www.navsource.org/archives/08/tnsubs.htm

History of the Canopus by Captain E. L. Sackett
http://as9.larryshomeport.com/html/history.html

History of the USS Squalus
http://www.navalhistory.org/2014/05/23/remembering-the -uss-squalus-75-years-later

List of Submarines in World War II
http://www.fleetsubmarine.com/sublist.html

Naval History and Heritage Command Website
http://www.history.navy.mil/

Understanding WWII Submarine Propulsion Systems
http://www.fleetsubmarine.com/propulsion.html

United States Navy
http://www.navy.mil/

USS Tang
National WWII Museum
http://www.nationalww2museum.org/see-hear/collections
/focus-on/the-uss-tang.html

MORE ABOUT THE USS WAHOO

Interview with Forest J. Sterling, Yeoman on the Wahoo
http://archive.defense.gov/specials/heroes/sterling.html

The map made of Wewak Harbor by the crew of the Wahoo
http://www.warfish.com/gaz_wewak-map.html

The Wahoo-Buyo Maru controversy
http://www.warfish.com/patrol3con.html

Discovery of Wahoo
http://www.navy.mil/submit/display.asp?story_id=26378
http://www.bowfin.org/uss-wahoo-ss-238

ATTACK ON PEARL HARBOR

Pearl Harbor Raid
Naval History and Heritage Command
http://www.history.navy.mil/browse-by-topic/wars-conflicts
-and-operations/world-war-ii/pearl-harbor-raid.html

Submarines at Pearl Harbor during the attack
USS Bowfin Submarine Museum and Park
http://www.bowfin.org/december-7-1941

Infamy: December 1941
National WWII Museum
This online exhibition includes images, oral histories, and radio broadcasts from the first month of America's involvement in World War II.
http://infamydecember1941.org/philippines.html

USS Arizona Memorial Virtual Tour
National Park Service
http://home.nps.gov/valr/learn/photosmultimedia/uss-arizona -memorial-virtual-tour.htm

GENERAL RESOURCES ON WORLD WAR II

The Bataan Campaign
https://bataancampaign.wordpress.com/author/371fg/page/4/

Loss of Sealion at Cavite, December 1941
http://www.history.navy.mil/research/library/online-reading -room/title-list-alphabetically/u/united-states-submarine-losses /sealion-ss-195.html

BIBLIOGRAPHY

BOOKS

Alden, John D. *The Fleet Submarine in the U.S. Navy: A Design and Construction History.* Annapolis, MD: Naval Institute Press, 1979.

——— and Craig R. McDonald. *United States and Allied Submarine Successes in the Pacific and Far East during World War II.* 4th ed. Jefferson, NC: McFarland, 2009.

Beach, Edward L. *Salt and Steel: Reflections of a Submariner.* Annapolis, MD: Naval Institute Press, 1999.

———. *Submarine!: The Classic Account of Undersea Combat in World War II.* New York: Holt, 1952; Annapolis, MD: Naval Institute Press, 2003. Citations and page numbers refer to the Naval Institute Press edition.

Blair, Clay, Jr. *Silent Victory: The U.S. Submarine War against Japan.* Philadelphia: Lippincott, 1975; Annapolis, MD: Naval Institute Press, 2001. Citations and page references refer to the Naval Institute Press edition.

Brinkley, Douglas, and David Rubel, eds. *World War II: The Axis Assault, 1939–1942.* New York: Times Books, 2003.

Bureau of Naval Personnel, Standards and Curriculum Division Training. *The Fleet Type Submarine.* Reproduction of June 1946 training manual as *The Silent Service in WWII: The Fleet Type Submarine* by Periscope Film. Print on demand, May 13, 2015. http://periscopefilm.com/the-fleet-type-submarine

Calvert, James F. *Silent Running: My Years on a World War II Attack Submarine.* New York: John Wiley, 1995.

Campbell, Douglas A. *Eight Survived: The Harrowing Story of the USS* Flier *and the Only Downed World War II Submariners to Survive and Evade Capture.* Guilford, CT: Lyons Press, 2010.

Chambliss, William C. *The Silent Service.* New York: New American Library, 1959.

Christley, Jim, with illustrations by Tony Bryan. *US Submarines 1941–45.* Oxford: Osprey, 2006.

Conner, Claude C. *Nothing Friendly in the Vicinity: My Patrols on the Submarine USS* Guardfish *during WWII.* Annapolis, MD: Bluejacket Books, Naval Institute Press, 1999.

DeRose, James F. *Unrestricted Warfare: How a New Breed of Officers Led the Submarine Force to Victory in World War II.* New York: John Wiley, 2000.

Enright, Joseph E., with James W. Ryan. Shinano! *The Sinking of Japan's Secret Supership.* New York: St. Martin's Press, 1987.

Finch, Edward W. *Beneath the Waves: The Life and Navy of Capt. Edward L. Beach Jr.* Annapolis, MD: Naval Institute Press, 2010.

Fluckey, Eugene B. *Thunder Below! The USS* Barb *Revolutionizes Submarine Warfare in World War II.* Urbana, IL: University of Illinois Press, 1992.

Frank, Gerold, and James D. Horan, with Joseph M. Eckberg. *U.S.S.* Seawolf: *Submarine Raider of the Pacific.* New York: G.P. Putnam's Sons, 1945.

Friedman, Norman. *U.S. Submarines through 1945: An Illustrated Design History.* Annapolis, MD: Naval Institute Press, 1995.

Galantin, I. J. *Take Her Deep!: A Submarine against Japan in World War II.* Chapel Hill, NC: Algonquin, 1987.

Grider, George, with Lydel Sims. *War Fish*. New York: Pyramid Books, 1959.

Hoehling, A. A., ed. *They Fought under the Sea*. Derby, CT: Monarch Books, 1963.

Holmes, Wilfred Jay. *Undersea Victory: The Influence of Submarine Operations on the War in the Pacific*. Garden City, NY: Doubleday, 1966.

Jackson, Stephen Leal. *The Men: American Enlisted Submariners in World War II; Why They Joined, Why They Fought, and Why They Won*. Indianapolis, IN: Dog Ear Publishing, 2010.

Jopling, Lucy Wilson. *Warrior in White*. San Antonio: Watercress Press, 1990.

Keith, Don. *Final Patrol: True Stories of World War II Submarines*. New York: NAL Caliber, 2006.

———. *Undersea Warrior: The World War II Story of "Mush" Morton and the USS* Wahoo. New York: NAL Caliber, 2011.

———. *War beneath the Waves: A True Story of Courage and Leadership Aboard a World War II Submarine*. New York: NAL Caliber, 2010.

Kershaw, Alex. *Escape from the Deep: The Epic Story of a Legendary Submarine and Her Courageous Crew*. Philadelphia: Da Capo Press, 2008.

Knoblock, Glenn A. *Black Submariners in the United States Navy, 1940–1975*. Jefferson, NC: McFarland, 2005.

La Forte, Robert W., and Ronald E. Marcello, eds. *Remembering Pearl Harbor: Eyewitness Accounts by U.S. Military Men and Women*. Wilmington, DE: SR Books, 1991.

LaVO, Carl. *Back from the Deep: The Strange Story of the Sister Subs* Squalus *and* Sculpin. Annapolis, MD: Bluejacket Books, Naval Institute Press, 1994.

Layton, Edwin T., with Roger Pineau and John Costello. *"And I Was There": Pearl Harbor and Midway—Breaking the Secrets*. New York: William Morrow, 1985.

Lockwood, Charles A. *Sink 'Em All: Submarine Warfare in the Pacific*. New York: Dutton, 1951.

Marcello, Robert E. "Interview with Martin Matthews." Denton, TX: North Texas State University, Oral History Collection, Number 430, 1978.

Marston, Daniel, ed. *The Pacific War: From Pearl Harbor to Hiroshima*. Oxford: Osprey, 2005.

McCullough, Jonathan J. *A Tale of Two Subs: An Untold Story of World War II, Two Sister Ships, and Extraordinary Heroism*. New York: Grand Central Publishing, 2008.

Mendenhall, Corwin. *Submarine Diary: The Silent Stalking of Japan*. Chapel Hill, NC: Algonquin Books of Chapel Hill, 1991; Annapolis, MD: Naval Institute Press, 1995. Citations and page references refer to the Naval Institute Press edition.

Monahan, Evelyn M., and Rosemary Neidel-Greenlee. *And If I Perish: Frontline U.S. Army Nurses in World War II*. New York: Alfred A. Knopf, 2003.

Monroe-Jones, Edward, and Michael Green, eds. *The Silent Service in World War II: The Story of the U.S. Navy Submarine Force in the Words of the Men Who Lived It*. Havertown, PA: Casemate, 2012.

Moore, Stephen L. *Presumed Lost: The Incredible Ordeal of America's Submarine POWs during the Pacific War*. Annapolis, MD: Naval Institute Press, 2009.

———. Spadefish: *On Patrol with a Top-Scoring World War II Submarine*. Dallas: Atriad Press, 2006.

Morison, Samuel Eliot. *The Two-Ocean War: A Short History of the United States Navy in the Second World War*. Boston: Little, Brown, 1963.

Morris, Eric. *Corregidor: The End of the Line*. New York: Stein and Day, 1981.

Norman, Elizabeth M. *We Band of Angels: The Untold Story of the American Women Trapped on Bataan*. New York: Random House, 1999.

O'Kane, Richard H. *Clear the Bridge!: The War Patrols of the U.S.S. Tang*. Chicago: Rand McNally, 1977.

———. Wahoo: *The Patrols of America's Most Famous WWII Submarine*. Novato, CA: Presidio Press, 1987.

Padfield, Peter. *War beneath the Sea: Submarine Conflict during World War II*. New York: John Wiley, 1995.

Prange, Gordon W. *At Dawn We Slept: The Untold Story of Pearl Harbor*. New York: McGraw-Hill, 1981.

Raymer, Edward C. *Descent into Darkness: Pearl Harbor, 1941: A Navy Diver's Memoir*. Novato, CA: Presidio Press, 1996.

Roscoe, Theodore. *United States Submarine Operations in World War II*. Annapolis, MD: Naval Institute Press, 1949. Citations from the ninth printing, 1972.

——— and Richard G. Voge. *Pig Boats: The True Story of the Fighting Submariners of World War II*. New York: Bantam Books, 1958.

Ruhe, William J. *War in the Boats: My WWII Submarine Battles*. Washington, DC: Brassey's, 1994.

Ruiz, Kenneth C., with John R. Bruning. *The Luck of the Draw:*

The Memoir of a World War II Submariner from Savo Island to the Silent Service. St. Paul, MN: Zenith Press, 2005.

Russell, Dale. *Hell Above, Deep Water Below.* Tillamook, OR: Bayocean Enterprises, 1995.

Sasgen, Peter. *Hellcats: The Epic Story of World War II's Most Daring Submarine Raid.* New York: NAL Caliber, 2010.

Schratz, Paul R. *Submarine Commander: A Story of World War II and Korea.* Lexington: University Press of Kentucky, 1988.

Schultz, Robert, and James Shell. *We Were Pirates: A Torpedoman's Pacific War.* Annapolis, MD: Naval Institute Press, 2009.

Scott, James. *The War Below: The Story of Three Submarines That Battled Japan.* New York: Simon & Schuster, 2013.

Sheridan, Martin. *Overdue and Presumed Lost: The Story of the USS Bullhead.* Francestown, NH: M. Jones, 1947; Annapolis, MD: Naval Institute Press, 2004. Citations and page references refer to the Naval Institute Press edition.

Sloan, Bill. *Undefeated: America's Heroic Fight for Bataan and Corregidor.* New York: Simon & Schuster, 2012.

Smith, Steven Trent. *The Rescue: A True Story of Courage and Survival in World War II.* New York: John Wiley, 2001.

Sterling, Forest J. *Wake of the* Wahoo*: The Heroic Story of America's Most Daring WWII Submarine, USS* Wahoo. Philadelphia: Chilton Book Division, 1960; New York: Popular Library, 1961. Citations and page references refer to the Popular Library edition.

Stevens, Peter F. *Fatal Dive: Solving the World War II Mystery of the USS* Grunion. Washington, DC: Regnery Publishing, 2012.

Sturma, Michael. *Death at a Distance: The Loss of the Legendary USS* Harder. Annapolis, MD: Naval Institute Press, 2006.

————. *Surface and Destroy: The Submarine Gun War in the Pacific.* Lexington: University Press of Kentucky, 2011.

————. *The USS* Flier*: Death and Survival on a World War II Submarine.* Lexington: University Press of Kentucky, 2008.

Trumbull, Robert. *Silversides.* New York: Henry Holt, 1945.

Tuohy, William. *The Bravest Man: Richard O'Kane and the Amazing Submarine Adventures of the USS* Tang. Stroud, UK: Sutton Publishing, 2001; New York: Presidio Press, 2006. Citations and page numbers refer to the Presidio Press edition.

Whitlock, Flint, and Ron Smith. *The Depths of Courage: American Submariners at War with Japan, 1941–1945.* New York: Berkley Caliber, 2007.

Wilkes, James W. *Down Under: My Life as a WWII Submariner.* Philadelphia: Xlibris, 2007.

JOURNAL ARTICLES & INTERNET SOURCES

Copeland, Kevin. "Submarine Force Will Begin Integration of Enlisted Women." Press release. Story number NNS150121-17; release date 1/21/2015 2:27:00 PM. Web. http://www.navy.mil/submit/display.asp?story_id=85274.

Enriquez, Elizabeth L. "Coping with War: KGST 'Radio' and Other Media Strategies of Civilian Internees in the Philippines in World War II." *Social Science Diliman* 6, no. 2 (December 2010): 1–28. Web. Accessed 5/16/2015. http://journals.upd.edu.ph/index.php/socialsciencediliman/article/view/2025.

Galvani, William. "Sea Dogs." *American Heritage* 45, no. 6 (October 1994). Web. http://www.americanheritage.com/content/sea-dogs.

Gleason, Bill. "Penny, a Sub Sailor." *Polaris*, August 1987. Web. http://www.subvetpaul.com/SAGA_8_87.htm.

Hornfischer, James D. "Revisiting Samuel Eliot Morison's Landmark History." *Smithsonian Magazine*, February 2011. Web. http://www.smithsonianmag.com/history/revisiting-samuel -eliot-morisons-landmark-history-63715/?no-ist.

Sackett, E. L. "History of the *Canopus*." Distributed to the men and families of the *Canopus*, May 12, 1943. Web. http://as9 .larryshomeport.com/html/history.html.

Stout, David. "Frederick Burdett Warder, 95; Decorated Submarine Skipper." *New York Times*, February 4, 2000. Web. http://www .nytimes.com/2000/02/04/us/frederick-burdett-warder -95-decorated-submarine-skipper.html.

Submarine War Reports. Historic Naval Ships Association. Web. http://www.hnsa.org/resources/manuals-documents/ submarine-war-patrol-reports/.

SOURCE NOTES

The following pages tell you where to find the sources of the quotations in this book. A quotation enclosed in double quotation marks (like this: "...") means the quoted words are from a direct or primary source, perhaps a book, an interview, or a war patrol report. When you see single quotation marks inside double quotation marks ("'...'"), that indicates a quotation or dialogue that appears within a source.

EPIGRAPH
"All ships have souls...": Beach, *Submarine!*, 4.

A LIQUID CHESSBOARD
"The U.S. Navy fought...": Enright and Ryan, *Shinano!*, xi–xii.

PART ONE
"To the Congress of the United States...": "Day of Infamy" Speech by Franklin D. Roosevelt, December 8, 1941; SEN 77A-H1, Records of the United States Senate; Record Group 46; National Archives.

"'Washington, Dec. 11...'": Brinkley and Rubel, *World War II*, 268.

"EXECUTE UNRESTRICTED AIR AND SUBMARINE WARFARE...": Roscoe, *United States Submarine Operations in World War II*, 5.

CHAPTER ONE
"He was wearing...": Matthews, Oral History Interview (hereafter Matthews), 2.

"Anybody fifteen years...": ibid., 5–6.

"It was to bed early...": ibid., 7.

"The chow was good...": ibid.

"'I wish I could get duty...'": ibid., 21.

"We heard noise...": ibid., 21–22.

The best drill: Prange, *At Dawn We Slept*, 510.

"'Oh, oh...'": ibid., 507.

"'I knew right away...'": ibid.

183 Japanese planes ... miles away: ibid., 490–491.

The attack's mastermind: ibid., 9–17.

"Pandemonium broke loose...": Matthews, 23, 25.

"I can't remember . . .": ibid., 25.

"I was just more or less . . .": ibid., 29.

"All I can remember . . .": ibid.

"When the *Arizona* . . .": ibid., 31–32.

"indescribably fearful . . .": Prange, 513.

"'the ship was sinking . . .'": ibid.

"There was steel in the air . . .": Matthews, 28, 33.

"I never got hit . . .": ibid., 32.

"'I'm Navy! . . .'": ibid., 34.

"Ships were still blowing up . . .": ibid.

"sitting ducks . . .": ibid., 36.

"to rescue people . . .": ibid., 35.

"We were told . . .": Matthews, 37.

"Every now and then . . .": ibid., 36–37.

"I knew then that even . . .": ibid., 41.

DISPATCH: Trapped on the USS California

"'So I leaned against . . .'": La Forte and Marcello, *Remembering Pearl Harbor*, 85–86.

"'All at once I heard . . .'": ibid., 86.

"'Nobody panicked . . .'": ibid., 88.

"'Smoke and fire . . .'": ibid., 90–91.

"'I couldn't believe my eyes . . .'": ibid., 87.

"'There was a dent in it . . .'": ibid.

CHAPTER TWO

"Probably no man in Japan . . .": Prange, 10.

"'fiercely attack . . .'": ibid., 16.

Japan boasted: Japanese Navy statistics from Blair, *Silent Victory*, 85–86.

the Atlantic Fleet: Roscoe, 3.

the Atlantic submarines . . .: ibid., 85–92.

US submarines; Asiatic Fleet; Pacific Fleet: Roscoe, 4. Roscoe lists five submarines at Pearl Harbor including the *Cuttlefish*, but her official records show she had departed for repairs at Mare Island Navy Yard near California at the time. See "Submarines in Pearl Harbor on December 7, 1941," USS *Bowfin* Submarine Museum & Park. Web. Accessed 5/14/2015. http://www.bowfin.org/december-7-1941.

"a concentration of effort . . .": ibid., 3–4.

Navy Department issued an order: Blair, 106, 58–60.

BRIEFING: The Japanese War Plan

"First, prior to a declaration . . .": Morison, *The Two-Ocean War*, 41.
"This scheme of conquest . . .": ibid.

CHAPTER THREE

to protect the Philippines: Blair, 81.
"'What's the matter . . .'": Frank, Horan, and Eckberg, *U.S.S.* Seawolf, 25–26.
"'Going to the docks . . .'": ibid., 26.
"The port was as busy as . . .": ibid., 25.
"The air was mild . . .": ibid., 26.
"I read the flashes . . .": ibid.

USS SEAWOLF

This story has 80 heroes: Historic Naval Ships Association, Submarine War Reports. Web. Accessed 5/20/2015. http://issuu.com/hnsa/docs/ss-197_seawolf_part1. Hereafter SWR with submarine number and name.

CHAPTER FOUR

"'Kid, why don't you come into this outfit? . . .'": Frank, Horan, and Eckberg, 7.
"We know we're different . . .": ibid., 6–7.
"Yard workmen were laying . . .": ibid., 1.
a nickname he didn't much like . . . : Stout, "Frederick Burdett Warder, 95," *New York Times*, February 4, 2000, http://www.nytimes.com/.
"I'd be her eyes and ears . . .": Frank, Horan, and Eckberg, 3.
"A submarine such as the *Wolf* . . .": ibid., 5.
"Each of us had to know . . .": ibid., 11.
"I'd seen a lot . . .": ibid., 7.
"Seated at this table . . .": ibid., 8.
"The first thing I did . . .": ibid., 11.
"a wizard softball player . . .": ibid., 12.
"Black, shining black . . .": ibid., 12–13.
"familiar odor . . .": ibid., 13.
"Marjorie and I . . .": ibid., 19.

SUBMARINE SCHOOL: Boat Names, Numbers, and Classes

"diving speed, cruising range . . .": Roscoe, 14.
These submarines could: Theodore Roscoe provides an analysis of the Japanese strategic error in ignoring the potential role of the US Submarine Force and a description of the building program. Roscoe, 12–16.
"embodied the best features . . .": ibid., 14.

CHAPTER FIVE

"'What are we waiting for?'. . .": Frank, Horan, and Eckberg, 28.

"a fluid front . . .": Roscoe, 50.

"'Needless to say, you all . . .'": Frank, Horan, and Eckberg, 29.

"'*You will sink* . . .'": ibid.

"Under way . . .": SWR, SS-197 *Seawolf*.

"We had no chance . . .": Frank, Horan, and Eckberg, 29.

"We were constantly . . .": ibid.

"As the sun rose . . .": ibid.

Whenever the *Seawolf* ran: Submarine engines from Roscoe, 14.

"sitting ducks" as shells: Discussion of Clark Field from Blair, 132, 129–131.

"We did not have a gun . . .": Monroe-Jones and Green, *The Silent Service*, 29.

Thirty miles away: Sloan, *Undefeated*, 43.

bombs hit the *Sealion*: Cavite attack from Naval History and Heritage Command, USS *Sealion* (SS-195). Web. Accessed 5/16/2015. http://www.history.navy.mil/research/library/online-reading-room/title-list-alphabetically/u/united-states-submarine-losses/sealion-ss-195.html.

"Topside there was chaos . . .": Blair, 134.

"'Man, this is the place . . .'": Jackson, *The Men*, 70.

"'The Skipper was watching . . .'": ibid., 73.

The *Sealion* would never: Destruction of *Sealion* from Naval History and Heritage Command. Web. http://www.history.navy.mil/research/library/online-reading-room/title-list-alphabetically/u/united-states-submarine-losses/sealion-ss-195.html.

"While I was rushing . . .": Monroe-Jones and Green, 29.

Seadragon and *Pigeon*: Roscoe, 30.

"We had many holes . . .": Monroe-Jones and Green, 29.

the *Pigeon* became: Roscoe, 30.

"'Right now Cavite is . . .'": Frank, Horan, and Eckberg, 31.

"'Ladies and gentlemen . . .'": ibid.

Don Bell's real name: Enriquez, "Coping with War," 2–3. Web. Accessed 5/16/2015.

attack at Cavite killed: Cavite death toll from Sloan, 43.

"The British had failed . . .": Blair, 135.

DISPATCH: Ernie Plantz . . . POW

"'half a cup of rice . . .'": Jackson, 79.

CHAPTER SIX

"We had missed . . .": Frank, Horan, and Eckberg, 31.

"I was too geared up . . .": ibid., 30.

"'Eck! Eck! . . .'": ibid., 31.

"'I can't figure it out . . .'": ibid.

"'Give me a bearing . . .'": ibid.

"I turned my wheel . . .": ibid., 31–32.

"Submarines can ram . . .": ibid., 32.

"I racked my brains . . .": ibid.

on these first patrols: Pioneering patrols from Roscoe, 31.

"Foraying in this fortnight . . .": ibid., 32.

called "the overwhelming forces . . .": ibid.

to enter Manila Bay: *Canopus* and Manila Bay from Blair, 134–135, Roscoe, 31.

"As soon as the hatch . . .": Frank, Horan, and Eckberg, 32–33.

"Groups of men . . .": ibid., 33.

CHAPTER SEVEN

"'Sound has something . . .'": Frank, Horan, and Eckberg, 34.

"'Up periscope,'" followed . . .": ibid., 35.

"'What do you have . . . ?'": ibid.

the order: "'Battle stations.'": ibid.

"Half-naked . . .": ibid.

"This was the telltale . . .": ibid., 36.

"Two full minutes . . .": ibid., 37.

"'Secure battle stations . . .'": ibid.

"With nightfall . . .": ibid.

"Captain Warder and Lieutenant Deragon . . .": ibid.

"The *Wolf* was going . . .": ibid.

"The approach was a delicate matter . . .": ibid., 38.

"the sense of shock . . .": ibid.

"a roaring, snapping . . .": ibid., 39.

"To hear the beating . . .": ibid.

"'Forward torpedo room, make ready . . .'": ibid., 40.

"'Open outer doors . . .'": ibid.

"In the control room below . . .": ibid.

"'Forward tubes ready . . .'": ibid., 41.

"'No, no, wait a minute! . . .'": ibid.

"Torpedoes are fired . . .": ibid.

"There was a sudden *whoosh!* . . .": ibid.

"An erratic fish . . .": ibid.

"'Stand by to fire two . . .'": ibid.

"As each fish left . . .": ibid.

"'Sound, do you hear . . .'": ibid., 42.

"The *Wolf* shook . . .": ibid., 43.

"'Initially, of course . . .'": Jackson, 102.

went to the *Swordfish*: Alden and McDonald, *United States and Allied Submarine Successes*, 27.

"'I can't understand it . . .'": Frank, Horan, and Eckberg, 43.

CHAPTER EIGHT

"There wasn't much we could do . . .": ibid., 47.

"The first inkling I had . . .": ibid.

"'Well, boys, she's finished . . .'": ibid.

"'What's finished? . . .'": ibid.

"He'd made tinsel . . .": ibid.

"the wildest collection of junk . . .": ibid., 49.

"There was a lump in my throat . . .": ibid., 50–51.

"Gus Wright came into the mess hall . . .": ibid., 51.

events in the Philippines: Morison, 83–86.

"Should he abandon . . .": Blair, 153.

"'We arrived late Christmas afternoon . . .'": ibid.

"'This was a very tough decision . . .'": ibid., 154–155.

"At dusk we surfaced . . .": Frank, Horan, and Eckberg, 56–57.

"'Here's the dope . . .'": ibid., 57.

"'These are slow-burning,' . . .": ibid.

"As I crossed . . .": ibid.

"It seemed we were taking . . .": ibid., 58, 60.

"The first moment I had . . .": ibid., 59–60.

BRIEFING: The Submarine War

Division 202: Asiatic Fleet from Blair, 82.

"The functions of the tender . . .": Roscoe, 16–17.

"The two submarine commands . . .": Blair, 203.

TIMELINE

Timelines: Data for timelines is drawn from the works of Blair and Morison.

PART TWO

"You say I'm punchy? . . .": LaVO, *Back from the Deep*, 75.

"The torpedo scandal . . .": Blair, 879.

CHAPTER NINE

"'Are we a sub or a transport? . . .'": Frank, Horan, and Eckberg, 64.

"You will remove . . .": SWR, SS-197 *Seawolf*.

"We packed ammunition . . .": Frank, Horan, and Eckberg, 65.

"'If they get us . . .'": ibid.

intercom: "'Call the Captain!'": ibid.

"'Captain, I see something . . .'": ibid.

"'Well, I'll be . . .'": ibid., 66.

"'How we going to . . .'": ibid.

"We were gliding . . .": ibid., 69.

"We were already . . .": ibid.

Seawolf docked: *Seawolf* at Corregidor from SWR, SS-197 *Seawolf*.

"I saw men sleeping . . .": ibid., 72.

"'You can set your watch . . .'": ibid., 71.

"All I knew was . . .": ibid.

"I could see searchlights . . .": ibid., 73.

"Our men were now making . . .": ibid., 70.

DISPATCH: Gold "Sandbags"

"'Our weight condition . . .'": Roscoe, 79.

"'We requested . . .'": ibid., 79–80.

bar of gold was missing: Blair, 207–208.

USS CANOPUS

"A less likely candidate . . .": Sackett, "History of the *Canopus*," Ch. I. Web. Accessed 7/21/15. http://as9.larryshomeport.com/html/chapter_i.html.

CHAPTER TEN

"The defenders of Bataan . . .": Morris, *Corregidor*, 394.

"The tough old girl . . .": Sackett, Ch. IV.

"We had refrigeration . . .": ibid., Ch. VIII.

"'She was one fine . . .'": Sloan, 107.

"The *Canopus* seemed reluctant . . .": Sackett, Ch. IX.

"I tore down . . .": Jopling, *Warrior in White*, 35.

"We had nothing to eat . . .": ibid., 36.

"Here I was put in the Operating Room . . .": ibid., 38.

"drank unboiled water . . .": ibid., 39–40.

"Walking out . . .": ibid., 42.

"'Those eyes just followed us,'": Norman, *We Band of Angels*, 87.

"At times we would be . . .": Jopling, 44.

"I was so sick . . .": ibid., 45.

"'Get up and get out . . .'": ibid., 47.

"the world was bright . . .": ibid.

"Suppose something had happened . . .": Sackett, Ch. X.

"the dark bulk of Corregidor . . .": ibid.

USS SPEARFISH

"War Patrol Report . . .": SWR, SS-190 *Spearfish*.

CHAPTER ELEVEN

"The hatch was such a small opening . . .": Jopling, 47.

"They had a single-layer chocolate cake . . .": ibid.

"later one of the crew members . . .": ibid.

"'Almost immediately after our boarding . . .'": Monroe-Jones and Green, 63–64.

One hundred and seventy-three . . . : Blair, 197.

"Our inability . . .": ibid., 78.

"'Your self-sacrifice . . .'": Norman, 221.

"'You have served . . .'": ibid., 222.

"Everyone was very quiet . . .": Jopling, 50.

"'There were three heads . . .'": Monroe-Jones and Green, 64.

"The submariners were so good to us . . .": Jopling, 50.

"sounded like a Model T Ford car horn . . .": ibid., 50–51.

"All we saw . . .": ibid., 51.

"The crew was very ingenious . . .": ibid.

"Working on the sympathies . . .": ibid., 53.

"who had just . . .": ibid., 52.

"One pint-sized girl . . .": Lockwood, *Sink 'Em All*, 11.

"'We spent our lives . . .'": Norman, 272.

SUBMARINE SCHOOL: Operating the Head

"The water closet installation . . .": *The Fleet Type Submarine*, 102–103.

SUBMARINE SCHOOL: Women Can Now Serve . . .

"'We are the most capable . . .'": Copeland, "Submarine Force Will Begin Integration of Enlisted Women." Web. http://www.navy.mil/submit /display.asp?story_id=85274.

CHAPTER TWELVE

improvised song: "'*Sink 'em all . . .*'": Lockwood, 2.

"These fighting words . . .": ibid.

"'The boys here . . .'": Blair, 274.

"The thin faces . . .": Lockwood, 5.

"Beyond a doubt . . .": ibid., 3.

"The submariners needed . . .": ibid., 4.

magnetic exploder: Torpedo exploders at Aparri from Blair, 136.

"'torpedoes were no . . . good . . .'": ibid., 290.

"During the thirty five minutes . . .": SWR, SS-188 *Sargo*.

"To make round trips . . .": SWR, SS-184 *Skipjack*.

"So much evidence . . .": Lockwood, 8–9.

"'It took Charlie Lockwood . . .'": Blair, 275.

"incompetent dunderheads.": Beach, *Salt and Steel*, 142.
"Bringing our torpedo runs closer . . .": Lockwood, 9.

USS TRIGGER
USS *Trigger*: SWR, SS-237 *Trigger*.

CHAPTER THIRTEEN
"There she was, a great . . .": Beach, *Submarine!*, 4.
" 'Stay in the big ships . . .' ": Beach, *Salt and Steel*, 57.
"leaning, leaking, lopsided . . .": ibid.
"To me, she certainly wasn't . . .": Beach, *Submarine!*, 4.
"two and a half . . .": ibid.
"If they lack judgment . . .": ibid., 5.
"All ships have souls . . .": ibid., 4.
"Fill her up . . .": ibid., 7.
"Our chance came suddenly,": ibid., 8.
"The success of this battle . . .": Morison, 148.
US fleet . . . Japan's forces: Japanese and American forces from ibid., 148–149.
attack on Midway: Battle of Midway from Blair, 234–249; Morison, 147–163.
"and maybe—*maybe* . . .": Beach, *Submarine!*, 8.
"All night long . . .": ibid.
"There were great black rocks . . .": Beach, *Salt and Steel*, 93.
" 'Sound the collision alarm!' ": ibid.
"Disaster was on us . . .": ibid., 93–94.
"We backed . . .": Beach, *Submarine!*, 8.
"And then came dawn . . .": ibid.
"We hoped for . . .": Beach, *Salt and Steel*, 95.
"At this point," said Ned . . . : ibid.
" 'She's moving!' ": Beach, *Submarine!*, 9.
"Incredulously we look . . .": ibid.
"When our skipper reported . . .": Beach, *Salt and Steel*, 97.

CHAPTER FOURTEEN
"It took *Trigger* . . .": Beach, *Submarine!*, 10.
an absolute zero: Beach, *Salt and Steel*, 130.
"upbeat, 'let-me-at-'em' . . .": Finch, *Beneath the Waves*, 25.
"With his arrival . . .": Beach, *Salt and Steel*, 131.
"He was steaming along steadily . . .": Beach, *Submarine!*, 11.
" 'Get right astern . . .' ": Beach, *Salt and Steel*, 132.
"It would soon be time . . .": ibid.
" 'Captain!' I yelled . . .' ": ibid.
" 'Collision Alarm! He's trying . . .' ": ibid.

"'Watertight doors shut . . .'": ibid., 133.

"one of the steadiest men . . .": ibid.

to Wilson. "'Right full rudder!'": ibid.

"'Rudder is right full.'": ibid.

"It was like driving a car . . .": ibid., 133–134.

"If Wilson's muscles . . .": ibid., 134.

"We would pass clear . . .": ibid.

"'Ned, are you a hero?' . . .": ibid.

"'If we're going to have . . .'": ibid., 135.

"behind the wisecracks . . .": ibid.

SUBMARINE SCHOOL: "I Have the Conn"

"Navy doctrine prescribes . . .": ibid., 91.

BRIEFING: African American Submariners . . .

"Few thrills . . .": Knoblock, *Black Submariners in the United States Navy, 1940–1975*, 3.

CHAPTER FIFTEEN

"About four hours . . .": Beach, *Submarine!*, 218.

"We'll be lucky . . .": ibid.

"*My God!* We see . . .": ibid., 218–219.

"Our tanker should be . . .": ibid., 219.

"'Wow! It's a destroyer . . .'": ibid.

"We are at 300 feet . . .": ibid., 220–221.

"How *Trigger* manages to hold together . . .": ibid.

"With each succeeding shock . . .": ibid., 220–221.

"No matter which way . . .": ibid., 221.

three hundred feet below: ibid., 222.

"Two or three men are near collapse . . .": ibid., 222.

"We wonder why the six escorts . . .": ibid., 223.

"Our battery and oxygen . . .": ibid.

"We head for the biggest gap . . .": ibid., 224.

"All at once he stops . . .": ibid.

"There is nothing to compare . . .": ibid.

"Wilson served two more . . .": Beach, *Salt and Steel*, 154.

"Since there would be some planning . . .": ibid., 159.

"The third night was a . . .": Beach, *Submarine!*, 267–268.

"Three days we waited . . .": Beach, *Salt and Steel*, 159.

"With submarines there is . . .": Beach, *Submarine!*, 268.

Walter Pye Wilson: Knoblock, 381–382.

"nothing in her worked . . .": Beach, *Salt and Steel*, 224.

DISPATCH: Waiting for Word
"is not the sudden realization . . .": ibid., 182.

CHAPTER SIXTEEN
"might have chosen to . . .": Blair, 353.
"It was a ticklish business . . .": Frank, Horan, and Eckberg, 168.
"throwing out depth charges . . .": ibid., 176.
"'Oh, here's another one . . .'": ibid., 177.
"It seemed as if . . .": ibid., 178.
"'He apparently doesn't see us . . .'": ibid.
"'Yes, Captain, I have him . . .'": ibid.
"'This is a 5,000 . . .'": ibid.
"'I can see them . . .'": ibid.
"It suddenly dawned on me . . .'": ibid., 181.
"We'd settled on dinner . . .": ibid., 170–171.
"For many weeks I hadn't . . .": ibid., 185.
"I climbed topside . . .": ibid., 186.
"The harbor on both sides . . .": ibid.
"When it came time for me . . .": ibid., 195–196.
"'I have been very fortunate . . .'": ibid., 196.
"'Good-by, Captain . . .'": ibid., 197.
"The tension of these last . . .": ibid., 191.
"He was big and brawny . . .": ibid., viii.
"By the autumn of 1944 . . .": Roscoe, 417.

SUBMARINE SCHOOL: A Bit about Tonnage
Tonnage is: Alden and McDonald, 21.
"Displacement is calculated . . .": ibid.
"A Japanese freighter of 5,000 . . .": Jackson, 24.

USS WAHOO
"The ship was called . . .": SWR, SS-238 *Wahoo*.

CHAPTER SEVENTEEN
"After exhausting months of drills . . .": Grider and Sims, *War Fish*, 33.
"Dudley greeted each of us . . .": O'Kane, Wahoo, 71–72.
"'Don't call me Mister . . .'": Sterling, *Wake of the* Wahoo, 26.
"It was one of life's touchy moments . . .": O'Kane, Wahoo, 84.
"I loved this ship . . .": ibid., 104.

PART THREE

"Mush was in his element . . .": Grider and Sims, 57.
"Morton feared nothing . . .": Roscoe, 205.

CHAPTER EIGHTEEN

"Everybody liked Mush,": Grider and Sims, 51.
"'Now, you're going to be . . .'": O'Kane, Wahoo, 114.
"I could feel the stirring . . .": Sterling, 81.
"'Every smoke trace . . .'": ibid., 86.
"'Any customers, Yeo?'": ibid.
"'That's the kind of stuff . . .'": ibid.
"'Wait a minute . . . I'm going . . .'": ibid., 88.
"This was the first time . . .": ibid.
"The thing that caught . . .": ibid., 89.
"'Any of you men ever. . .'": ibid.
"'We have a special mission . . .'": ibid.
"'Would you guys . . .'": ibid.
"'Guess I'll go back . . .'": ibid., 90.
"'Rowdydow.'": ibid.
"'Do you think he's crazy? . . .'": ibid.
"It was an awe-inspiring night . . .": ibid., 91.
"The whole universe . . .": ibid.
"This was another innovation . . .": ibid., 92–93.
"'Clear the bridge.'": ibid., 93.
"all two thousand pounds . . .": ibid.
"'I bet you don't . . .'": ibid.
"'Attaboy, Yeo . . .'": ibid.
"'We clipped three seconds . . .'": ibid.
"Most of them could be . . .": ibid., 93.

SUBMARINE SCHOOL: Dive!

"There's no such command . . .": Sheridan, *Overdue and Presumed Lost*, 13.
"It's an uncomfortable feeling . . .": ibid., 19.

CHAPTER NINETEEN

"Our charts simply showed . . .": O'Kane, Wahoo, 133.
"How could we reconnoiter . . . ?": Grider and Sims, 54.
"'It means we take a cautious . . .'": ibid.
"'The only way you can . . .'": ibid.
"Now it was clear . . .": ibid., 54–55.
"'Hey, Mr. Grider . . .'": ibid., 55.
"A couple of months before . . .": ibid.

"The outline of Wewak . . .": O'Kane, Wahoo, 133.

"When I thought . . .": Grider and Sims, 56.

"Mush was delighted . . .": ibid.

"Normal prudence . . .": O'Kane, Wahoo, 133.

"It was a strange . . .": Grider and Sims, 53.

"He wandered up . . .": ibid., 53–54.

"'All right, George . . .'": O'Kane, Wahoo, 134.

"'We've been laying off . . .'": Sterling, 94.

"'The Old Man spotted . . .'": ibid.

"'How's things up there? . . .'": ibid., 95.

"'I guess he's like me . . .'": ibid.

"The atmosphere was heavy . . .": ibid.

"'Every person is the center . . .'": ibid.

"*Wahoo* was my cocoon . . .": ibid.

"What kind of Japanese warships . . .": ibid.

CHAPTER TWENTY

"We spent the entire morning . . .": Grider and Sims, 57.

"all of us in the conning tower . . .": ibid.

"few captains other than Mush . . .": ibid.

"For all the tension within us . . .": ibid.

"'I have the periscope . . .'": ibid., 58.

"'Dick . . . you're in low power.'": ibid.

"'Down periscope! . . . All back . . .'": ibid.

"'Well, Captain . . .'": ibid.

"We would not leave . . .": O'Kane, Wahoo, 136–137.

"The two of them . . .": Grider and Sims, 58.

"'We'll take him . . .'": ibid., 59.

CHAPTER TWENTY-ONE

"We had the element of surprise . . .": ibid.

"Now our plan to catch . . .": ibid., 60.

"'She's up-anchored . . .'": Sterling, 96.

"I believed it was . . .": O'Kane, Wahoo, 135.

"*Wahoo*'s hull bucked . . .": Sterling, 96.

"'All hot . . .'": O'Kane, Wahoo, 138.

"The situation had changed . . .": Grider and Sims, 61.

"'All right,' said Mush . . .": ibid.

"We had talked about down-the-throats . . .": ibid.

"Now I remembered . . .": ibid., 62.

"For a fleeting moment . . .": O'Kane, Wahoo, 138.

"'Stand by to fire . . . five!'": Grider and Sims, 62.

"'Bring her up, Hank . . .'": ibid.

"'He's still coming . . .'": ibid.

"How many were left? . . .": Sterling, 97.

"utterly cool"; "had been lost . . .": Grider and Sims, 62.

"I watched her come . . .": O'Kane, *Wahoo*, 138.

"'When shall I fire . . .'": Grider and Sims, 62.

"'Well, for heaven's sake . . .'": ibid.

"'Fire six! . . .'": ibid.

"I couldn't take her . . .": ibid., 62–63.

"The first explosion was loud . . .": ibid., 63.

CHAPTER TWENTY-TWO

"Ten, twenty, thirty . . .": ibid.

"'Jeez . . .'": ibid.

"'Well, by God . . .'": ibid.

"a mighty roar and cracking . . .": O'Kane, *Wahoo*, 139.

"It's a hit!'": Sterling, 97.

"'Bring her back up . . .'": Grider and Sims, 63.

"Bedlam broke loose . . .": ibid., 63–64.

"A line had formed . . .": Sterling, 97–98.

"'Chow will be spoiled . . .'": ibid., 98.

"'The war is one Japanese destroyer . . .'": ibid.

the destroyer . . . *Harusame*: Holmes, *Undersea Victory*, 199.

"'All my nerves are tied up . . .'": Sterling, 99.

"'Get your depth-charge medicine . . .'": ibid.

"We were still celebrating . . .": Grider and Sims, 64.

"Three blasts sent us . . .": O'Kane, *Wahoo*, 141.

"'George, you take over . . .'": ibid., 142.

"The conduct and discipline . . .": SWR, SS-238 *Wahoo*.

"When the sun balanced . . .": Sterling, 100.

"I came below decks . . .": ibid.

SUBMARINE SCHOOL: Attack Strategies after Pearl Harbor

"Ideas about what a submarine . . .": Grider and Sims, 29.

"The 'skipper problem' . . .": Personnel figures from Blair, 818.

CHAPTER TWENTY-THREE

"Our crew pitched up . . .": O'Kane, *Wahoo*, 142.

"The great weakness . . .": Grider and Sims, 68–69.

"We were entering . . .": ibid., 70.

"Before the day ended . . .": ibid.

"Let's finish him off . . .'": ibid., 71.

"Our battery was getting . . .": ibid., 72.

"'Every one who does . . .'": O'Kane, *Wahoo*, 153.

"Some Japanese troops . . .": ibid., 154.

how many people died: Death toll from DeRose, *Unrestricted Warfare*, 94.

"To some submariners . . .": Blair, 386.

"We made quite a stir . . .": Grider and Sims, 82–83.

"put a crack in . . .": O'Kane, *Wahoo*, 175.

"Mush had talked to her . . .": Grider and Sims, 83.

"'Tenacity, Dick . . .'": O'Kane, *Wahoo*, 162.

"'You're not leading enough . . .'": Sterling, 135.

"Morton had demonstrated . . .": O'Kane, *Wahoo*, 177.

"In round figures, we had . . .": ibid.

"Only one question . . .": Grider and Sims, 83.

"I groaned . . .": ibid.

"I never saw him again,": ibid., 85.

"I left the *Wahoo* . . .": ibid., 91.

"the homemade chart of Wewak . . .": ibid., 86.

"A big controversy . . .": ibid.

CHAPTER TWENTY-FOUR

"Mush was boiling mad . . .": Lockwood, 98.

"All Morton wanted . . .": ibid.

"'Yeo, I'm going to ask . . .'": Sterling, 229.

"'Why, you're Gene Tunney . . .'": ibid., 232.

"I thought, Oh brother, . . .": ibid., 233.

"'The Commander has a fine idea . . .'": ibid.

"'The men will receive it . . .'": ibid.

"'We've got an hour . . .'": ibid., 236.

"I had been complimented . . .": ibid., 237.

"I heard the diesels . . .": ibid., 238.

"Days dragged by . . .": Lockwood, 110–111.

"This makes her final total . . .": ibid., 111.

"'What happened, George?'": Grider and Sims, 87.

"By now virtually all . . .": ibid., 88.

"I like to think . . .": Beach, *Submarine!*, 65.

PART FOUR

"It is one thing to be . . .": Grider and Sims, 131, 133.

"O'Kane is the fightingest . . .": SWR, SS-238 *Wahoo*.

"Submariners are always asked . . .": Beach, *Salt and Steel*, 87.

USS TANG

USS *Tang*: SWR, SS-306 *Tang*.

CHAPTER TWENTY-FIVE

"My beloved *Wahoo* . . .": O'Kane, *Clear the Bridge!*, 50.
"*Tang* had no bugs . . .": ibid., 27.
" 'Why, only the Chief . . .' ": ibid., 25.
"It was the answer I had expected . . .": ibid.
"If a steward became adept . . .": ibid., 26.
"I had to shake my head . . .": ibid., 89.
"a vibrant ship . . .": O'Kane, *Clear the Bridge!*, 52.
" 'All hands are aboard . . .' ": ibid.

DISPATCH: The Officer in Charge of Ice Cream

" 'We think we know where . . .' ": Beach, 90.
"Stinky—now known as . . .": ibid., 92.
"Even if the Captain . . .": ibid., 94.

DISPATCH: Heads or Tails? . . .

"We had prepared a can . . .": ibid., 167.
"Instead," reported *Flasher*'s . . .": ibid.
"Too little has been written . . .": ibid., 167–168.
"No one on *Flasher* ever knew . . .": ibid., 167.

CHAPTER TWENTY-SIX

"a name was to be had . . .": Monroe-Jones and Green, 133.
"he was flabbergasted . . .": ibid.
"While we were talking . . .": ibid.
" 'Steward, what . . . did you spill . . .' ": ibid., 134.
" 'Gleason to the captain's cabin . . .' ": ibid.
" 'Where is it . . .' ": ibid.
"The skipper's eyes . . .": ibid., 135.
" 'I just couldn't throw . . .' ": ibid.
" 'I have no idea, sir . . .' ": ibid.
" 'Although it's very unusual . . .' ": ibid.
"We finally found her . . .": ibid., 136.
"When my mother saw . . .": ibid.
"The dog, LUAU, . . .": SWR, SS-411 *Spadefish*.
" 'The whole ship was awake . . .' ": Moore, *Presumed Lost*, 185.
"22:48 FLASH NEWS . . .": SWR, SS-411 *Spadefish*.

DISPATCH: The Stowaway Rat

"a real monster . . .": Monroe-Jones and Green, 122.

"prove that I still had . . .": ibid.

"I gave up . . .": ibid., 123.

"By now I had grown . . .": ibid., 124.

"I imagined him enjoying . . .": ibid.

CHAPTER TWENTY-SEVEN

"Sometimes the ships . . .": O'Kane, *Clear the Bridge!*, 101.

"When a person walks down . . .": ibid., 102.

" 'It's all in here . . .' ": ibid., 104.

"The enemy closed . . .": ibid., 106.

"In a few minutes it would be . . .": ibid., 106–107.

" 'We're right on,' ": ibid., 107.

"I had," he said later . . . : ibid., 108.

"The destroyer had crossed . . .": ibid.

"If we were sighted . . .": ibid., 108–109.

" 'Constant bearing—mark . . .' ": ibid., 109.

" 'Level off at five . . .' ": ibid., 110.

CHAPTER TWENTY-EIGHT

" 'Blow safety . . .' ": ibid., 111.

"We held on, waiting . . .": ibid.

"The scene was not . . .": ibid.

" 'Stop pumping,' ": ibid., 112.

"An axiom of antisubmarine . . .": ibid., 114.

"Perhaps it was wishful thinking . . .": ibid.

"The destroyer would be getting . . .": ibid.

"their fast *swish-swish-swish* . . .": ibid.

"a highly agreeable parting.": ibid., 115.

"The sea was all ours . . .": ibid., 116.

"Gone was the former glossiness . . .": ibid., 130.

"To a man they were . . .": ibid.

"Submarines were an unknown . . .": Lockwood, 252–253.

" 'I thought that I had been . . .' ": ibid.

" 'We picked him up . . .' ": ibid.

During her second patrol . . . air strikes: Truk strategy from Blair, 607.

"Lifeguard was our mission . . .": O'Kane, *Clear the Bridge!*, 161.

"*Tang* lit out . . .": ibid., 170.

" 'Thar she blows!' ": ibid.

"an old-fashioned man-overboard . . .": ibid.

"Time and time again, it seemed . . .": ibid., 182–183.
"There had been sub-air . . .": ibid., 191.
"*Tang* was a happy ship . . .": ibid., 187.

DISPATCH: A Historic Operation at Sea
"'I can do it . . .'": Blair, 291.
"Lipes devised surgical instruments . . .": ibid., 292.
"The seaman came into . . .": Lockwood, 37.
"'Good Lord . . . will a shot . . .'": ibid.
"His courage, resourcefulness . . .": ibid.

CHAPTER TWENTY-NINE
"'You've got some small broken bones . . .'": ibid., 384.
"The torpedo, our very last . . .": ibid., 456.
"'All ahead emergency . . .'": ibid.
"All stories seemed . . .": Beach, *Submarine!*, 183.
"'All I could do . . .'": DeRose, 226.

CHAPTER THIRTY
144 airmen: Lockwood, 244.
"Ever since the loss of *Wahoo* . . .": Roscoe, 478.
Getting in and out . . . : Sea of Japan from Blair, 857.
FM sonar gear: Mine detection from Roscoe, 479.
Lockwood was eager: Lockwood training from Blair, 858.
"'There was a scraping . . .'": ibid., 861.
"'Had *Sea Dog* or *Crevalle* . . .'": ibid., 860.
"'All hands breathed . . .'": Blair, 861.
"The Hell Cats turned out to be . . .": ibid., 863.
Over the next ten days: Hellcats statistics from ibid.
"'When I came out here . . .'": Sasgen, *Hellcats,* 56.
"'our country, the place where . . .'": ibid., 68.
"'so deeply and completely . . .'": ibid., 220.
"'Dearest Sweetest Love . . .'": Sarah Edge's letter from ibid., 233–234.

EPILOGUE
"The valiant efforts . . .": Roscoe, 494.
"'The long-awaited day . . .'": Sasgen, 241.
"'Cease offensive operations . . .'": Blair, 870.
"'Captain, I talked it over . . .'": Blair, 871.
"Thirty of us had been . . .": O'Kane, *Clear the Bridge!,* 466.
"Just when everything seemed its darkest . . .": ibid.
"We all weighed in . . .": ibid.

"He was just skin and bones . . .": Lockwood, 327.

"In just over four . . .": Blair, 769.

"There was no assurance . . .": O'Kane, *Clear the Bridge!*, 466.

" 'Let us pray . . .' ": Blair, 873.

AFTER SECTION

"What we saw and did . . .": Mendenhall, *Submarine Diary*, xvi.

ON ETERNAL PATROL

The first confirmed . . . attack number 4,735: First and last sinkings of
Japanese ships from Roscoe, 490; Blair, 870; Alden and McDonald, 334.

FACTS AND FIGURES

4,472 separate attacks: Alden and McDonald, 335.

Although figures have continued . . . reduction in tonnage: Blair, 80, 82,
877–879.

PHOTO PERMISSIONS

Photos ©: i: Bureau of Ships Collection/Naval History and Heritage Command; iii: U.S. Navy/Naval History and Heritage Command; vi: Mike Smolinski/NavSource.org; ix-xi background, 2-3: U.S. Navy/Naval History and Heritage Command; 4: Library of Congress; 10, 13, 16, 21, 28, 32: U.S. Navy/Naval History and Heritage Command; 34: U.S. Navy/navsource.org; 36: Courtesy of Harry S. Truman Library; 38: Darryl L. Baker/navsource.org; 48: Lt. Cmdr. Fred Freemen/navsource.org; 51: Army Signal Corps Collection/Naval History and Heritage Command; 55, 64, 71: U.S. Navy, Courtesy of Harry S. Truman Library; 82-83: National Archives; 86: Courtesy of Harry S. Truman Library; 89: National Archives; 90: AP Images; 94, 99, 101: U.S. Navy/Naval History and Heritage Command; 106-107: Dr. Diosdado M. Yap, Editor-Publisher, Bataan Magazine, Washington, D.C., 1971/NHHC; 116: Chief Mass Communication Specialist Ahron Arendes/U.S. Navy; 118: National Archives/NHHC; 124-125: U.S. Navy/Naval History and Heritage Command; 128: Mike Smolinski/NavSource. org; 131: Rick Connole/navsource.org; 138: Naval History and Heritage Command; 140: Courtesy of Harry S. Truman Library; 145: U.S. Navy/Naval History and Heritage Command; 146: Army.mil; 152: National Archives/Naval History and Heritage Command; 157: ussubvetsofworldwarii.org/navsource.org; 160: U.S. Navy/Naval History and Heritage Command; 166: Naval History and Heritage Command; 170, 176-177: Bureau of Ships Collection/Naval History and Heritage Command; 179: U.S. Navy/Naval History and Heritage Command; 181: U.S. Navy, Courtesy of Harry S. Truman Library; 185: Courtesy of Harry S.

INDEX

Note: Page numbers in *italics* refer to illustrations.

ACKNOWLEDGMENTS

THANKS TO THE CREW

Teamwork was an enormous part of being on a World War II submarine crew. And I'm fortunate to have an extraordinary team of people at Scholastic, without whom this book wouldn't have been launched. Thanks, as always, to my dedicated and exceptional editor, Lisa Sandell, who takes her editing responsibilities so seriously she edits in the wee hours and even visited a submarine museum herself to learn more about the subject—and came away with some great ideas!

Thanks also to the rest of the Scholastic crew, with a special commendation to Phil Falco for once again bringing his extraordinary design talents to bear for this book. Just as the tender *Canopus* helped to keep submarines operating smoothly, I'm grateful to the production team for all their work, especially production editor Maya Frank-Levine, photo researcher Emily Teresa, and copy editor Joy Simpkins. Thanks also to Laura Beets, Ellie Berger, Lori Benton, Bess Brasswell, Michelle Campbell, Saraciea Fennell, Caitlin Friedman, Antonio Gonzalez, Emily Heddleson, Robin Hoffman, David Levithan, Christine Reedy, Lizette Serrano, Brooke Shearouse, Janet Speakman, Tracy van Straaten, and many more.

I owe a debt of gratitude to Alice Watts, Education Coordinator at the San Francisco Maritime National Park Association, for taking the time to read and comment on the manuscript. I'm grateful to Steven Malk, my agent, for his support, and to Michele Kopfs of Provato Marketing for all her help. I'm also thankful to the parents, teachers, and librarians whose own love of history inspires them to put books like this into the hands of young people. I want to especially acknowledge all the schools who have hosted me for author visits, and for the wonderful response and ideas from students (who are never shy about offering advice on what I should write next).

Special thanks to authors Deborah Wiles, for her encouragement (especially when deadlines loomed), and Iain Martin, for sharing his expertise in military history (and for bringing my attention to Forest Sterling). I'm grateful to Sheridan Mosher for her gracious hospitality, and for accompanying me on visits to the Naval Undersea Museum in Keyport, Washington, and the Puget Sound Navy Museum in Bremerton, Washington. I'm extraordinarily lucky to have the support of friends and family, including Janice Fairbrother, Bonnie Johnson, Vicki Hemphill, Elisa Johnston, Ellie Thomas, Deniz Conger, Candace Fleming, Maya Abels, Sara Wright, Sheridan Mosher, Kristin Hill, Bill Carrick, Barbara Noseworthy, Cyndi Howard, Judy Sierra and Bob Kaminski, Jane Kurtz, Candy Smith, Deborah Correa, Eric Sawyer, Teresa Vast and Michael Kieran, Greg and Becky Smith, and the great instructors and my fellow members at ClubSport Oregon.

Stowaways and mascots were a big hit on some boats, and so it seems only fitting to give a shout-out to my canine office mates, Brooklyn and Rue, who could take only so many hours of napping next to me before dragging me out for a walk (probably a good thing). Finally, to my husband, Andy, and children, Rebekah and Dimitri, I wouldn't want to be on a submarine crew with anyone else. You are the joy of my life.

Deborah Hopkinson

ABOUT THE AUTHOR

Deborah Hopkinson is the acclaimed author of over forty award-winning books, including, most recently, *Courage & Defiance: Stories of Spies, Saboteurs, and Survivors in World War II Denmark*, a Sydney Taylor Notable Book, an NCTE Orbis Pictus Recommended Book, and a Bank Street Center for Children's Literature Best Children's Book of the Year selection; *Shutting Out the Sky*, an NCTE Orbis Pictus Honor Book and a Jane Addams Peace Award Honor Book; *Up Before Daybreak*, a Carter G. Woodson Award Honor Book; and *Titanic: Voices from the Disaster*, a YALSA Award for Excellence in Nonfiction Finalist and a Sibert Medal Honor Book. Deborah lives with her family near Portland, Oregon.

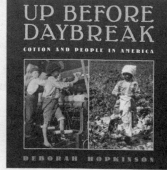

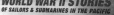